MEMOIRS OF M. THIERS

MEMOIRS OF M. THIERS

1870—1873

Translated by

F. M. ATKINSON

HOWARD FERTIG

NEW YORK · 1973

222635

First published in 1915

HOWARD FERTIG, INC. EDITION 1973
Published by arrangement with George Allen & Unwin, Ltd.

All rights reserved.

Library of Congress Cataloging in Publication Data

Thiers, Adolphe, 1797–1877.
    Memoirs of M. Thiers, 1870–1873.

    Reprint of the 1915 ed., which is a translation of Notes et souvenirs de M. Thiers, 1870–1873.
    1. France—Politics and government—1870–1940. 2. Franco-German War, 1870–1871—Sources. 3. France—History—Third Republic, 1870–1940—Sources.
DC344.A32   1972   944.081′092′4   [B]   79-80598

PRINTED IN THE UNITED STATES OF AMERICA
BY NOBLE OFFSET PRINTERS, INC.

CONTENTS

	PAGE
M. THIERS IN LONDON	7
A DIPLOMATIC JOURNEY	23
NEGOTIATIONS FOR AN ARMISTICE	66
THE PEACE PRELIMINARIES	102
PRESIDENCY OF THE REPUBLIC	117
APPENDICES	333
INDEX	377

MEMOIRS OF M. THIERS

M. THIERS IN LONDON

SEPTEMBER, 1870

[M. Thiers, in his tour of the European capitals on behalf of France, came to London in the first place. Here follow his letters to M. Jules Favre, taken from the latter's "Histoire du Gouvernement de la Defense Nationale." They form an integral part of these MEMOIRS, though not included in the French arrangement.]

LONDON, 13*th September*, 1870.

MON CHER ANCIEN COLLÈGUE,—I set out yesterday evening as I had promised you, and was, I think, the last person to use the Northern Railway, for the engineer officer charged with the task of cutting communications told me that he had waited for me to pass before blowing up the bridge at Creil.

I reached London at seven in the morning, and finding no lodging anywhere, so great is the number of foreigners here, and especially French, I was obliged to stay at the Embassy, where, thanks to M. Tissot, a kind of camping-place has been got ready for me. I have had an opportunity of observing, while receiving various people this morning, that public opinion is moving in our favour, and even that the news of my arrival had given a distinct fillip to men's minds, a circumstance that has reassured me a little as to the usefulness of my mission, which, to my mind, was very doubtful. So much the better, I am told, the Ministers will be obliged to declare themselves. The *Times* itself has changed its tone for the better. M. Tissot having placed himself fully at my disposal, I made use of his services to inform the English Cabinet of my arrival in London. Precisely at noon Lord Granville came to see me, wishing to spare me the trouble of going to the Foreign Office. Our conversation was lengthy and on my side urgent, but always very friendly. It is impossible to recount its inevitable repetitions. I give you herewith a summary as accurate as possible.

First of all I took pains to prove, by an exact account of the events leading up to the war, that France had not desired this war, that the Chamber itself had not desired it, and had only yielded to the pressure of the Imperial power, which it could never resist, and that on the last day especially, the 15th of July, it had only allowed itself to be drawn in by a most culpable falsehood with regard to a pretended insult to France.

My account seemed to dispel more than one erroneous impression in Lord Granville's mind, for he appeared to think, from what the agents of the Empire had told him, that at heart France had desired war, and that the dynasty had merely taken the initiative. I think I have convinced him upon this point. On this occasion we touched on a matter that preoccupied us a little when I left Paris: an intrigue of the Bonapartes towards setting up the Empire again upon the head of the Prince Imperial under the regency of the Empress. Lord Granville treated this as a chimera that could not be realized, and beneath any one's attention. Information I have received from other quarters proves that there is nothing serious in it, that the Imperialist refugees here do not themselves believe in it, and are taking no steps in the matter. For the moment they are frightened and inert. Bonapartist intrigue, if it exists, would be much more likely in the Prussian camp. Lord Granville told me that the Prussian Court, not wishing, or appearing not to wish, to treat, would perhaps use this as a pretext, alleging that in its view the Imperial Government alone had a regularly constituted character, that the new Government was the outcome of a popular movement, that it had no legal being, and that in treating with it they might find themselves treating with nobody.

This objection, which Lord Granville did not offer as his own, gave me an opportunity of saying that the Chamber might have seized the power if it had had sufficient decision; but that through its hesitation it had left the way clear for a popular movement, that from this movement had sprung the present Government; that it was idle and dangerous to argue about its origin, and that we should look to its actions, which were excellent. (Lord Granville several times nodded approval of my assertions.) I added that at the moment the Republic was everybody's accepted Government; that since it brought despair to no party because it did not finally realize the idea of any, it suited all for the present; that reasonable men were united in maintaining it, because, to the merit of not exasperating party feeling it added that of being at the moment the veritable Government of National Defence, for all parties could rally to the common defence, without the vexation of feeling that they were working for an opponent; that finally it was in the hands of honourable men of the best aims, who had till now directed all their efforts to the maintaining of order; that for my own part I held this opinion, since I was in London, and prepared to go elsewhere to persuade all the

European Courts that for France and for Europe the best thing to do was to help the present Government of France.

Lord Granville fully accepted all I said on this matter, and if he had paused upon it it was as an objection, not on the part of England, but of Prussia seeking pretexts not to treat. He even asked me why the next Constituent Assembly had not been summoned as quickly as possible. I replied that the nature of the circumstances of the moment made it impossible, and in any case he seemed in this to wish to prove that he spoke not for himself but for Prussia, whose ill-will we have to neutralize.

At length we came to present circumstances, and I asked what England was willing to do; I asked it in the most urgent manner, reminding him of our forty years' alliance, our brotherhood in arms in the Crimea, and the loyalty of our behaviour during the war in India. I asked if England would refuse all support at a moment when the madness of the fallen Government had left us disarmed before a Power that in no way disguised its passion for aggrandizement.

Hereupon Lord Granville uttered many expressions of affection for France, and tried with the utmost gentleness to evade my importunities. He reiterated continually that England would be eager to come to our aid, but that not wishing to go so far as war, since at the moment she had not the means, she exposed herself, if she insisted in the name of the neutral Powers, to the displeasure of Prussia, who would not hear of their intervention, and thenceforward she would harm rather than help our cause. As I rejoined that by keeping to this she would do nothing, absolutely nothing, and that she would fall from her high place by allowing the greatest revolution of modern times to take place without her and in spite of her; he defended himself by saying that the Germans, on the contrary, complained that she was doing too much on our behalf, and that she was wholly partial to France. I answered that without doubt in her situation one was exposed, whatever one did, to accusation from both sides, but that of the two complainants one must needs be right; that this was clearly France, for she was not the conquering Power seeking to change the face of Europe, and that nevertheless it was only Prussia that was given a free hand, and that simply to do nothing was the greatest possible partiality to her. "Besides," I added boldly, "do you know what they say everywhere in France? That your Queen is so dominated by family affections, and that in this affair the Cabinet is influenced by her."

"I am profoundly devoted to my Sovereign," answered Lord Granville, "but I am a Minister of England, and my country's will is the only one I consult."

In London it is thought that Lord Granville is influenced by the Queen's maternal feelings; but I must say that he seemed to be guided chiefly by a policy of inertia, which consists in avoiding all considerable affairs. In other days England would have shuddered with indignation at the idea of allowing so great a revolution as was accomplishing itself under our eyes to be fulfilled without taking a part in it proper to a great Power. To-day, while recognizing that Prussia is becoming formidable, she prefers to shut her eyes and ears rather than to see it or hear it said. She is vexed and troubled; but the idea of a great war dismays her, and the thought of taking a step that might meet with a rebuff and offer her the alternative of enduring an affront or taking up arms, dismays her almost as much as war itself. I said so just now to Mr. Gladstone, my interview with whom I shall recount to you in the course of this dispatch; I said to him: "England, which once was angry when Napoleon told her that she was exclusively a maritime Power, leaving her legitimate rôle when she took part in continental affairs, England to-day acknowledges that he was right, for certainly she is doing as he wished, and leaves the Continent to itself without venturing to have an opinion on what takes place there." Mr. Gladstone said nothing and preserved a grieved and uncomfortable silence.

Yet public opinion is awaking little by little, the old English pride is murmuring, and would break out if Parliament was assembled. But there is no one in London except Mr. Gladstone and Lord Granville, who have been brought here on account of my presence and my errand. Ministers, therefore, do as they please, and yield to this inertia, displaying annoyance when they are shown what they are permitting to happen.

For the rest, personally I can only felicitate myself upon the way they received me, and the interest they express in France. When I said to Lord Granville that after all this interest came to nothing, he replied that they had done something, that they had made themselves our intermediary in transmitting to Prussia a communication equivalent to a proposal to treat, and that we must wait for the answer. I replied that this was a very small matter, that without doubt we must await this answer, but that it was of no more importance than the request (I did not yet know the answer, which has arrived); that something

M. THIERS IN LONDON

else was needed, and something that would give more character to England's intervention. He replied that doubtless if there was anything useful to be done (apart from any thought of war) he would not reject it, but that he was sure that the intervention of neutrals in this affair was supremely disagreeable to Prussia, and that much better conditions would be obtained by negotiating direct with her than by importing neutrals into the matter. "And why," he added, "would not M. Jules Favre confer directly with Count Bismarck? What objection could he have to such a step?"

Recalling then what you had told me, that you were prepared to brave every danger, every distress, in order to visit the Prussian Headquarters, I replied, without binding you in any way, that while I did not know what resolve you might take I nevertheless did not believe that you would be opposed to such a step, but that we must beforehand assure ourselves of a favourable answer and a reception befitting the representative of France; that England would have to be the intermediary of this proposal by recommending it strongly, and thus guaranteeing its faithful accomplishment.

Thereupon Lord Granville said he would consider it and consult Mr. Gladstone upon it. I then requested him either to convey a letter from me to Mr. Gladstone, asking for an interview, or to ask it for me by word of mouth. He replied that it was unnecessary to write, and that he would give me an immediate answer. A quarter of an hour after I received a word from Lord Granville announcing that Mr. Gladstone would visit me at six o'clock.

At six o'clock, then, Mr. Gladstone came to the

French Embassy, where I told you I was established. I found him grave, friendly, gentle, but profoundly saddened by events in Europe. " The answer we were expecting has come," he said; "here it is, read it." I need not reproduce it since it is in your hands. This answer, you may imagine, made me shudder. In affecting to be unable to treat with the French Government, because it would be incapable of exacting obedience, Count Bismarck lets it be seen what he would demand. Mr. Gladstone and I were both very careful not to say a word of the conditions insinuated rather than expressed in this reply. I would not, of course, have wished to bring them under discussion. I confined myself to saying that the present Government would be obeyed by the troops as by the civilians so long as it would demand nothing of them that could offend their patriotism. We then immediately went back to the idea mentioned this morning by Lord Granville as the most practicable, that M. Jules Favre should visit the Prussian Headquarters. "When they are face to face," he said, "it will no longer be asked whether they can or cannot treat." " Yes," I replied, " but I cannot answer for M. Jules Favre; I can only say one thing: he has often declared to me, that in order to bring about an honourable peace he would be ready to brave the greatest dangers, or if not dangers, the most extreme annoyances, and especially that of visiting the enemy's Headquarters. We must accordingly await his answer. But this is not all: England must come away from her inertia, she must herself propose the suggested interview, and claim it as a thing due to Europe and the whole of humanity." " Without doubt," said Mr. Gladstone, "England will become the intermediary for this proposal." "Intermediary, yes," I replied, "but she cannot confine herself to the part of a mere messenger; she must speak as befits her greatness, her dignity, the lofty sentiments she professes. Bearing this message of peace, she must claim its acceptance as a duty towards humanity, revolted at the blood poured out by two great civilized countries." "Yes," said Mr. Gladstone, "Lord Granville will say that." "That is not enough," I added. "England must not keep to the language of a pastor preaching charity; she must speak in the name of Europe, must express the feeling of Europe upon what is taking place at this juncture. England," I added further, "must say that humanity desires peace, but she must also say a word on the nature of that peace, and add that shedding of blood must be brought to an end, by means of an equitable and lasting peace, which should deal the balance of Europe no more blows than it has already endured."

Mr. Gladstone said, "Yes, Lord Granville shall say that." I insisted and obtained that he should be still more decided, repeating with the utmost fervour that if England did not speak as a European Power, she would abdicate before the whole world, and in presence of the blood that would flow under the walls of Paris, in presence of the colossus that would rise up in the centre of Europe, she would seem to say that it matters little to her, and to shut herself up in her insular position to let the bloodshed go on and Europe manage for herself as best she can.

It was eight in the evening; I begged Mr. Gladstone, who was about to rejoin Lord Granville, to ask him for another interview for me before midnight, and at any hour he wished. Lord Granville was dining in town.

I then wrote an urgent letter to him (you see all the importunities called for by the situation, that one would never employ for one's self), asking him to see me again. Broken with fatigue, for I had spent the last forty-eight hours in going to and fro, or in travelling, I bade one of our young attachés to stay on guard, and to come and wake me if an answer arrived. It came only this morning, and explaining his last night's silence by a dinner at Holland House, and his receiving my letter too late, Lord Granville announces his visit for eleven o'clock. I am expecting him, and shall add the details of the interview to this dispatch.

WEDNESDAY, 14*th September*, 11 A.M.

I have just seen Lord Granville again. I found him still more friendly than yesterday, but still afraid of compromising England by going too near the conflagration that is devouring the centre of the Continent. He told me he had written to Lord Lyons on the step that M. Jules Favre might take by going to the Prussian camp, which England would support with all her power. He first of all asked me if M. Jules Favre would take this step, especially after yesterday's reply from Prussia. To this I answered as I did yesterday, that I thought M. Jules Favre was prepared for the most painful sacrifices in the interests of a speedy and honourable peace, but that I could not make in his name a pledge for which I had no authority. I then went back to our conversation of yesterday, and again I urged that England in asking that M. Jules Favre should be received in the Prussian camp, and honourably received, should not play the part of mere messenger, a part

M. THIERS IN LONDON

too lowly for her; and I urged that the English Cabinet should recommend, *in the name of humanity*, the stopping of this dreadful bloodshed, and *in the name of the general interest*, a peace that should not inflict on the balance of power in Europe more loss than it had received. I added that Mr. Gladstone had approved this double recommendation in the name of humanity and in the name of the balance of Europe.

Lord Granville here appeared to be still anxious not to thrust his finger into machinery that might seize the finger, then the arm, then the whole body. He did not say *no*, but he desired to consult with Mr. Gladstone, whom he had not seen yesterday evening, and I have to meet him at the Foreign Office at half-past four.

My credentials being on the table, and bearing the address of Lord Granville, he said to me: "I think this packet is for me." "Yes, my lord, it is for you. It is my credentials, which I did not present to you yesterday, since I was so eager to enter upon affairs." He smiled as he said that such formalities were superfluous at the moment; he opened the packet, read it, and added: "I receive it, though strictly I should not, as our Government has not recognized yours. But you see that in reality our relations are just as they would be if this recognition had taken place."

I had intended this very day to take up the question of recognition, and I seized the opportunity that offered itself. "My lord," I said, "you continually speak of moral support, as material support is out of the question; but here is a way of affording the French Government a powerful moral support, to recognize it." "Without doubt," replied Lord Granville, "you see by our relations with you that we act precisely as we should towards a recognized Government; but so far nothing has given the Government established at Paris on the 4th of September a fixed character, and we should fear to go too far and too hastily in recognizing it. If to-morrow, for instance, a shock overthrew it, what sort of figure should we cut? Oh! if any vote had given your country an opportunity to sanction the new Government, we should not hesitate. But why put off the elections so long?" I repeated that circumstances had prevented holding them sooner, that their result was assured; that they would return a majority of Conservative-Liberals, disposed, like myself, to uphold the present Government; that if it was such a manifestation that England desired before recognizing the French Government, she might recognize it instantly, for the Government would be as indispensable in a month's time as it is to-day. "Yes," answered Lord Granville, "but a shock? Who can answer for that?" "The shock," I rejoined, "depends more on Europe than on us; if the Moderate Government now in charge of affairs is not properly treated, if it is driven, or allowed to be driven to extremity, no one can answer for what might happen." This brought up again all the points already discussed, and I did not insist. But Lord Granville did not seem wholly opposed to recognizing us. I am to see him again at the Foreign Office at half-past four.

A. THIERS.

WEDNESDAY, 14*th September*, 1870.

I have just left the Foreign Office after seeing Lord Granville for the second time to-day. He showed me your reply to Count Bismarck's communication,[1] which reply I find here on my return to the Embassy. It is excellent. Lord Granville wholly approves it. After a few minutes' talk on this subject he told me of his conversation yesterday with Mr. Gladstone. I had foreseen that he would retract something of the concessions Mr. Gladstone had made yesterday, and I wished to regain them, but in vain, and the following are the final resolutions of the English Cabinet. If at a moment, which it is for you to select, you think it useful to confer with Count Bismarck at the Prussian camp, England will be your intermediary, will convey the expression of your desire to the Prussian camp, and will strongly recommend it as the simplest way of placing the belligerents in a position to explain themselves and come to an understanding, and will express in the name of humanity the prayer that we may speedily see the end of this bloodshed, and calm

[1] Bismarck inquired: "What guarantee is there that France, or at this moment the troops of Metz and Strassburg, will recognize the arrangements into which we might enter with the Government at present existing in Paris, or with those which will probably succeed it?"
M. Jules Favre replied as follows:
"The guarantees properly demanded by Count Bismarck can be furnished from both a political and military standpoint. From the political point of view, the Government of National Defence will sign an armistice and will at once convene an Assembly which shall ratify the treaty of peace agreed upon by the Prussian Government and that of France. From the military point of view, the Government of National Defence offers the same security as a regular Government, since the Minister of War is obeyed in all the orders he gives. All that may be agreed upon in an armistice would therefore be punctually carried out without any delay."

restored in Europe by a peace equally honourable for both sides.

I was about to begin my remonstrances afresh, when Lord Granville stopped me, saying : "Do not insist further. You have already made us change our plans, you are forcing us to do more than we meant, for we intended to be merely intermediaries without supporting any solution; but to make us recommend a peace which should not inflict more harm upon the balance of Europe than it has already sustained is to make us enter into the negotiation and take sides for one solution against another. I do not know if later we may not have to go further; but to-day we are going a step beyond the bounds we had set for ourselves. Be satisfied with this, and do not ask us to do what we cannot do."

I let it be seen that I was sad, unsatisfied, discontented with an old alliance that ended in so little help in our great danger; but I did not wish to run the risk of irritating without gaining anything. I certainly believe I have conquered their inertia to some extent, that I have moved them, but without drawing them out of their obstinate abstention. I told them they were behaving to-day as France did in 1866. They feel this is the case; but to throw themselves boldly into present danger to prevent a greater one in the future is beyond the courage of Europe at the moment, and we must admit that the state of unpreparedness of all the Powers explains their inertia, without justifying it. All I shall have obtained will be that Lord Lyons will find somewhat less hindrance to his goodwill for us.

* * * * * *

I am convinced that they would prefer keeping me

M. THIERS IN LONDON

here to letting me go to Saint Petersburg. This is a reason for not delaying my departure. However, I think it best to await your reply to my present communication.

Thank you for to-day's dispatch. I am happy even in the midst of so much distress to know that Paris is so right-minded and so well disposed.

With renewed assurance of my regard and esteem,

A. THIERS.

A DIPLOMATIC JOURNEY

URGED by the telegrams I receive from Paris to leave London in order to go to Saint Petersburg, I decide to take my passage, on Sunday the 18th of September, 1870, upon the steamboat that runs between England and Russia; but at the moment of my departure there arrives the *Desaix* (the old *Prince-Jerôme*) with Commandant Bruat, detailed to bring me to the Dunes, where the *Solferino* and the fleet have been ordered to come to meet me.

We reach the Dunes at break of day, in a heavy fog. After waiting and hunting about for several hours and not catching sight of any ship, we make for Cherbourg, where we find the *Solferino* and the fleet, their orders having been countermanded when I had reported my intention of going by passenger steamer.

On Admiral de Gueydon's telling me that with the large ships of his command he could not escort the *Solferino* as far as the point where I should be beyond reach of the Prussians, I resolve to go to Russia overland.

Travelling all night we arrive at Tours on Tuesday, September 20th, and stay at the Archbishop's palace, a part of which had been placed by the Archbishop at the disposal of M. Crémieux, the delegate from the Government of Paris. We resume our journey the same day.

On our way, the railway-stations are thronged with the people of the neighbourhood, who all come to tell me how ardently they pray for peace. We pass Mont Cenis (Wednesday the 21st), and during the night we reach Turin, where we only pause for a few hours.

Thursday the 22nd, at six in the morning, we set out for Vienna. A wonderful day. As we cross Lombardy we see the lovely lake of Garda, Verona, the towers of Maximilian. From Mestre, where we must wait for the train, we go to spend the evening in Venice, more abandoned than ever.

On the night of the 22nd we cross the Julian Alps in a terrific north-east wind, and come into Styria. Wild aspect. Going down into the valley, the country is rich and the inhabitants prosperous. Wide expanse of meadows. One of the richest and most happy districts to the eye that I have ever seen. The Save and the Drave issue from it to run into the Danube, and the Soemmering shows as a long outwork of the Alps, rising up to separate Styria from Austria and Vienna.

At length, at 11 p.m. on Friday the 23rd, we arrive at Vienna, where we find the French legation waiting in the station. I go to the Hôtel Cour d'Autriche.

Saturday morning, September 24th, I have a conference with Count Beust.

Tall, with a certain claim to good looks, always smiling, subtle, intelligent, among all the men I have known the one who has the least air of believing what he says, readily admitting Austria's former blunders, forgetting only the one he led her into when he brought her, by bringing Saxony, to interfere with

Danish affairs, Count Beust, whom I had previously met, but whom I failed to recognize, received me most cordially. With him, as with the other personages I had seen during the previous six days, I began by a very clear account of the declaration of war, and I showed that it was not France that had willed it; that the Government itself had only acted in submission to the Bonapartist party, on which lay the sole and entire responsibility for this fatal war.

I then said that in the circumstances the Republic was the one form of government possible, and for a period that no one could estimate, if it understood how to conduct itself.

"Now," I added, "we must see what the Powers can do for us: if they realize how greatly it is to the interest of Europe not to leave Prussia free to do what she pleases, and whether they are not, each in what concerns herself, about to make the same mistake as Napoleon III made after Sadowa."

Here Count Beust interrupted me in order to express his views on the past, and I listened with a silent attention that sometimes embarrassed him, for he was asking himself whether I approved his narration and his comments or not. But to make what he said to me quite clear, I must explain the situation of the political parties in Austria.

Count Beust is the subject of attack from nearly everybody. He is accused of being deep in the intrigue that helped to bring about the present war. The Emperor would have wished to be revenged, the army shared his feeling, the nobility too: the Austro-Germans were inclined the same way before the latest Prussian victories. Our Ambassador, M. de Gramont, had fostered these feelings as far as he could, and Count Beust, seeking to conciliate both Paris and Vienna, had showed no sign of opposing them. The Hungarians had, on the contrary, made almost unconditional objections.

"When Germany is threatened with fresh invasions from Prussia," they had said, "it will be time enough for us to meddle with the affair."

They had declared as much to M. de Gramont; and so to-day they assert that if Count Beust had only spoken as decidedly, Europe would not be in the throes of war.

Count Beust was clearly seeking to defend himself against this reproach. According to him, the war had been a mere piece of insanity. Doubtless the Emperor, the army, Austria even, wished to have their revenge, but they did not want it quite so soon. The country saw its material prosperity in process of rebirth.

"We are beginning to have more ease; buildings are rising from the ground, as you see," said Count Beust, "but our finances still need time to re-establish themselves. Our army is being reorganized; we too, like the Prussians, will be able to have a million soldiers; but we have not completed our reorganization, and if our first line army is complete and in being, the army that is to be made up of our whole people is not yet in existence. For all these things time is essential. I have at various times said so to M. de Gramont: I was of opinion that he had understood that this country could not be an effective ally for some years. It seems that M. de Gramont announced that we would mobilize a hundred and fifty thousand men towards the Silesian frontier. If we had done so, what difficulties we should have had with Hungary and Russia! As soon as we disclosed our feelings in the matter, the Russians said: "If you intervene, you will oblige us to intervene as well, and that will not be the way to help France. Leave it to us, and we will bring our influence to bear upon the King of Prussia."

Coming back to the origin of the war, Count Beust satirically cited this instance of Bonapartist infatuation:

"Imagine," said he, "that at the very moment when we heard the news that war was declared, the French Government asked us to inquire and to inform them without delay whether the declaration had arrived in Berlin, for, they asserted, they were ready to invade Germany on the same day. A fortnight later, not a shot had been fired! Hearing you reiterate that you were ready, we counted upon immediate and decisive action. The Prussian press always said that in such a war they must expect reverses at the outset, but that by persevering they would triumph. Judge our astonishment, then!"

Count Beust then spoke of every one's amazement at the news of our earliest reverses: the Hungarians, though full of sympathy for us, less than ever disposed to intervene; then among the Austro-Germans those who were favourable to us losing confidence in us, and those who had not already avowed their preference for the Prussians no longer hiding it, since they could explain it by a certain pride of kinship; nearly all the Press, won over by Count Bismarck, and the Court itself, whose wishes and sympathies were with us, no longer, in prudence, venturing to do anything that might bring the storm upon Austria.

What Count Beust did not say, is that, after having begun to take up arms, they turned again to lay them down. They have bought, in the meantime, about thirty thousand horses for the cavalry; more for the artillery; the army has been brought out of the wretched condition imposed upon it by the necessities of the budget; but they dare not make any use of it for fear of the Prussians and the Russians. While the English, thinking themselves sheltered from the storm, because they look on it from the shore, wish to keep out of war, the Austrians on the contrary clearly see the danger that threatens Europe, but they fear they will bring it on themselves if they intervene to lay it. That is what makes this a very delicate question to treat of with them. I only touched the subject therefore with the greatest circumspection and without dwelling upon it, when Count Beust broached it himself.

"We feel this danger," said he; "but what can we do? It is all in the hands of Russia."

"The Hungarians being for us and the Austro-Germans against us," I answered, "would it not be difficult for you, even if the Russians showed the example, to adopt a decided attitude in our favour?"

"We will not be behind them," replied Count Beust. "I am very much attacked at the moment, but when I propose that Austria shall do something that is her plain duty to herself, I do not doubt that I shall be listened to."

He then went on to insist that Italy should take sides with us; he thought that this, by making the Prussians uneasy as to the disposition of other neutrals, would give the latter more weight. He came back to this several times. With regard to the Republic, he said the apprehensions of Austria were now somewhat allayed.

I arranged with him to stop at Vienna on my way back from Russia. I begged him to lay my homage at the feet of the Emperor, from whom I shall request the honour of an audience on my return.

" You must come back," said Count Beust, " to let us know what the Russians mean to do ; we shall then be in a better position to bring into line with them the conduct you look for from us."

Immediately after my interview with Count Beust I saw Count Andrässy.

Count Andrässy is a man of some fifty years, tall, with a face full of character and a piercing eye. My first impression of him was a favourable one.

From the first, with him as with all the others I have conversed with, I spoke of the misfortunes of our country.

" What an unforeseen course of events!" he said. " Who would have believed that such reverses could come on the French army, always so heroic, even at this moment still heroic!"

After these signs of interest on his part, I explained the reason of our reverses in the field, which I wished very much to make clear, especially to one to whom, as a Hungarian, affairs of war certainly came home more than to anybody else.

Count Andrässy then desired to prove to me at once that he had not been implicated in the intrigue that had helped to bring the war about. What he said, which was slightly inclined to accuse Count Beust, though without mentioning him by name, was specially aimed at Metternich and M. de Gramont.

"For a long time," he said, "I watched certain tendencies appearing among us. Those who dreamed of taking revenge for Prussia's success were numerous (Andrässy never named or indicated the Emperor). I did not blame this feeling, but I fought against it.

"I have always maintained that we were not a German nation, but a European nation placed upon the borders of all nationalities and composed of all; that we must not adopt a policy of rancour, but one of equilibrium, in a word, of common interest, and only to intervene when the interests of Europe absolutely demanded it; that this was my own deliberate opinion and that of all my Hungarian fellow-citizens. On every occasion when I have seen the idea of war for the sake of war beginning to peep out, I have fought against it, and I have had to fight against it in Count Beust himself (an allusion to the latter's hatred of Bismarck). When I saw that M. de Gramont was being egged on, I resisted, though the best way to gratify him was to decry Prussia and to declare that we must before long make war on her.

"For my own part, I explained myself very freely and fully to M. de Gramont. I told him I had two motives for putting off the war, which might perhaps one day be unavoidable; the first, to give Austria time to re-establish herself; the second, to wait till we had right on our side against Prussia.

"As for the first of these motives, I maintained that for some years Austria would not have either her forces or her finances in a proper state of preparedness. 'Austria,' said I, 'is an ally whom you cannot do without, of whom you will have the very greatest need, but who will be of no service to you whatever if you involve her too soon.' As to being in the right, that is of no less importance. The Hungarian people does not wish to serve mere hatred, but the moment will come when Prussia will put herself in the wrong; she will put out her hand to

Baden, Würtemberg, Bavaria. Then all our Austro-Germans will be justly angry, our Hungarians will have an interest in supporting them, all Europe will approve our action, and Austria-Hungary joined with France will be at once and completely victorious."

Count Andrässy thus set forth precisely the policy I have always upheld. Then continuing:

"I said to M. de Gramont: 'Do not be deluded; whoever promises you the support of Austria is deceiving you. Your Government should know this and must not be ready to count on this support; it will be found wanting.' We must not then be accused of deserting you, for we have promised nothing. And if certain persons at Vienna have spoken otherwise, they were wrong to do so. In any case, after what I have said, there can be no further illusion. I quite suspect that Metternich, whose career is ended, did not tell the whole truth at the Court of the Tuileries, but he will have to bear the penalty, and that Court with him.

"M. de Gramont's conduct was no surprise to me. It was calculated to please his Government, and even before your visit, my dear M. Thiers, I conceived affairs to be as you have explained them to me."

So much said, we considered the actual situation.

"We are not in a position to make war," said Count Andrässy. "We are, however, prepared to some extent, but that would not be enough: far from it. The Austro-Germans have yielded to the glamour of success, a certain number of them, at any rate. They are divided. Our Hungarian compatriots are not: they all deplore the misfortunes of France; but what can be done?"

I then came back to the idea of not lagging behind Russia, if Russia declared herself.

"Yes," said Count Andrässy, "if Russia declares herself, we shall not leave her to stand alone; but she cares no more for, the idea of co-operating with us than we with her; if she speaks in the name of European interests, we will speak too. You have excellent chances of winning a hearing. All Europe honours your conduct and your political acumen. Your country could not do better than make you its representative. You did not follow your Government in its policy of barren and disloyal agitation with regard to the Poles. That is to your credit. The Russian nation is friendly to France, and if this feeling triumphs over the Emperor's weakness for his uncle you will obtain something from Russia. We shall follow her lead, without, of course, committing ourselves to war, but we will show that we still count for something in the world. Visit us here on your return; we shall receive you as a friend and as a great patriot."

I then took leave of Count Andrässy, and at half-past eight on the same evening, September 24th, I set out for Saint Petersburg.

On the 25th, from Oderberg to Cracow we skirted Prussian territory—a beautiful country, and well cultivated, as long as we were in Silesia. Entering Poland, wooded sand dunes appear in wide plains to the horizon. Arrived in Warsaw on the 25th at evening. At the station a silent, sympathetic crowd, all with heads uncovered. Deep interest among the Poles and Russians for France; the first time the two populations are united in sympathy.

In spite of very great fatigue, we gave up the idea

A DIPLOMATIC JOURNEY

of sleeping in Warsaw, so that we might reach Saint Petersburg on Tuesday morning instead of Tuesday night.

The whole night of Sunday the 25th and all day on the 26th we spent travelling. Tuesday the 27th, in the morning, in delicious weather, hardly even chilly, I arrive in Saint Petersburg, having journeyed day and night without a break except in Vienna, where I spent twenty hours. I find M. de Gabriac at the station. He tells me that Prince Gortchakow thinks I must be too tired to go to see him, but that he is at my service. I send him word that I will be with him at two o'clock, at Tsarkoé Sélo.

At the hour indicated, I presented myself at Prince Gortchakow's house. He lives in a pavilion of the palace, with only a door to pass in order to be with the Emperor. I had known the Chancellor before, when he was simply the Minister at Stuttgard. He was then lean, modest, reserved. I found him now full of health, confident, having acquired the habit of domination since he had held Europe in check in the deplorable Polish business, so imprudently stirred up by the broken dynasty; he had grown ripe, in a word, with long years of uninterrupted and successful power. I have never had a more cordial reception. My accurate foresight of the course of events, my opposition to the war were assets the value of which in the eyes of foreign Courts I could now perceive.

The Prince told me he had shut his doors to everybody, that the Emperor was hunting, and that he could devote himself to me.

Once again, as in London and in Vienna, I began my recital of what had occurred, in order to prove that it was not France on whom lay the guilt of the war.

He listened attentively, and I touched upon the events of 1866 in recounting the mistakes made by the Empire.

"Allow me," he said, "to add something to your narrative. In 1866, when I perceived that the Germanic Confederacy was about to be left to perish, I wrote to Paris that, as guarantors of the constitution of this Confederacy, we were prepared to denounce those who should take up arms to destroy it; and the only reply was blank silence."

I remembered the blunder, which was partly Baron Budberg's, for at that moment he had to some extent shared in the mistakes of the Court of the Tuileries.

From those responsible for the war we passed to the question that was preoccupying every one in Russia —the question of the Republic. Prince Gortchakow, who has the sagacious and lofty mind of a true statesman, and who likes to show himself free from prejudices, avowed to me that the Republic caused him no apprehension and that he knew of good republics.

"Yes," said I, "it is a republic that is your best friend to-day, and perhaps there will soon be two of them in your affection: at least that is my wish."

He replied, smiling:

"I should greatly wish it; but here we ask whether with you the Republic is a really serious thing, and you cannot assure us that it will exist for long."

The Russian Chancellor seemed to be specially preoccupied by the elements of instability in any relations that might be entered upon with the French Government. I repeated then to the Prince that this Government, born of necessity, was not the triumph of one party over another, and if it did not satisfy all, it was the despair of none. Besides, for the greater part it was made up of clever and moderate men.

Hereupon the Prince declared that he found what M. Jules Favre said and did most satisfactory. But he repeated once more:

"Negotiating with this Government, can we hope to achieve something solid? How long will it exist?"

"The Government is sincere," I replied, "and I affirm that the next elections will place the reins of government in moderate hands. Treating with us to-day, then, you may rest assured that our agreements would stand; and if it should happen one day that I should no longer be your interlocutor, you would find in my successor the same way of thinking."

"Ah! if it were you!" exclaimed the Prince. "But it will be you; I like to hope so."

He told me then that our reverses had greatly astonished Europe and distressed those who could not without grave disquiet view the portentous aggrandizement of Prussia. It is feared that France, heretofore so great, may never again be capable of any manifestation of energy.

I immediately gave him, with regard to our armies and the most recent military operations, the details necessary to explain our reverses and to convince him that France, as soon as she should be wisely ruled, would recover her place in Europe. I then cited the army of Metz, and he agreed with me that where the soldiers have been well led they have displayed all their ancient quality.

The true facts with regard to our political and

military position having been established, I entered upon the examination of our present difficulties. I told the Chancellor that it would be very fitting for Russia to put herself at the head of the Powers to arrest Prussia's ever-increasing ambition, that Russia's lead would be followed by all the neutral countries, and that without the necessity of having recourse to war this unanimous and determined attitude would be enough to preserve the balance of Europe.

"Let your Sovereign," I said, "but speak for us with an insistence that means his determination to be heeded."

"Menaces!" cried the Prince, "the Emperor will employ none. When one makes a threat, one must be ready to strike the blow. Our ideas do not move that way! Already the Emperor has spoken on your behalf; he will speak again, even though he has already gone as far as possible on this path. It is to him you owe the Ferrières interview and the admission of the idea of an armistice."

Here the Prince was mistaken, for it was England who at my instance had asked and obtained for M. Jules Favre an interview with Count Bismarck.

Prince Gortchakow added that there were two versions of this interview: that of M. Jules Favre and that of Count Bismarck; that he did not take the latter's account for gospel; but that if only Strassburg, Toul, and Verdun had been asked for as hostages, and no mention of Metz or Mont-Valérien, he regretted that the proposal had not been accepted, since it was a way of gaining time, and perhaps of appealing to a congress, which might have been the salvation of France and of Europe.

A DIPLOMATIC JOURNEY

I replied that, like him, I did in fact regret the rejection of the armistice, but that I explained it to myself by the bitterness of having to give up Strassburg at the moment when it was defending itself so magnificently, and also by the twistings and turnings of Count Bismarck.

"Yes," replied the Chancellor, "that is possible, and I fully understand; but I regret it. Now you are both of you out of your reckoning."

Now to get more closely to work with him, I spoke of an alliance. I said that I was fully empowered to propose it; that both in the present and for the future we retained enough strength and wealth to make us such an ally as could not be met with twice, an ally most of all against Germany, now so nearly formidable, and I set forth the picture of Europe on the morrow.

"We have always been promised this alliance," he replied; "General Fleury spoke to us of it constantly, and we never saw it come to pass. But I believe you, I know you are a man of your word; however, to-day is not the moment to conclude it. Later we will take measures for uniting France with Russia; for the moment, let us consider the question of how to save her from the evil case in which she finds herself."

"But," I insisted, "time presses, and brooks no delay. To save her an immediate effort is needed, and if you were boldly to take the lead, Austria, England, and Italy, who only need the encouragement of your example, would follow you, and in the face of a Europe inspired by you Prussia would show herself much more moderate."

"Ah, collective action, collective action!" exclaimed the Prince. "I understand you, but we don't wish for that. It would only serve to irritate Prussia, which does not admit of the intervention of neutrals in the present war, and we should lose the very real influence we enjoy at Berlin."

Still I insisted very warmly. Our conversation had lasted more than two hours, and we deferred it until another day.

"You are here," said the Prince; "we shall await the development of events; for till they are more in relief it is impossible to do anything effective. You will see the Emperor. To-morrow I shall ask him for a day and an hour. You and I, we are both much of an age; but you are the more vigorous, and I am sure that you would find it agreeable to go over the palace. Give me your arm and let us go round."

For more than an hour the Prince showed me the splendours of Tsarkoé Sélo, and talked to me of his master's character and the might of Russia. I took leave of him overwhelmed by his friendly behaviour.

Wednesday, the 28th.—While awaiting my audience with the Emperor, which has been appointed for to-morrow, I am to visit the Hermitage. During the day we hear of the capitulation of Strassburg.

On Thursday the Emperor, who had come to Saint Petersburg, received me in the Winter Palace. As soon as I entered, he gave me his hand, saying he was delighted to receive me in his Empire, and made me sit beside him.

The Emperor, who is simple and natural in manner, and expresses himself with ease in French, led me at once to the matter that brought me to Russia.

"M. Thiers," he said, "if we had been listened to, if you yourself had been listened to, we would not be in the presence of this terrible war that is rending

A DIPLOMATIC JOURNEY

and horrifying Europe. I have had recounted to me your explanations of the origins of this war: they interested me very profoundly."

He then invited me to lay before him freely everything I might think useful for him to know.

Not having to tell him who were the real authors of the war, I explained to him how the present Government was formed, and I was advised that details on this point would be valuable.

The Emperor listened attentively, and when I had said that this Government, born of necessity, was the only possible one, that it was moderate, and that it would become more moderate still if it were supported, he replied:

"As for myself, I have no objection to make to a republican form of government. And that too does not concern me, and concerns only France. I only fear men given to disorder, and most of all, the instability that is so little of an inducement to treat with a Government."

To reassure him with regard to this danger of instability, I repeated what I had already told Prince Gortchakow: that the coming elections would most certainly give a majority of moderates, and that, even if modifications were to take place later in the Government, these modifications would involve no change in its policy.

"So you have no uneasiness about the maintenance of order?" asked the Emperor.

"No, sire; and the proof that my confidence is justified is the calm that rules in Paris, in very grave circumstances."

"So much the better," went on the Emperor; "but now, let us come to the situation at the moment."

I enumerated then the various enterprises of Prussia, from the despoiling of Denmark to her intentions, now boldly announced, of dismembering France, and I asked His Majesty if he could without perturbation see arising in the centre of the continent in the place of the old peace-loving Germany a conquering Power extending from the Sound to the Danube, even to the Inn; for she would not respect Denmark for long, would presently reduce Bavaria, Würtemberg, and the Duchy of Baden to the same condition as Saxony, and would thus unite forty millions and more under the sceptre of a Germanic Emperor, who would certainly be proclaimed before many months had passed.

Only touching very delicately on the danger that might threaten the Russian Baltic provinces, and on Prussian aims with regard to the German provinces of Austria, I asked the Emperor if, in order to arrest such an overflowing ambition, he would not consider it prudent to oppose the action contemplated against France, and thus to make a faithful ally of this France, which under a good Government would speedily recover all her former might.

His Majesty having listened seriously, interrupted me with some emotion:

"I know, M. Thiers, how grave a matter for Europe, and for my Empire, is the creation of such a power as you describe. I should most gladly obtain such an alliance with France, an alliance for peace, not for war and conquest" (and the Emperor emphasized these last words). "Show me the way to help you; I shall gladly adopt it. Already I have intervened, and with warmth; I intervened spontaneously, and before you had invoked my good offices; I have spoken with no uncertain voice, believe me. I will do so again; but

I can neither go so far as war, nor the threats that lead to war; for above everything my duty is to my own country. Like you, I am convinced of the need of peace, and a peace that France can accept, and Europe can ratify. I have said this, and will say it again; in a word, I shall do everything that lies in my power; but as for war, you must not ask it of me."

I hastened to reply that I asked not for war, but for good offices, effective in the interest of all Europe; good offices that in no way could make Prussia decide to run the risks of another war, most of all with such a Power as Russia.

"I have given my word," said the Emperor; "you may rely upon it."

He was visibly moved, and I had come to the point that must not be overpassed. Besides, the Emperor was on the point of setting out for Tsarkoé Sélo. He took leave of me with the same cordiality as he had shown at the beginning of the interview.

Scarcely had I returned when Prince Gortchakow arrived to call on Mme. Thiers, and to find out my impressions.

"What did you think of my Emperor?"

"As the best and most upright of men, and I believe I should become friendlier to the idea of personal government if I was called on to serve such a man."

The Chancellor's face beamed at this praise of his master. He then wished to know if I was satisfied.

"I am, most assuredly; but I have a great deal to say in answer to the Emperor's remarks upon the subject of war. It is not war I ask for, merely firm and clear language on the part of the neutral Powers.

"I am always told that they have spoken, that

they will speak again; but something more effective is wanted."

"What?" replied the Prince. "War?—we cannot make war."

"Then Europe is going to emulate France's behaviour in 1866."

"Not quite; for in 1866 a word would have been enough to stop Prussia, and to-day it would need a great war."

"No," I rejoined; "if the whole of Europe spoke out definitely, even without threats, she would influence the behaviour of Prussia."

"Prussia has no intention of paying any heed to neutrals," replied the Prince. "She would only give way before neutrals if they were in arms, and they will not go so far as that. Nothing now can be of any avail but what we say as a friendly Power, from which she cannot refuse a recommendation or a word of advice. We shall strongly condemn and reprove, and we shall beforehand invalidate any peace that might be imposed on unjust terms, and that, we think, is no little thing."

Always accepting what was promised me, I tried to get some explanation from the Prince with regard to Austrian affairs. I asked why he was opposed to the armaments of this Power.

"You do not wish to take action," I said, "but at least do not prevent others from doing so. Why do you stand against Austria's arming herself? By this you are in reality allying yourselves with Prussia against us. I understand that when he might have feared the entry of the French into Berlin, the nephew might well have come to his uncle's assistance. But to-day it is Paris that is threatened; it is, then, the time to turn your shield, to leave Austria free to succour Paris. You say at heart you are our allies, but your behaviour contradicts your words!"

"You are touching," replied Prince Gortchakow, "upon one of the most delicate of subjects, one of the hardest to approach. . . . It involves a pledge of the Emperor's with which we must not clash. Let us leave the subject, I beg you; it is impossible to handle it profitably at this moment. Besides, we are not depriving you of anything. When the Austrians make out that we are keeping them from arming, by ourselves threatening to arm, it is merely a pretext, for under no circumstances would they arm."

"Well, then," I replied, "leave them free; in this way you will confound them." And, carrying audacity still further, I added, "If I were Chancellor of Austria, I would not trouble in the matter; I should arm, and defy you to make war on me!"

Embarrassed, the Prince confined himself to replying that that would depend on the frontier towards which the Austrian mobilization might be directed.

This reply convinced me that the veto of Russia was simply admonitory, and that if the Austrians were to disregard it they would be in no danger. Afterwards the Prince complained bitterly of Count Beust's inconsistency, and allowed me to perceive very keen feelings of resentment, which went back to the Crimean War and the refusal to heed him at that time.

Leaving this delicate subject, I led him to speak to me of the Italians. He assured me, in very precise language, that they might do all they had a mind to without any opposition from Russia.

"Ah! if you had the smallest success," the Prince continued, "how everything would arrange itself. Do not go away; you would seem to be dissatisfied, and that would be tactless. Besides, Petersburg is well worth seeing. As for myself, I live in Tsarkoé Sélo; you will find me there when you please. Come to see me, and we shall in this way be always in a position to seize the opportunity if circumstances give birth to one."

Next day, September 30th, I spent the morning at the Hermitage and the afternoon at Tsarkoé Sélo, where we had afterwards a very interesting evening with the highest personages in Russia. On Saturday, October 1st, I dined at Tsarkoé Sélo with M. de Gabriac.

Sunday, October 2nd.—I went back at nine o'clock in the morning to Tsarkoé Sélo. I had an appointment with the Heir-Apparent at half-past ten, and with the Grand Duke Constantine at one.

When I arrived, I was brought into the presence of His Imperial Highness. The young Prince came to me holding out his hand, and with an air of complete sincerity expressed his pleasure in seeing me, a feeling on which I had counted, for I knew that the Prince was wholly French in sympathy.

He is a handsome, manly young man, intelligent and resolute. I spoke to him quite frankly. When I told him that my urgent representations were met with the fear of war, and that I did not admit that Russia, by speaking out with a proper firmness, would expose herself to war:

"War," he answered proudly, "I should be glad to know who would dare to make war on us! For my own part, I should not hesitate to communicate our opinion to Prussia, and I am certain that without declaring war on her I should oblige her to heed it."

The Prince promised to repeat to his father what I had just said, allowing modestly that he had very little influence because of his youth.

As I was leaving the Prince's quarters, a chamberlain came to inform me that the Tsarina would like to see me, and would receive me next day, Monday.

The hour of my rendezvous with the Grand Duke Constantine having arrived, I went to the Paulowski Palace, where he lives. After a few minutes' waiting in a library that might almost have been French, I was brought in to him.

He made me be seated, told me that he had time at my disposal, and at once led me to speak of the principal aim of my mission.

I insisted then, more than when with the Tsarevitch, on the necessity of paying for an alliance with France by an immediate service.

The Prince did not contradict me. "The whole of Russia," said he, "is full of sympathy for you and of the opposite feeling for Prussia. We must not forget, however, what is the prevailing trend of ideas to-day among us. We think we should dream, not of aggrandizing the Empire, but of civilizing it, and I have come to the conclusion, in the exercise of my duties in the State, that under this head there is an immense amount of work to be done. Much has been done already: the serfs have been given their liberty, we are busy with railways, and all these things involve heavy expenses. At the moment, a war would be a total interruption of this policy, and all men of intelligence would be profoundly affected."

Taking me by the hand, the Prince added: "I have

very little influence in affairs. In the Imperial Council over which I preside we only deal with legislation, and the Emperor does not allow us to go beyond our prescribed functions; but I can speak of any subject with Prince Gortchakow, and I shall not fail to bring before him what you have just said."

In my last interview with the Chancellor, I had seen that he was troubled over the silence of the Court at Berlin, which had made no answer to his last instances on behalf of peace. Our common friend, M. de Jomini, had already said to me:

"You have no idea to what lengths we have gone, and we have no answer!"

Before returning to Saint Petersburg, I accordingly determined to call on Prince Gortchakow. He came to me eagerly, and as though he had good news for me. He seemed, so to speak, almost gay.

"We have heard from Berlin," said he. "They are beginning to feel the burden of the war, and would not be displeased to bring it to an end. We must seize this opportunity to make peace."

The Prince was completely changed, radiant with hope. On the advice he had given me, and relying on the protestations of regard addressed to me on every side, I proposed to him that he should ask the Emperor to mediate.

"Do not speak of that," he hastened to reply. "Our Emperor is too modest to allow himself to be tempted by the greatness of such a part beyond the bounds within which he wishes to remain; but we shall be your intermediaries, without so much ceremony, and we will do our very best in the matter. You will bring your Government to reason, we the Prussians, and we shall in the end bring them together."

A DIPLOMATIC JOURNEY

"I cannot attempt anything from here," I said. "First I would have to communicate with the Government of Paris and know definitely what I can propose."

"Yes, most assuredly," replied the Prince. "This is what must be done: the Emperor himself will ask for safe-conducts for you, and then everything will go smoothly. We shall make the peace by our own two selves!"

The Chancellor appeared delighted with this idea. The project, however advantageous it might be for us, since the negotiations would be opened by Russia, none the less called for ripe reflection. I said, therefore, to the Prince:

"I always like to sleep on my resolutions, and I ask you to allow me to put off my answer until to-morrow. I shall come back, and we will examine the whole matter closely."

"You are right," said he.

He shook hands with extreme satisfaction, and I came away.

Next day, Monday, as had been agreed, I went again to Tsarkoé Sélo to pay my visit to the Tsarina, and was presented to the young Danish princess destined one day to be Empress of Russia.

Seeing her so gentle, so agreeable, with a shyness full of grace, and comparing her with her husband, I was struck by the contrast shown in this union of weakness and strength. She thanked me for my efforts on behalf of Denmark in 1866, reminded me that her brother, then in Paris, had come to see me, expressed good wishes for France, and gave me an incommunicable impression of goodness and charm.

I arrived at Prince Gortchakow's at half-past two,

and stayed until half-past five. I found him alone, still very cordial, but not so happy as the day before. He had in his hand a packet of dispatches from London and Tours, and said to me:

"Come, let us read them together."

He reads very well, in a clear, strong voice, with a pleasant Russian accent. He read first of all one from Baron Brunnow.

"It is excellent for me," I said to him, "but really one might imagine it an English voice."

"You are right," he answered.

Baron Brunnow approved England's inaction, and thought Russia should imitate her. Then came two telegrams from Tours—from M. Okouneff, friendly but grave: Paris could not, he said, defend herself, and Tours presented an aspect of hopeless disorganization.

"Well," I said, "all these people make me think of a coterie deaf to any way of thinking but their own, and falsifying everything. These two Russian ministers are certainly not malign, but they have accustomed themselves to view French affairs from the dark side, and they paint everything black. There is, alas! only too much that is black in our affairs, but there are also brighter hues in the picture, and to my mind here is a proof that it is most difficult for a prime minister to have precise information if he does not continually test and rectify the reports of his agents."

"Without doubt," replied the Prince; "we should always mistrust those who send us reports in writing."

At length we came to our business of the day before.

"I have considered everything you said to me yesterday," said I, "and I understood that your latest news from Berlin seemed more satisfactory to you. Would it be indiscreet to ask you whence and from whom it reached you, and if it would be possible for me to have it *in extenso*?"

The Prince answered with some embarrassment.

"It must suffice you to know that this news, which is beyond suspicion, establishes the fact that in Berlin there is felt the need of putting an end to the war; and it would be well to bring about fresh negotiations as a result of this excellent disposition. I should be glad if you, who are a sensible man and a patriot, should have the honour of raising your country out of the abyss into which she has been cast. I confess that I have forebodings. I distrust fortune, and above all I distrust the Prussians. It would be better to bring the business to an end at once than to expose yourselves to fresh reverses, which your enemy would cruelly abuse. The Prussians want to keep Strassburg and Metz—that is to say, Alsace and Lorraine. By taking advantage of this opportunity you might perhaps save Lorraine. The more you hold out the more you will increase your losses. It would, then, be better to give way now. This would only be a sacrifice which might be merely temporary, and from which you may one day recover, if the opportunity should arise for seizing back what you had lost."

These things, though said in a friendly way, were bitter to hear.

"Prince," I said, "these are sacrifices too cruel to be endured. It is possible that it might become necessary to resign ourselves to them, but we must first of all know the true condition of affairs, which I cannot believe to be as desperate as you think. In any case, it would be essential to judge for oneself, on the actual spot, and to know also the opinion of those who are responsible and in whom is vested the burden and the power of deciding.

"As for me, I had the fullest powers in the case of a real, immediate co-operation, which would have entailed the making of engagements; but I have no powers whatever to treat of peace."

"That," said the Chancellor, "is why yesterday we both were of opinion that you ought to go to Versailles."

Here he rose, and moving to his desk he read a paper written with his own hand. It was a telegram from the Emperor to the King of Prussia asking for safe-conducts for me. I give it from memory, since Prince Gortchakow was unwilling that I should take a copy.

Here is the gist of it: "M. Thiers is here. He is both wise and moderate; he alone can get France to make the concessions necessary for peace. Send him safe-conducts."

I objected to this wording.

"To begin with," I said, "you give me the rôle of negotiator for peace, a rôle that has not been assigned to me, and further, I seem to admit that my countrymen are wrong not to be willing to make concessions. Now what are the concessions they refused? The surrender of Alsace and Lorraine? Well, I am with them there; we need not speak of it. Present me merely as what I am, as a man of common sense, who having seen the internal condition of his country and knowing the feeling of Europe, might perhaps find a way of bringing both sides together, if he were authorized to enter Paris and to leave again."

"Very well," said the Prince, "but the object of

your entry and your leaving must be expressly stated, and this object can only be peace."

I consented to this, provided it should be clearly understood that I was not taking on myself the quality of negotiator of peace, which I was in no way entitled to; that the telegram asking for safe-conducts for me should be held back until the word should come from me; that, if when I reached Tours I found the Délégation disposed to reopen negotiations, if I thought it would be desirable to confer with M. Jules Favre and his colleagues shut up in Paris, I could then give the signal agreed on, and the telegram would be dispatched, and that if the safe-conducts were sent, I should use them to go immediately to Paris.

The impression I had from these long days of conversations was that the Chancellor desired peace, that his sovereign desired it no less than he did, and that they would both exert every effort to obtain moderate conditions for us. They wished to serve us, in compliance with the feeling in Russia, without giving up their friendly relations with Prussia, because of engagements we knew of, and perhaps others of which we knew nothing.

Next morning, October 4th, we started for Vienna. As we were very tired, we stopped at Warsaw on the 6th. During the day visited the Château de Villanof, which had belonged to Sobieski. On the 7th we go on our way for Vienna, where we arrive at daybreak on the 8th. Again I saw Counts Beust, Andrássy, and Potocki, and on the Sunday I was received by the Emperor Francis Joseph.

The Emperor greeted me very kindly; he expressed his grief for France's misfortunes, and his desire to be able to help us. I had not seen him since 1863. I found him grown thin, aged, profoundly sad. It appears that he is eaten up with cares. The triumphs of Prussia and the dislocation of the monarchy plunge him in despair.

I then saw Count Beust and Count Andrássy. They told me again that, in the present divided mind of the country, Austria could not adopt a strong unanimous attitude in our favour; and that on the other hand her preparations are too inadequate for her to expose herself to reprisals from Prussia and the attacks of Russia by declaring war. And so Count Beust would have the Italians be first to take action, and he is urging them to do so.

"Our territory shields them," he said, "as far as Switzerland. To enter their country ours would have to be crossed. We are, then, their allies of necessity, and I should be glad if an attempt was made to fall upon them, for war would be declared in fact, without my having to declare it myself. The intervention of Italy is the only way to make the war universal. If it becomes universal, you are saved."

He furnished me then with arguments to draw in the Italians.

We agreed that he should preserve his attitude in favour of common action; and if the English, forced by Parliament, found that nothing but such action was possible, perhaps the Russians in the end would join in it. In the meantime, we would take advantage of whatever the latter might do by themselves, and Count Beust does not deny that this may have excellent results, especially in case of a success under the walls of Paris.

We asked each other also why the Russians show

themselves so strongly opposed to any collective action on the part of neutrals. Count Potocki and Count Andrässy believe, perhaps rightly, in a secret agreement in virtue of which Russia, in order to settle the Eastern question to her own advantage, may have ensured the concurrence of Prussia by guaranteeing them against such collective action.

Count Andrässy then asked me if we had taken any engagements with the Russians.

"I could understand it," he said, "for in your dangerous situation you would be within your right; but for us the union of France and Russia in the East would be our ruin."

I answered that in Saint Petersburg I had been given the most positive assurances of an active intervention in favour of France, whose engagements with regard to Russia would be subordinated to the effectiveness of this intervention.

To sum up, Austria, best of all disposed toward us, is impotent, England thinks she has no interest in taking our side, and Russia is held back by her engagements to Prussia. The Italians are left; I shall see what they can do.

Wednesday, October 11*th.* — I leave Vienna for Florence, and arrive in the evening of Wednesday the 12th. . . . Great crowd in the station. Marked signs of sympathy. Long conversation with M. Senard, our Envoy Extraordinary at Florence. He thinks I shall not be able to obtain anything. I share his fears, without giving up my intention to make a supreme effort.

Thursday, October 13*th.*—In the morning, my first interview with Marquis Visconti-Venosta. The same day, at four o'clock, a long conversation with the King, who during my stay at Saint Petersburg had sent me an invitation to come to see him.

After depicting the situation exactly, I spoke to him, modifying it a little to make it more acceptable, of the military operation which the Government of Tours had, in its letters, charged me to propose to him. This intervention seemed to attract him, and perhaps if he were free he would attempt it; but he fell back upon his Ministers and the Parliament. I asked him to bring me into contact with his Ministers and a representative of the Army. He consented, and sent for General Cialdini, who is at the moment the most highly esteemed general in Italy.

Saturday, October 15th.—Conference at the house of Marquis Visconti-Venosta, the Foreign Minister, with Signors Lanza, the President of the Council, Sella, the Minister of Finance, Ricotti, Minister of War, General Cialdini, M. Senard, and myself.

I made the greatest efforts to convince them, without succeeding, their decision being made beforehand. To begin with, I reassured them with regard to their fear of pressure from outside, for I had it from Prince Gortchakow that he would not oppose the arming of Italy. As for Austria, I know from Count Beust that she would view this arming with feelings of satisfaction, and that besides, the Austrian states completely enveloping Italy, they would be a protection to her, and she would thus be sheltered from any danger of attack. The prudent and supposed wise counsels from London and Saint Petersburg were then concerned with dangers of which Italy could not speak seriously. To the objection raised on the grounds of expense, I took it upon me to reply by the offer of a subsidy, an offer I was convinced would not be repudiated.

A DIPLOMATIC JOURNEY 55

As for the danger of a conflict with the Prussians, I said there was no question of their going to face them on the plains of Champagne. Out of the two hundred and ninety thousand Italian troops, highly organized, according to the very positive details given by our military attaché, only one hundred thousand would be detached. From Turin to Chambéry the Italians and the French are in a regular granite trench, sheltered from any attack. From Chambéry to Lyons, where they would find an encampment of fifty thousand French, the Italians would be covered by the fortifications of Lyons, as strong as those of Paris, and the camp of Verona. So far, then, nothing to fear. No one contested this. I added that this army of a hundred and fifty thousand men would have a considerable effect on the Prussians, already wearied by the sieges of Metz and of Paris, and that it might decide them to make an honourable peace with France, who desires it. Supposing that he were to follow the course of the Saône, Victor Emmanuel would be covered by the Saône itself, by the Jura and the neutrality of Switzerland, and advancing towards Haute-Saône, he would find about ten thousand men at Langres, twelve thousand at Besançon, thirty-five thousand at Belfort. Threatening without invading Southern Germany and the army blockading Metz, without risking an encounter he would draw to him a part of the German forces and would in this way relieve Paris or Metz, which might see their sieges raised; and peace would follow, peace that we should owe to the Italians, at no risk to them, for if they were to fall in with too great masses of the enemy (and that would in any case mean that Paris or Metz was freed) they would easily, sheltered by Langres,

Belfort, Besançon and the Saône, regain the impregnable camp of Lyons.

No one made us, M. Senard and myself, anything but the feeblest answers. The most serious was that it would be going too far to take steps without the Parliament, which could not be got together before a month's time. I replied that the King, taking advantage of his popularity, might presume to take action without waiting for Parliament to meet. But that would involve a change in the Cabinet, for the Ministers of the day have taken neutrality as their political platform, and they are not willing to resign for the sake of France.

I tried to awaken their gratitude, but very circumspectly. "France," I said, "is perishing through having brought about the unity of Italy, which provoked the formation of a united Germany. While helping Italy we reserved Rome for ourselves, for reasons of state, and Italy takes advantage of the moment when we are overwhelmed by our foes to ravish Rome from us. And to crown all, when France asks for help that would save her, from Italy who could give it without risk, Italy refuses!"

I spoke also of the future Will Prussia leave Europe at rest after this war? Who knows whether the unity of Italy can continue without our support? Our only answer was a prodigality of protestations of friendship and of regret that they could not help France.

Sunday, October 16th.—Visits from the Ministers. Fresh conversations. Before writing my report for the Government, I inform M. de Chaudordy of my conversations with the King and his Ministers in a private letter which he will read to the members of the Délégation, without placing in the archives. In this letter I also recommend that General Bourbaki's and General Montauban's offers of service should not be refused. I regret the delay in the elections. I had done everything in order to obtain them; they had been promised and announced everywhere, and if they had taken place Europe would have recognized the Government the very next day.

Tuesday, October 18*th.*—Departure for France. The Minister of Justice and the Minister of Public Works accompanied me to the station with Signor Ratazzi.

Wednesday, October 19*th.*—Reached Suze, Wednesday, 19th. . . . Pass Mont Cenis. . . . We are at Macon at one o'clock in the morning. A special train to Moulins, via Chagny. (I had been telegraphed to from Tours not to come by sea, and not to pass through Nevers, but by Moulins, Montluçon, Poitiers.) The special train cannot go beyond Montchanin.

Thursday, October 20*th.*—Leave Montchanin at halfpast six for Montluçon, by ordinary train. All along the way, the mayors and chief people come to thank me for what I am doing for France. We reach Tours at two in the morning on Friday, October 21st. M. de Chaudordy is waiting for me at the station. Two hours' conversation with him.

Friday, October 21*st.*—Great numbers of visitors: Admiral Fourichon, M. Glais-Bizoin, all the Diplomatic Corps. M. Gambetta and M. de Chaudordy tell me that Lord Lyons came several times to ask what news I was bringing; that the English are preoccupied by the dread of allowing themselves to be forestalled and outstripped by Russia, and that my arrival will decide them to do something very marked. We agree that it is most useful to arouse the feeling of emulation in England. I go to the session of the Government, where MM. Crémieux, Gambetta, Glais-Bizoin are present.

After giving an account of my mission, I set forth the serious question of reopening negotiations, and what was agreed with Prince Gortchakow in the matter. At this point M. de Chaudordy arrives. He reports the contents of a dispatch from the British Cabinet, in which England, on her own initiative, proposes to each of the belligerents an armistice, to enable France to elect and convoke a Constituent Assembly. It is fully established that England has acted of her own accord, not at the instance of France. The Council is almost unanimous in its satisfaction. M. Gambetta holds aloof. M. de Chaudordy says that it is in emulation that England takes the same path as Russia. We proceed to deliberate. It is admitted, without dispute, that the English proposal should be accepted with thanks. But, they said presently, we must certainly accept Russia's proposal too, and not depend solely on England. I read the draft of the telegram I had brought from Russia, which is to be sent by the Emperor Alexander to the King of Prussia, to ask for safe-conducts for me to go to Paris, and from Paris to the Prussian Headquarters, if the Government of Paris thinks fit. The telegram is in these terms:

"M. Thiers has shown himself moderate, and has appeared to appreciate the situation justly. Direct contact with him might perhaps offer the possibility of shortening a struggle whose end you, myself, and Europe equally desire. Would you be disposed, if the appropriate circumstances should come about, to grant him a safe-conduct to enter Paris and to leave it immediately, and thus to create the chance of relations being entered into with your Headquarters?"

Question the first: Should I go first of all to the Prussian Headquarters? No; I must first go to Paris to inform and consult the Government, and, if they are of opinion that I should go to Headquarters, I must go. With the unanimous assent of all four voices, it is decided to telegraph to Saint Petersburg asking for the safe-conducts.

Question the second: According to the English proposal, which is to be the basis of future negotiations, the armistice is meant to facilitate the election of a Constituent Assembly. What is the mind of the Government on this point?

MM. Crémieux, Glais-Bizoin, Fourichon vote formally that this basis be adopted.

"If the whole of France, including Paris, is free to vote, there is no longer any reason for not having recourse to universal suffrage."

M. Gambetta thinks that an Assembly is of no value towards bringing the war to an end. He adds that he will nevertheless fall in with the opinion of his colleagues at Paris and in Tours, if the Government of Paris shares that of the Délégation of Tours, and adopts the proposal to conclude an armistice in order to convoke a Constituent Assembly.

The question of the armistice to permit of the convocation of a Constituent Assembly is put to the vote. It is carried by three voices. M. Gambetta is alone in opposing this convocation. I shall inform the Government of this posture of affairs, if I am able to go to Paris. The conditions of the armistice remain to be examined, but cannot be determined beforehand. There is, however, one that can be fixed on the spot: this is that Paris is to be revictualled! Otherwise, Paris might be taken by armistice. This is received with the liveliest approval on the part of M. Gambetta. Before we separate, it is decided that the minutes of this discussion shall be put in writing and sent to me signed by the members of the Délégation.

At Tours, great agitation of deputies asking to have the elections. Among them M. Grévy is extremely ardent. I try to calm them by announcing that the elections would probably take place speedily, but without disclosing our plan to them. I recommend them to hold together in harmony.

Saturday, October 22nd.—The English having spoken, their proposal is quickly known to the public. I receive a visit from Lord Lyons. He is glad to see that I am supporting the English proposal. I tell him I have from my side worked to the same end, and add, without going into any details, that I had provided myself on my way with the means of success, and that safe-conducts had been asked for me. Lord Lyons thinks that I am the only person to carry through such a negotiation, and says he will telegraph to London and ask, on his side also, for safe-conducts for me. I thank him, and accept.

The evening of the same day I learn that an attack is intended towards Beaugency. I find this unwise; for on the one hand, if we are beaten, we may draw the enemy on Tours, and on the other hand, we are putting ourselves in flagrant discord with a proposal for an armistice. I beg Admiral Fourichon to inform M. Gambetta of my apprehensions. The latter is strongly dissatisfied. He says that in his view the projected negotiations are nothing, and so forth. Then he grows calmer, and assures me that there is no question of engaging in battle between Orléans and Tours.

A DIPLOMATIC JOURNEY

Sunday, October 23rd.—If there was any idea of attacking from the Orléans side, there is none now.

Monday, October 24th.—Meeting at the Archbishop's palace, where the Government sits. M. Gambetta expounds the military situation. I discuss it, and give certain advice. It is recognized that no attack should be made at the present moment, but that we must make a really good army before we think of fighting.

After, on the question of the armistice, we discuss what is to be done if the Prussians ask that the electors of Alsace and of Lorraine will not be called upon. It is agreed that we must oppose such an exclusion; but we must not ourselves raise the difficulty. If we say nothing, we shall in nowise have recognized Prussian pretensions, and their refusal to summon the electors of Alsace and Lorraine will be an act of violence on their part.

In the press something has been said of a peace supposed to be signed by Bazaine. If this is the case, if the truth is that the Marshal has confined himself to stipulating certain peace conditions for France, the examination of these conditions will be referred to the sovereign people.

Tuesday, the 25th.—News is brought to me of the capitulation of Marshal Bazaine.

At half-past eleven I go to the Archbishop's palace to inform the Délégation of this great blow that has fallen upon us. M. Gambetta feels it more terribly than his colleagues, for this capitulation seriously compromises the military situation, for which he claims the responsibility. He is shattered by it.

After futile dissertations on Marshal Bazaine's action, which cannot be properly weighed as long as we do not know the determining circumstances, I read them a letter M. Cochery had just brought me from the Bishop of Orléans, and my reply sent off immediately by the same messenger:

"In this letter," I said, "the Bishop of Orléans has sent me on, from the Prussian Headquarters at Versailles, safe-conducts sent him for me, on behalf of Count Bismarck, by General Baron von der Tann, commanding the Bavarian Army at Orléans. Count Bismarck then would seem to wish to bring me to Versailles before I see the Paris Government; and if it is the case that Count Bismarck has conquered the military element in the person of Marshal Bazaine, perhaps in me he hopes to conquer the civilian element. I have therefore returned these safe-conducts to the bishop, informing him that I could not avail myself of them, and that I was awaiting others which would allow me to go first to Paris to ask the Government to give me the necessary powers to conclude an armistice. It is only when I have been invested with these powers that I will be allowed to go to the Prussian Headquarters at Versailles. It was with this intention that the neutral Powers, and especially Russia, procured these safe-conducts for me."

M. Gambetta, after reading the bishop's letter and my reply, rose and said to me:

"M. Thiers, you are correctness itself; your letter cuts Count Bismarck's ruse at the very root, and he will not be able to derive any advantage from it."

Once more we approach the examination of the military position, so terribly aggravated by the surrender of Metz.

"We had two pivots," said I, "Metz and Paris. Now we have but one, and the defence of Paris has no support. We must create a fresh one with the army of the Loire; but it is a difficult matter, and the month this armistice would give you is more than ever indispensable."

M. Gambetta recognizes this, though it costs him something to do so, for the armistice involves the necessity of convoking the Constituent Assembly.

"You have talked of two armies," I added: "one, the army of the Loire, the other, the army of the East. Doubtless it would be all the better if you could assemble two of sufficient strength, and it could have been done if Victor Emmanuel had sent us a hundred thousand men. But lacking this help, what you can do in the east will be no great matter. Leave at Besançon, Belfort, Langres, and Lyons good garrisons that will hold the enemy busy in sieges, and bring everything that can keep the field to Tours. Bring together in your army of the Loire the many elements of resistance that are held back, in the centre and the north, by the mania of local defence. Make this army strong in numbers and quality, and above all be careful not to split up into several sections the forces you manage to assemble. If you can arrive at a hundred and fifty thousand men, you will then have something the enemy will have to reckon with, and Paris will no longer be destitute of support. Once you have got your army together, take care not to risk it in a battle which you might lose. Put your men into camp, accustom them to face the enemy in skirmishes, never in a general engagement. Furthermore, do not take it on you to move on Paris with flags flying. You must in a fashion steal to Paris. The enemy will not set up a long cordon of investment: but he will make huge entrenched camps round Paris to act as bases for the columns whose task will be to prevent all attempts at provisioning the city. Organize a good spy service. If one of these camps gives the chance, try to seize it. Such a success would open your way to Paris, and you would be able to join hands with the garrison. Outside this way of working, as delicate as it is difficult, there is no chance for anything but disaster. We have still to hear what has become of Marshal Bazaine's army, what freedom of action it has retained, and what can be done with it."

M. Gambetta approves these counsels, calling them invaluable directions, and recognizes that in order to follow them the armistice is indispensable.

"Since that is your opinion," said I, "write it, and I will take your letter to Paris." I insist, and every one insists with me. Impossible to extract a word from M. Gambetta. At length, urged to answer, he says:

"I have written to Paris; I will send you a copy of what I have written."

I go back to my lodging; M. Spuller brings me this copy. It is of no significance whatever.

Wednesday, October 26th.—A great diversity of news about Marshal Bazaine. The established opinion is that he has not yet capitulated, but that he will in the end. The Government sits. M. Gambetta recovers confidence, and sends me a dispatch contradicting the news of the surrender of Metz.

M. Okouneff visits me, to show me a telegram from Prince Gortchakow announcing the assent of the King of Prussia to the Emperor Alexander's request with regard to sending safe-conducts.

"Accordingly," runs the telegram, "M. Thiers has only to ask for the safe-conducts necessary to enable him to go to Paris."

Thursday, October 27th.—M. Okouneff comes to tell

me that the King of Prussia is disposed to grant a satisfactory armistice.

At midnight, M. Cochery arrives from Orléans with the safe-conducts, this time drawn up in terms that permit me to make use of them.

Friday, October 28th.—I set out for Paris, passing through Orléans.

NEGOTIATIONS FOR AN ARMISTICE

Friday, October 28*th*, 1870.—Leave Tours with M. Paul de Rémusat and M. Cochery. We reach Orléans. Most sympathetic reception at the bishop's palace. A visit from General von der Tann. He telegraphs to Versailles in order that the advanced posts may facilitate our entry into Paris.

Saturday, October 29*th.*—We start, in the bishop's own carriage. A young Bavarian officer accompanies us. Everywhere, hideous traces of the war—burned-out villages, torn-up roads. Great difficulty in pursuing our journey. We arrive at Arpajon very late. Dreadful quarters littered with officers and soldiers. We have supper with Prince Wittgenstein, the Russian military attaché in Paris.

Sunday, October 30*th.*—We are on our way well before daybreak. The horses refuse to go farther. We go a long way on foot. At length a gun team is sent to us. We pass through numerous bodies of troops on the march, and get to Versailles at nine o'clock. My fellow-travellers go with the Bavarian officer to the German staff-office. There they meet Count Moltke, who asks if I will not see Count Bismarck. On their report, fearing to annoy the Chancellor by not going to see him, I pay him a visit of a few minutes.

"I must not talk to you except to tell you that I must not talk to you," I said to him.

He approves of my scruples. Count Moltke comes

NEGOTIATIONS FOR AN ARMISTICE

to tell me that all arrangements are made to pass me through the outposts. Count Bismarck walks down the street with me and confirms the news of the capitulation of Metz. An officer, Herr von Winterfeldt, is told off to accompany me. About two o'clock we come to the bridge of Sèvres, the last outpost. Sèvres is deserted. The manufactory is riddled with balls from Mont-Valérien, still firing at this very moment. The Prussian soldiers are behind a barricade built in front of a bridge. We go forward. Numbers of officers surround us, showing every sign of respect. The white flag of truce is waved, and a trumpet sounded. One of these officers, in the uniform of the hussars, goes forward. I shudder to see him expose himself in this way. At length the white flag makes its appearance on the opposite bank. A boat is cast off, and draws near. I cross the Seine. I am announced. The post turns out, and I go to the French Headquarters established in the Bois du Boulogne, in the beautiful house of the Rothschilds. From there to the Foreign Ministry. Arrive at five o'clock. Interviews with MM. Jules Favre and Picard, and General Trochu. My friends arrive: Mignet, Saint-Hilaire, Calmon, Piscatory.

The Government is summoned for ten o'clock at night, at the Foreign Ministry. They assemble there. Present: General Trochu, the President, MM. Jules Favre, Picard, Ferry, Emmanuel Arago, Garnier-Pagès, Jules Simon, Rochefort, General Le Flô, the Minister for War, Adam, the Prefect of Police, and a member whom I do not know.

Nothing definite was known about Metz, and they were ignorant, not merely of the details, but even of the results of my late mission to the principal European Courts.

I tell them for certain that Metz has capitulated, and that the Marshals and a hundred and seventy-three thousand men have been made prisoners. This news fills every one with consternation.

I then announce that England and Russia advise the two belligerent Powers to sign an armistice whose declared object will be the convoking of a National Assembly, in order to invalidate Prussia's contention that she does not know whom she can negotiate with.

As for the military situation, I say that the members of the Government must know how much longer Paris can hold out. As for what concerns the provinces, I know the army of the Loire is eighty thousand strong. From what I am told by the authorities at Tours it will soon be a hundred to a hundred and ten thousand men, who, like the troops in Paris, have taken advantage of the time that has elapsed to train and organize; but could this army, in its present condition, take the field? No one, not even M. Gambetta, ventures to think so. In twenty-five days (if we get them by an armistice), this army, augmented by the forces in the North, and by what could be taken from the East, might perhaps amount to a hundred and fifty thousand men; but it has not the confidence that victory gives. In any case, it would have to deal with a hundred and fifty or two hundred thousand Prussians set free by the capitulation of Metz. I think, therefore, that the provinces might draw off a part of the enemy, without achieving the relief of Paris, and without preventing it from falling through hunger.

Another factor in the situation remains to be considered: the internal Government of France. This Government at the moment is practically non-existent. Under the influence of circumstances, and ideas of decentralization, there is a frittering away of power and resources. Our first interest should be to reestablish the unity of this power and the concentration of these resources. For instance, at this moment, at Tours a loan of two hundred and fifty millions is being raised at the usurious rate of $7\frac{1}{2}$ per cent. without the Government of Paris having been consulted.

I sum up as follows:

The armistice proposed by the neutral Powers cannot be refused without offending them; it is indispensable to permit of the election and convocation of an Assembly; it would afford our provincial armies the means of increasing their numbers and organizing in the best way possible; it would obtain a revictualling Paris cannot do without; and finally, the armistice would give satisfaction to the country, which desires to be called on to take up once more the direction of its destiny.

I add that at Tours all were unanimous in recognizing the military value of the armistice (four votes out of four); that upon the political question, that is to say, on the convocation of an Assembly, there were three voices for, and one (that of M. Gambetta) against, and I end by saying that Russia and England, having asked for safe-conducts to allow me to enter Paris to make the report that had just been heard, the Government must make up its mind without delay, for I have to meet the Prussian officers at four o'clock next afternoon at the Sèvres outposts.

After this account of affairs, several members speak. Nearly all support the idea of an armistice. They ask what its conditions will be, and insist on the necessity of the revictualling.

I answer that this is the absolutely essential condition, otherwise, as I said before the Délégation at Tours, "Paris would be captured with the armistice."

Questions are next asked whether the elections will be free and uncontrolled, and if Paris will be allowed to hold them.

I reply further that the whole of France will share in the elections; that as for Paris, I venture to think I shall succeed by making them an absolute *sine qua non* in case of dispute.

"Will they be possible, too, in Alsace and Lorraine?"

The majority of the members present would not, at any cost, have this point raise a difficulty that might wreck the armistice; besides, we must avoid prejudging in the armistice the question of the cession of territory. If we could make use of a general expression to include the whole of France, without mentioning such and such a province expressly, I should be disposed to content myself with it.

This opinion is adopted. We also discuss the length of the armistice. Finally we decide on these three conditions:

> An armistice in order to hold the elections.
> A revictualling proportioned to the duration of the armistice.
> Freedom of the elections throughout the whole of France.

The question of the internal condition of France and the necessity of making provision for it comes up several times. General Trochu speaks at great length, energetically and effectively, upon this subject. The armistice seems to him indispensable from a military and political point of view. From the military aspect he thinks it so useful, if we obtain the

NEGOTIATIONS FOR AN ARMISTICE

revictualling, that he doubts whether the Prussians would consent to this condition. Politically, he is persuaded that without the speedy meeting of an Assembly, social dissolution in France is imminent. He complains of M. Gambetta, but without attacking him personally, and reproaches him with being too much obsessed with the interests of his party. Especially he criticizes the loan of two hundred and fifty millions raised without the knowledge of the Government of Paris, and calls it an act of usurpation. This vehement speech ends the discussion.

From this moment the members occupy themselves only with drawing up a resolution. Some would wish to have all the conditions stipulated for the armistice published, which according to them would silence all objections. I answer, and M. Jules Favre with me, that this would make any negotiation impossible, for the Prussians would not allow conditions to be dictated to them publicly. This argument is accepted, and M. Jules Favre is given the task of formulating instructions for the French negotiator conformably with the decisions just arrived at by the Government.

There will besides be printed in the *Gazette* a few lines to announce my arrival, the result of my mission, and the steps I am about to take to obtain an armistice to open the gates of Paris for its revictualling and to allow all France to elect an Assembly. This announcement will be followed by another, distinct from the first, to make known the capitulation of Metz, which is still doubted.

Next day I spend an hour in our home, which I had left two and forty days before, and I return to the Foreign Office, where M. Jules Favre hands me my powers as negotiator. I see again Barthélemy-

Saint-Hilaire, Mignet, Vitet, Piscatory, Calmon, Bocher, d'Haussonville, de Lasteyrie.

They tell me there is great disturbance in Paris, and that the Hôtel de Ville is threatened! The Government had denied that Metz had fallen, and the contradiction administered by events is a triumph for Felix Pyat and the revolutionaries. The armistice is not understood. Ill-disposed persons say that M. Thiers comes to impose it on behalf of Prussia. M. Ferry fears trouble during the day.

We lunch, interrupted continually by people bringing news and by telegrams urging M. Jules Favre to come to the Hôtel de Ville. He goes off, arranging with me that if he has not come back I shall take my departure at two o'clock.

At two, as no one has returned, I set out with M. Roger, who has procured a safe-conduct for the gates of Paris. On our way we see General Ducrot, who gives me his chief of staff and an escort of excellent volunteer horse. About four o'clock we are at the bridge of Sèvres—the trumpets had sounded already; the two flags of truce were hoisted. We cross the Seine in gusts of wind and rain. The Prussian officers were punctual to their hour. Herr von Winterfeldt accompanies me, as on the previous day. At six o'clock we reach Versailles. Herr von Winterfeldt leaves me and returns a moment later to congratulate me, from Count Bismarck, on my return without any mishap, and to ask what hour will suit me to-morrow. I choose noon. At this moment the guns of the forts make themselves heard with extreme violence.

November 1, 1870.—I had entered Paris Sunday, October 30th. I had left again on the 31st. On the

1st of November, as soon as I have risen, I write to Mme. Thiers a letter with a note for the Government of Tours, a missive which I hope to have dispatched to Tours as a simple family letter.

Precisely at noon I am at Count Bismarck's house in the Rue de Provence. He receives me immediately. His face has a very changed expression from the time I knew him first, but his eyes are still keen and intelligent, and I ask myself if the gentleness he displays in my presence is the effect of age or deliberately meant to make me forget what took place at Ferrières. He hastens to say that Mme. Thiers must be reassured as to my journey and my health, for he has sent a dispatch to von der Tann, instructing him to inform her of my safe return. This thoughtfulness deprives me of any excuse for sending my letter.

We at once enter upon the great subject we are to treat of together. I tell the Chancellor that I have received from the Government sitting in Paris the necessary powers to conclude the armistice proposed by the neutral Powers, which has for its main object the convocation of a National Assembly with which peace could be discussed.

Count Bismarck does not reject the idea of an armistice; but he objects to the proposal emanating from neutrals, for he has never admitted their intervention in this war; and taking, for example, the English proposal, to which the other neutrals have rallied, he says that the English dispatch expatiates at great length on considerations of humanity, but comes to no precise conclusion.

I answer that the proposal addressed to France is precise and clear. I should be surprised if the proposal that has been made to Prussia is less so; for the rest, it is certain that the four neutral Powers— England, Austria, Italy, and Russia—advise us to conclude an armistice, and that is the subject which I have come to discuss with him.

Count Bismarck leaving these preliminary reservations, we pass to the discussion of the armistice. He pretends that he accepted the idea at Ferrières, that he would have been willing to arrange one then, which would have spared much bloodshed; that he continues to-day to be willing, but that an armistice being extraordinarily in our favour, we must expect military advantages to be exacted in return, and that we might, for example, be asked to give up one of the Paris forts.

I reply at once that such a condition is inadmissible, for it would be giving up Paris; that we must forgo any further negotiation if this were to be insisted upon. I say this so finally that Count Bismarck confines himself to repeating that pledges will nevertheless be exacted, and, failing a fort, it will be something else. He then dwells on the purpose of the armistice, viz. on the convocation of the Assembly.

"The motive is excellent," he said, "and perfectly agreeable to us, but is it agreeable to the Governments of Tours and of Paris? Originally the elections were ordered; then they were suspended, then ordered again, and finally suspended indefinitely. If they are ordered now, will they take place at Lyons, at Marseilles, at Toulouse?"

"There has been a fluctuation," I replied, "and that is not surprising, since the Government felt all the agitations of an immense city undergoing siege. However, in point of fact, the Government desires to have them. The chief objection they have met in the heart of the Government arose from the fear that there could be no election either in Paris or in the departments in the hands of the enemy. This fear once abolished by the armistice, the objection disappears, and far from meeting with opposition, the convocation of an Assembly will but fall in with one of the most pronounced wishes of public opinion. Possibly there will be selections that will not please us Moderates, but the majority will be Liberal and Conservative and attached to a policy of reason and justice."

Count Bismarck then said:

"We do not ask anything better than to deal with a proper body representing France and a Government with which we can treat authoritatively; but we have, if necessary, the choice between the restoration of the Empire, a Republican Government, and even a monarchy other than that of the Bonapartes."

"What!" I exclaimed. "The choice——?"

"Yes," went on Count Bismarck, "you know, doubtless, that the Emperor Napoleon has summoned to him the Marshals and other heads of the army who are our prisoners. They have answered the summons, the Empress has joined them, and they are deliberating at this moment. Our two or three hundred thousand prisoners might be formed into an army for them, they might summon the Senate and the Corps Législatif, and declare the Government sitting at the Hôtel de Ville null and void."

"What!" said I. "The Empress, who has informed us, by Prince Metternich, that she wished to keep aloof from all intrigue, who would not listen to General Boyer? . . ."

"The Empress," rejoined the Chancellor, "do not

trust her! We have had messages from her in quite the opposite sense, and I could show them to you."

I replied that in any case he was too much a statesman to lend himself to such ridiculous combinations; that he ought to be fully aware that France would never, at the hands of a few generals, an enemy's prisoners, and finally at the hands of the enemy himself, accept a broken-down dynasty that had plunged her into the depths.

"I am not," I added, "a party man, and if the Bonapartes had granted a sufficient measure of freedom, and followed a reasonable policy, I would not have served them, but I should not have fought against them; but after the calamities they have drawn upon France, no one would uphold them."

"I know," said Count Bismarck, "that you are not a party man, but a Frenchman solely attached to his country, and I understand your feelings. Besides, I am myself of the opinion that in order to treat of peace, an Assembly elected by the nation is better than a restoration of the Empire. I merely desired to let you see that we had a choice, that failing the Government at the Hôtel de Ville, we could find others to set their names to a peace."

We then returned to the subject of the armistice.

"You will doubtless also demand," said Count Bismarck, "that during the armistice Paris should be fed."

"Count, it is beyond dispute the regular usage of war, and the rule of armistices, to arrange matters so that the belligerents should in no way have impaired their respective positions at the end of the armistice."

"I quite agree," he replied; "but to provision Paris for thirty days, or even for fifteen, will be immensely difficult."

"I know it will, since I have helped to carry out a provisioning that will hold you many months longer, and I know the means of increasing it."

He objected that when this provisioning was effected the neighbourhood of Paris was teeming with every kind of food; but that now all was exhausted. Requisitions now brought in nothing, and Count Moltke only fed the army from distant markets. Besides, there were no railways now. Count Bismarck doubtless wanted to discover if we had definitely settled our ways and means of revictualling the city.

As for the necessary quantities, I told him they were already determined in a memorandum which I would send him. The provisions would enter in by three or four railway termini, commissaries of both nations would keep the tally, and there would be no false reckoning on either side. As for the railways, the rails were there, we had the locomotives, they would be made neutral and returned whence they came, after delivering the trains of provisions.

"You will give me your memorandum," said Count Bismarck, "and we shall go into it. Since the quantities depend on the length of the armistice, we must know how many days you would need."

I spoke of a minimum of twenty-five days. He thought a cessation of hostilities for forty-eight hours would be enough for the ballot.

I replied that it would, indeed, be enough for the ballot; but the preparations for the elections, the convocation of the Assembly, and the settlement of its powers would call for a minimum delay of five and twenty days.

"Be it so," said the Chancellor; "but the place where the Assembly will meet is a serious matter. At Paris it could not deliberate in peace, and if in the end it did not come to an understanding it would be cut off and in no position to govern."

I acknowledge these difficulties, and Count Bismarck added that perhaps he would ask for something on this head to be embodied in the conditions of the armistice.

After touching all these points, I thought I had attained my end in a single meeting, when Count Bismarck said further that he would have to take the opinion of the military staff on these different questions, who would doubtless demand a price for the sacrifice imposed upon their army by an armistice so advantageous for us.

He then opened the question of the freedom of the elections, and assured me that we should have more than under any form of government, but that he did not wish to have any elections in Alsace nor in German Lorraine.

"Ah, as to that, no, no," I replied. "The armistice is not the treaty of peace; never will we allow a question of territory to be prejudged in an armistice."

The Chancellor was struck by the fire of my reply.

"We do not want to prejudge this question," said he, "but if it is not to be prejudged against you, it must not be prejudged against us either."

"Do not let us say any more about it," I answered; "on this head I have positive instructions."

The reservations Count Bismarck had just made with regard to Alsace and Lorraine having given me the opportunity to broach the territorial problem, I said to him:

"The latest victories of the German armies will add to the Northern Confederation Bavaria, Würtemberg, the Grand Duchy of Baden. After so great an increase of territory what interest could Germany have in seizing a few square leagues and a few thousands of subjects from us, and so inflicting a wound on the very heart of France that we should never forgive?"

Count Bismarck replied that the Germans regarded the acquisition of a part of French territory as a matter of pride and a question of security. They had not forgotten the conquests of Louis XIV, and wished to guard against future incursions on the part of France. Territorial acquisitions, such as Metz and Alsace, for example, would satisfy these two feelings. And hereupon he repeated the supposed historic dissertation, so often published by the German press, on the insatiable ambition of France.

"Prussia," I replied, "less than any other Power can have any right to reproach France with her conquests. France, the Gaul of olden days, has always been a great Empire. She has her territory from Nature itself, not by war or diplomacy; and the necessary and legitimate conquest of her natural frontiers was never inspired by the ambition of aggrandizement. But you Prussians, on the contrary, from the Grand-Elector to your King to-day, you have only lived by taking something from some one. You were a million and a half in the time of the Grand-Elector. Half a century after you were brought by Frederick the Great up to ten or twelve million subjects; you reach fifteen millions by the partition of Poland, eighteen to nineteen millions in 1815; in the past six years you have gone on from twenty to thirty millions, for the Northern Confederation will be nothing but a compound of prefectures under your

King! And it is you who dare to reproach us with our spirit of conquest, and our ambition! But indeed, Count, one must imagine oneself dreaming, when one hears such an accusation in your mouth!"

"Well, let it be as it may," said the Count; "but all that would fade away if we had no territorial safeguards, if we had not the fortresses of Metz and Strassburg in our hands to cover us."

"These places are something, without a doubt," said I. "And yet, does starting from ten leagues nearer or farther make any great difference to invasions. If a long and formidable frontier like the Rhine is a safeguard, a few leagues added to the Palatinate will be no protection against the implacable feelings you will leave in our hearts. You have therefore more interest in policy to give us back those places than you have strategic interest in keeping them. However that may be, I repeat that I have neither the power nor the will to sign an armistice in which the solution of these matters would be prejudged."

Count Bismarck then asked me if, in order to avoid a prejudgment, we would not find it possible to adopt a middle way, which would be to choose leading men from the occupied provinces without having recourse to a formal convocation of the electors. Clearly what he wished was to avoid all election disturbances in Alsace and Lorraine. I accepted this proposal, and I took upon myself to draw up a memorandum to this effect.

Count Bismarck having repeated that he would have to consult the military authorities upon the placing of the armies during the armistice, and the importance of the provisioning I had stipulated for, we arranged a meeting for next day at noon.

I left the Chancellor with a little hope, for he seemed desirous of bringing into existence, through the elections in France, a Government with which he could treat. We then went, with my two companions, MM. de Rémusat and Cochery, to wander about the park and look again upon the places that had witnessed our ancient greatness. We came upon Prussians moving along the alleys on horseback, and French people, too, who questioned me sadly with their eyes.

In the afternoon, the Count came to ask me to put off my visit next day until two o'clock instead of noon. The King was to assemble the military chiefs to talk over the project of the armistice, and this conference would not end before two o'clock at least.

November 3rd.—At two o'clock I was at the Chancellor's. I found him irritable, not so calm as the day before.

"I have just been discussing the question of the armistice with the King and the Staff," he said. "There will be many difficulties still to solve. As for the elections in Alsace and Lorraine, what we agreed upon yesterday is accepted. You will have permission yourselves to choose in these provinces leading men to complete your Assembly. On the other points, have you prepared a formal document?"

"Here it is," I replied, "in the form of questions, followed by the indicated answers. With these elementary details to go on we can very speedily draw up an agreement ready to be signed by both of us."

He read the preamble.

"Bases of an agreement to put an end to loss of life, in conformance with the desire of the neutral Powers. . . ."

At these words, "the neutral Powers," Count Bismarck looked at me with an air that declared that these Powers did not exist as far as he was concerned. I said:

"I will delete the words, but the neutral Powers will none the less exist, and will not cease to count in Europe."

The Chancellor continued:

"Article 1.—Cessation of hostilities. Convocation of an Assembly."

No comment, except that a date is to be fixed for the elections so as not to waste the time of the armistice uselessly.

"Article 2.—Duration of the armistice: twenty-eight days."

"It was to be twenty-five," said the Chancellor; "this is an inconvenience: it increases the quantity of provisions to be brought into Paris. We shall see."

"Article 3.—The choice of place where the Assembly is to meet."

"As we have already agreed," remarked Count Bismarck, "it must not meet in Paris. Let us continue."

"Article 4.—Freedom of the elections."

Nothing to remark, after the solution already indicated on this point.

"Article 5.—Military operations during the period of the armistice."

My wording was not acceptable to the Chancellor.

"It would hamper the German army," he said. "We will trace a line of demarcation outside which the belligerents shall be masters of their movements."

He had already traced this line in red pencil on a map. According to him, a hundred and sixty thousand men, set free by the fall of Metz, were pressing for-

NEGOTIATIONS FOR AN ARMISTICE

ward to occupy Rouen, le Havre, and Normandy. They would only stop on the day the armistice was sealed. Our interest, then, was to sign it as soon as possible.

"Articles 6 and 7.—Revictualling of Paris."

Upon this head, serious difficulty.

"You ask too much of us," said Count Bismarck. "If we granted you what you ask you would last out two months longer, and we should be forced to remain here for the winter, for we do not wish to destroy Paris. We wish to wait for the exhaustion of your stores. Accordingly, this article is to be modified. If you were willing to surrender a fort I would let you have provisions, but you would still say I am demanding Mont-Valérien!"

"No," I replied; "provisions and no fort, otherwise no armistice."

Without insisting further Count Bismarck comes to the last article, relating to the third party as arbiter. He will not consent that a third party should be chosen from among the neutrals.

Next there was the question of the fleets, which I had not mentioned in my draft. Count Bismarck wished ours to have their limit fixed at the estuary of the Seine.

"What!" said I, "have Dieppe, Boulogne, Dunkirk ceased to be ours? The sphere of our fleet will be limited by Calais Straits."

As to the German fleet, whose position Count Bismarck did not know, it was agreed that it should stay wherever it was at the time.

At this point Count Bismarck spoke to me of the thirty-five merchant ships that we had taken, and whose captains had been made prisoners. That, he said, was an intolerable abuse of force. The Germans had therefore taken in our towns forty citizens whom they were equally holding as prisoners in Germany.

"And you have violated the law of nations," I said. "This law, which you cannot be ignorant of, since it arises out of international customs and treaties, authorizes the making prisoners of the crews of ships held lawful prize, but not the non-combatant inhabitants of occupied towns."

He pretended then that the Prussians, never having recognized prize law, could not admit the decrees of the law of nations on this head. Then, at the end of his arguments, he fell back upon the *francs-tireurs*, accusing them of atrocities, and of having killed a relation to whom he was greatly attached.

"That is their law of nations," he cried: "that's the law of nations according to the French army!"

At the word, I rose to go, and I said to the Chancellor:

"I have taken pains to avoid importing any bitterness into our painful discussions, and I am astounded that you should utter in my presence, with reference to the French army, a reproach that is not deserved and that I cannot consent to listen to."

He became calm then and assured me that he had no intention of insulting the French army, but that he regretted that it should admit such persons into its ranks, which made it responsible for their actions.

"It is possible," I said to the Count, "that there may have been excesses committed on both sides, and I reprobate them all alike. In all cases, if there have been deeds of violence, they would be more excusable in the invaded than in the invaders. Guerillas have always been recognized, and every means is justifiable to defend one's country."

I had sat down again when I saw the Count was on the defensive once more. He then took up a paper from the table and said to me it was an abominable proclamation that had come from Tours. It was, in fact, ridiculous, relating to the surrender of Metz, and couched in terms of extreme violence, possibly calculated by M. Gambetta to make the armistice impossible.

"You cannot imagine," said Count Bismarck, "the difficulties these violent explosions create for me. How after this sort of thing can I procure the signing of armistices?"

Coming up to me then and taking me by the hand: "Pray forget," he said, "my hasty expressions; they are provoked by all the difficulties I have to face, and I cannot wholly control them."

Seeing him so much softened, I spoke of an incident that had surprised me. The Prussian prefect of Versailles had on the 31st of October directed the President of the Civil Tribunal to administer justice in the name of Napoleon III. I pointed out to Count Bismarck that this showed an inconsistency, since, at the very moment, he was treating with a representative of the French Republic. When he replied that he had not recognized this Government, I asked him if he had not given up the thought of coming to terms with the Bonapartes. He then said expressly that he found the Cassel intrigues ridiculous and trivial, and that if he had to choose a party, outside Prussia, he would be with the Bourbons.

Taking advantage of this tone of confidence and cordiality he was adopting towards me, I questioned him as to the terms of the capitulation of Metz. He showed it to me and translated it. It dealt only with military matters and only arranged the fate of the army. Then he came back to talk of his preference for the Bourbons.

According to him, the proper thing would be to form a good Government by uniting the party of the Comte de Chambord and that of the Comte de Paris. He had in his possession, he said, a letter sent him by the Bishop of Orléans to be forwarded to the right address. He had been too scrupulous to read it, but as it was open and as the bishop was a friend of mine, he offered it to me to read.

"I am too scrupulous, also, to take notice of it," I replied.

"So, but you guess what it may contain. It is, most probably, on the lines of this linking up of the Bourbons of which I have just spoken to you. What are the Orléans princes doing? If you have any message to send them, I am at your service."

"I thank you, Count, and I would not hesitate to trust you, if there was any reason. I look upon the Orléans princes with respect and affection, but I think they would be wrong to do anything imprudent, and to be willing at this juncture to behave as claimants to the throne. My conduct, solely inspired by the interests of France, has always been loyal. It will be the same towards the Republic. I have told its heads that if they gave us a wise and well-ordered Government we should accept it; that otherwise we should return to our preferences. We shall be faithful to this promise. To-day the Republic allows Legitimist, Republican, and Orléanist to fight side by side in defence of their country; let us take advantage of this. Later we shall see. There are certain symptoms which indeed make one apprehensive lest

NEGOTIATIONS FOR AN ARMISTICE

the Republic of 1870 may follow the example of the Republic of 1848. In that case the return of the Orléans princes might be useful to France. But to-day I have nothing to send to them, and I thank you for your confidence."

We then returned to our discussion of the armistice.

"We are agreed upon nearly all points," said the Count; "but as the revictualling must needs prolong the resistance of Paris, the military authorities will not consent, and without them I am powerless."

I then said calmly but decidedly, that if he thought the refusal of the military authorities was final, it was better to say so frankly and to break off a negotiation that must come to nothing. I was ready to inform my Government of the fact and to leave Headquarters.

Count Bismarck found that I was in too great haste to abandon all hope of coming to terms. He would see the King again, and perhaps we might agree in the end if, for example, I would abate my demands in the matter of the revictualling.

"Give me until to-morrow," said he, "and at noon I will give you a final answer."

It was clear that the Prussians did not consider that the political advantage accruing to them from the convocation of an Assembly would counterbalance the military advantage we should derive from the revictualling of Paris. Perhaps, too, they had consented to embark upon negotiations merely in order not to alienate the neutral Powers, and without ever having had any intention to grant the armistice.

Next day precisely at noon I was at the Chancellor's house. He seemed preoccupied, and began by asking if I had news from Paris. When I answered in the negative, he then told me the Commune had been proclaimed, and that MM. Dorian, Delescluze, Félix Pyat, and perhaps Blanqui, made up the new Government.

My distress at this news was very great. I had many times uneasily asked myself what had been the result of the disturbance that had manifested itself at the moment of my leaving Paris. Count Bismarck read me his information; it agreed with my fears sufficiently to justify them all. I wished, however, to have more certain news; and accordingly I proposed to the Count to send one of my secretaries to the outposts at the bridge of Sèvres, to discover what had occurred. He welcomed the idea, and I dispatched M. Cochery immediately.

"If the revolution is a fact," said he, "the negotiations will *ipso facto* be broken off. If not, we shall take up our task again; there must be some truth in all this, and that will be enough to lessen greatly the political value of the point we are discussing. Let us put it aside until we are better informed. Your envoy will be back in the evening. You will let me know what he has heard, and we shall act accordingly."

"If the news of this revolution is confirmed," I replied, "I shall ask your permission to leave to-morrow."

"Yes, we shall give you every facility."

Our sitting, which like the former ones should have been for several hours, was very much curtailed. And so, seeing Count Bismarck disposed to talk, I led him to speak of 1866 and of all he had done at that time, which was so glorious for him. I took him in this way on the human side, and he yielded to the temptation.

First of all, he told me that at Biarritz he had

obtained nothing whatever, though he had made every suggestion that could engage Napoleon III to conclude an alliance. The Emperor had appeared convinced that Austria would gain the day, and determined to join with her to crush Prussia, or else with Prussia at a price for his help. He had calculated badly.

After Sadowa, the attitude of Napoleon III, and the fear of a coalition between France, Austria, and the little German states, had decided him to make the peace of Nikolsbourg. The King opposed it with indignation and called it cowardly; he would have liked to destroy Austria. Count Bismarck thought it too soon for that.

"We could not"—these are his exact words—" have filled the empty space from Prague to Constantinople."

He had had violent scenes with the King.

"I owe him my malady," said he; "one day when he had come to see me in my bedroom, he so exasperated me that I leaped out of bed and locked myself in my dressing-room, and refused to come out till he had gone."

He had, in a fashion, driven him out of his wits. He told me, further, that he kept in his family papers a copy of the Treaty of Nikolsbourg on which the King had written with his own hand:

"I sign, vanquished by the violence of my Prime Minister."

Prussia was lost, he said, if he had not put an end to the war, and he added:

"Monarchy makes one a republican!"

He was persuaded that in 1866 a single demonstration on the part of France would have altered everything. Von der Goltz, far from seconding him as I had believed, had run counter to him, obstinately desiring to keep at peace. To make the King Emperor, he will wait until Bavaria takes the initiative. It is clear that Count Bismarck is speculating on Hungary. She "will fill the empty space from Prague to Constantinople." He would like to make her a kind of intermediate empire, after taking all the German peoples for himself. He has all this in his dreams.

Six o'clock in the same evening.—I am waiting. M. Cochery does not come back. What a curious thing! this Paris, from whose very heart any piece of news once spread with the speed of light, is now so closely shut that a revolution in her midst can be several days old without being known!

A quarter to eight.—At last M. Cochery is here. He has made his way into Paris and heard everything. The members of the Government of National Defence were for some hours the prisoners of the Commune, whose followers had taken the Hôtel de Ville by surprise. The National Guard, rallied by M. Picard, drove off the rioters. M. Pyat and some others are, they say, arrested.

I go to see Count Bismarck and announce the victory of order over disorder. He seems none too well satisfied with the news. Might he be regretting the loss of an easy way of breaking off our negotiation?

"Yesterday," I said, "you had promised to make a last attempt with the King and the military staff to obtain an armistice with a reduced revictualling. What have they decided?"

"They will not permit a revictualling even on a reduced scale, unless you give them an equivalent return."

"But what equivalent?"

"Give up the revictualling, or surrender a fort."

NEGOTIATIONS FOR AN ARMISTICE

"In both cases, it is the surrender of Paris you demand," I exclaimed. "How could you have entered upon this negotiation with the idea that we should accept such terms?"

"Yet you ought to have foreseen them."

"We had seen that the advantage to you to be able to treat of peace immediately with a regularly constituted Government, was fully as great as our advantage in the revictualling of Paris."

"As a matter of fact, we were fully disposed to make sacrifices in the hope of arriving at a speedy peace; but the outbreak in Paris and the Tours proclamation have forced us to give up this hope."

I determined then to leave Versailles, and to announce to the Government of Paris that negotiations were broken off.

Before we separated, Count Bismarck said that, in the interests of both of us, to avoid making statements that would have to be corrected later, as had happened with M. Jules Favre, we might agree beforehand as to the statement we should each publish.

I replied that I should make my statement from my French point of view, that he would make his from his Prussian standpoint, that we should communicate them to each other, and in this way avoid contradictory accounts.

I went home and put off till next day the drafting of my account of this negotiation, undertaken in some hope and so unexpectedly broken.

November 4th.—Next day, after long reflection, filled with the feeling that it would be regrettable to break off finally without a last effort to obtain the elections, I asked Count Bismarck to receive me. I told him that in order to profit by the friendly disposition he had more than once showed in the matter of electoral freedom in the occupied provinces, I should like to propose to the Government of Paris to hold these elections under armistice, without revictualling, since this condition was categorically rejected, or even without an armistice; but for this, it would be necessary that when he went to Paris to announce the refusal of the revictualling, M. Cochery should be allowed to bring the members of the Government to the outposts where I would go to confer with them.

Count Bismarck accepted this proposal; he gave the proper orders, and M. Cochery started on his mission.

I then had the idea of risking a step that might have decisive results. If it was useful to form an Assembly, by means of an election, it was not less useful to have some idea of the peace this Assembly would be called upon to conclude. I wished then to press Count Bismarck to disclose his inmost thought on this matter.

"Well!" I said, "if we were to offer to treat with you at once, without holding you for two months before the walls of Paris, what would you ask from us?"

"A great deal, and a great deal more still," he replied, "if you wait until hunger reduces Paris to surrender like Metz. The two hundred thousand men who were investing the latter place are coming to us; you will see your country overrun to the coast, and France will be ruined up to the Loire. Better for you, then, to treat without delay. To-day we should ask Alsace (Haut-Rhin and Bas-Rhin); as for Lorraine, not a very great slice around Metz."

"And Metz?"

"If you treat at once, I promise to do my best with the King to have it given back to you." (At this I felt an immense relief that I took great pains to conceal.) "There remains," he went on, "the question of indemnity. You have cost us a great deal of money; so we will exact two budgets."

"Two budgets? What do you mean by that? You mean two Prussian budgets?"

"No, two French budgets."

"Impossible! Never!"

Count Bismarck, struck by the energy of my reply, perhaps felt he had gone too far. I showed him then that our budgets only reached two milliards, because of the insane expenditure of the late Government, that the real budget was only some fifteen hundred millions, which would still bring two budgets to three milliards, and that France would never be in a position to pay this sum.

He seemed to be giving way, and I thought I could guess that two milliards, with Alsace and part of Lorraine, without Metz, might be the conditions of a peace signed immediately. I then felt redoubled energy to do my duty, and increased desire to make the Government of Paris hold the elections at once, without the revictualling of the city, with the armistice or even without it.

I left Count Bismarck, promising to come back to see him during the evening; and I spent my afternoon in working to finish my account of the negotiation, which I was to read to him.

The same evening, November 4th, at half-past eight, I handed him my note. Before reading it, he began to speak again of the intrigues of the Court of Cassel; he recounted the capitulation of Sedan, the attitude of Napoleon III, his meeting with the King; he was inexhaustible on the subject of the King, the Prince

Royal, Moltke, the Court, the people at Court, etc. (I shall relate all this in another place.)

At midnight he was still talking, without so much as an eye cast on my work. At length he took it up and read it very closely.

We were agreed on all the facts, but he said, with a little temper, that he objected to our making our fundamental position the reproach against him of having opened negotiations with the intention of refusing the revictualling or else demanding the surrender of one of the Paris forts.

As I did not want to embitter our reports, fearing lest it might make peace more difficult in the future, I proposed to say simply that we had not been able to agree on the question of the revictualling, and that this was the reason for the fresh rupture. This he accepted.

We parted, arranging a meeting for the next day on my return from Sèvres.

Saturday, November 5th.—Precisely at eight o'clock in the morning I was on my way to the bridge of Sèvres. Arrived at the Prussian outposts, the series of formalities imposed upon bearers of flags of truce had to be gone through again. As these were lengthy, I had time to see the houses of the lower town, open, abandoned in a disorder that made me think of Pompeii, overwhelmed in full life and activity by a sudden catastrophe.

The boat I was waiting for at length came and ferried me across to the French outposts. M. Cochery, who had come to meet me, had told me beforehand that I should only find M. Jules Favre and General Ducrot at the rendezvous. Through fear of rousing the populace of Paris neither M. Picard nor General

Trochu had come. The insurgents had been put down, and the Government seemed to lack the courage of its victory.

I was little disposed to be explicit before General Ducrot, who was not a member of the Government, and whose character was little known to me. However, to refuse to speak in his presence was a serious thing, for it would have been an insult to an officer whose merit as a soldier inspired confidence. I decided then to describe the position of affairs before him.

I began by recounting my efforts to obtain an armistice with the revictualling of Paris, the refusal of the German Staff to allow any revictualling unless we gave up a fort, and the rupture of the negotiations upon this refusal. I then said that in spite of this rupture the elections might still be held in two ways, either under armistice without revictualling or without the armistice; for in each case Count Bismarck had promised to give every possible facility.

On the first question, of an armistice without revictualling, my two hearers exclaimed that it would be impossible to get the Parisians to accept it, since it would fan their revolutionary passions to a tremendous flame.

"I agree that it is difficult," said I, "but, in the end, where would be the difference between the elections held with an armistice without revictualling, and those held without an armistice? In the first case, they will be prohibited from fighting for a month, and will live upon their supplies; in the second case, they will consume the same quantity of food and will not fight either, unless you take the offensive, for the Prussians seem determined to await the surrender of Paris through famine, rather than to win it by force. The great advantage of the armistice would be to stay the march of the two hundred thousand men who are on their way from Metz; le Mans, le Havre, Amiens, the whole of Normandy and Picardy would be saved from invasion. These are the provinces into which all our stocks of cattle and provisions of every kind have been dispatched; the quantity is enormous; their seizure would enrich the enemy and be nothing short of ruinous for us. To facilitate the elections and save so much wealth are advantages not to be despised."

"Without doubt," said General Ducrot, "but we should lose the advantage of being able to give battle!"

"If you could give battle and win it, I should have nothing to say, but still, there can be no real victory unless the blockade is broken, that is to say unless we could immediately march on a point where supplies have been concentrated which could be brought freely into Paris. Now this point could only be Normandy, and the two hundred thousand troops from Metz are already on the march to seize it!"

General Ducrot's only answer was to assure us again that it would be impossible to get the people of Paris to accept an armistice without revictualling, and M. Jules Favre repeated his declaration.

"Confine yourselves, then," said I, "to the announcement that, the revictualling not being granted, the armistice has been refused."

And I went on to the second question, of holding the elections without the armistice.

"I believe that peace, if actually concluded, would cost us Alsace, part of Lorraine, and two milliards, a cruel price; but if you wait until Paris surrenders through exhaustion you will be reduced to signing a still more grievous peace. I carry out my duty to my own conscience in laying the situation before you, it is for you to do yours. You can choose between a well-calculated resistance, which is ended the moment it becomes more hurtful than useful, and the resistance of despair, carried to a point where total ruin is preferred to surrender. I absolutely deny that you have any right to choose the latter alternative. Only France has the right to decide this choice, for her fate depends on the fate of Paris. Your duty, then, is to appeal to France."

"We are completely of your opinion," exclaimed both my interlocutors; "we must immediately hold the elections without armistice."

I then said that if there was not to be an armistice, I was authorized by Count Bismarck to give them the following information. The Prussian Generals would have orders to allow the elections, and to afford the utmost freedom for them throughout the occupied territory. Only in Alsace and Lorraine, in order to prevent any election disturbances, the French Government would be able to select certain leading men, who would be left free to attend the Assembly when it met. Certain facilities of communication would be granted, and one or two persons would be allowed to leave Paris to go and issue orders at Tours. The Assembly would meet wherever it might please, but preferably not in Paris.

M. Jules Favre undertook to lay these proposals before the Government of Paris, whose answer M. Cochery was to bring me next day at Versailles.

We regained the bridge at Sèvres, and at four o'clock I was in Versailles.

The same evening I went to tell Count Bismarck of the incidents of the day. I told him that in all likelihood the Government of Paris would not accept an armistice without revictualling, and that it would be more disposed to hold the elections without the armistice. Our conversation was brief, and I carried away the impression that Count Bismarck was preoccupied by the effect, on the minds of the neutral Powers, of this second rupture of negotiations for the armistice.

Sunday, November 6th.—I am waiting for M. Cochery. He arrives at last about noon, and brings me an envelope containing two dispatches—one asking me to break off all negotiations and leave the Prussian Headquarters, the other addressed to the Délégation at Tours.

I go accordingly to Count Bismarck's house to notify him of the Government's decision putting an end to the negotiation.

After expressing to me his regrets, more or less sincere, he repeated that he was always ready to concede full freedom for the elections, without an armistice.

We took leave of each other, and he announced that he would come to make his adieus in the course of the evening, which he did, expressing the hope that he would before long see me again to arrange peace between our countries.

Monday, November 7th.—Greatly preoccupied by the fact that M. Jules Favre, from his dispatch, appeared not to have put before the assembled Government the question of holding the elections without the armistice, making use of the facilities promised by Count Bismarck, and considering it a mistake to reject this proposal, I determined to leave M. Cochery at Versailles, with the mission to go to Paris and formally propound the question at the Hôtel de Ville.

Count Bismarck, to whom I had spoken of this plan, showed himself ready to further it, and all being settled with M. Cochery for him to act accordingly, I left Versailles on Monday, November 7th, at half-past six in the morning.

The way was less difficult than on my previous journey. Everywhere the people flocked round in the villages, asking for news and expressing an eager longing for peace. We got to Orléans pretty early, where the Bishop greeted us with his accustomed kindness. We saw a great many people there.

Next day, November 8th, as we were on the point of departing, General von der Tann came to express his regrets at the failure of the negotiations. He told me a battle was imminent, that there had been a cannonade all day long, and that we would have some trouble to get clear of the outposts. When we got to the outposts we found M. de Villeneuve, of the Geneva Cross, who had preceded us in the morning and announced our arrival. A detachment of chasseurs à pied had come to meet us, and we passed from the Bavarians to the French. At five o'clock we were in Tours.

All who were rational and sincerely patriotic, more bent on the interests of France than on those of a party, came to express their regret at the breaking off of the negotiations, and their gratitude as well. The majority of the Government were distressed that the armistice had fallen through; M. Gambetta alone was perhaps not altogether sorry that the man he considered the head of the moderate party had failed to succeed in his mission; but he regretted, for the sake of the army of the Loire, to be deprived of the twenty-five days of the armistice.

November 9th.—Battle of Coulmiers. A success of excellent moral effect for the army. I should have preferred that it should have been won elsewhere. Orléans is a point too dangerous and too challenging for the Prussians, and will bring on an immense effort on their part. We must without doubt hold up against it, but in holding up we expose ourselves to be turned and hemmed in.

On November 12th or 13th, we hear of Russia's repudiation of the treaty of 1856. Count Bismarck goes hand in hand with Russia so far as is needed to keep the support of Saint Petersburg. All the diplomatists here have lost their bearings. I advise the Government not to write, for already they had thought of a note, and to confine themselves to a verbal answer to give Russia to understand that there are relations to be kept with everybody; that in the meantime we shall range ourselves with whoever shows himself most helpful to France.

From the 15*th to the* 20*th November.*—Public opinion coming forward more and more every day in favour of the elections, the Government begins to think of them. M. Gambetta alone opposes. They think of sending M. Glais-Bizoin to Paris in order to inspire a resolution to this end. They ask Count Bismarck for a safe-conduct for him, and hope to obtain it.

M. Cochery has come back to Tours four or five days after I left Versailles. Count Bismarck, who had seemed disposed to allow him to go to Paris, had sent him to Moltke. That was on the 7th, the second day before the Battle of Coulmiers. It was natural that Moltke did not wish him to enter Paris at such a moment, for fear lest he might bring with him some intelligence that would have made it possible to arrange a sortie of the besieged, in concert with the forward movement of the army of the Loire. Moltke, while refusing to allow him to go into Paris, offered to send him back by the East and through Switzerland. M. Cochery refused. Confined to his quarters for three days, he was liberated upon an order of the Crown Prince and sent back via Montereau.

And so M. Cochery has not been into Paris, and the question of holding the elections without an armistice has not been laid again before the Government of National Defence.

THE PEACE PRELIMINARIES

STARTING from Bordeaux during the evening of February 19th, to go to treat with Count Bismarck upon the terms of peace, I made my first visit at Versailles on Tuesday, February 21, 1871. M. Barthélemy-Saint-Hilaire very kindly accompanied me.

I arrived at Count Bismarck's house at a quarter-past one. On his chimney-piece stood two bottles carrying candles, playing the part of candlesticks. Count Bismarck, coming to meet me, says:

"It was not you upon whom such a task should have fallen! I do not know if France has done well by you; but I know she did enormously well by herself when she entrusted her destinies to you."

Before entering upon the subject we had to treat of, I wished to answer his complaints about the still unexploded mines that were in existence all around Paris. I said that the military engineers, the civil engineers, and the fleet engineers had made mines and planted torpedoes pretty nearly everywhere; that there was the greatest difficulty in finding them again, and that I had given orders to have them looked for and unloaded, in the interests of public safety and in deference to the principle of the armistice.

Immediately after we went on to the question of the armistice and its extension.

He began by flatly refusing any extension. He said

that our preparations for war were going on, witness the class of 1871 which at that moment was joining the various regiments. And as I had asked powers to send away the men of the garde mobile mustered in Paris, he added that these mobiles would go to reinforce the armies, which would aggravate the danger to the Prussians in case hostilities were taken up again; that the German army was ready to continue its operations to bring the business to an end at once.

What our enemies are everywhere doing falls in with this declaration. Everywhere, in fact, they are crushing the country under levies which they exact without respite. With two armies, each of a hundred or a hundred and fifty thousand men, one of which would march on Bordeaux, the other on Lyons, they would willingly bring the war to an end and obtain their terms as soon as possible.

I protested loudly that from to-day, Tuesday, to Thursday, the end of the armistice, was only forty-eight hours, and that a treaty of peace is not to be made in forty-eight hours.

Count Bismarck answered that to draw up the treaty was impossible without five or six weeks of continuous consultation on the single point of the new line of frontiers; but that it was possible to set down in a preliminary treaty the fundamental conditions of peace, and this would not call for more than forty-eight hours; for as regards the two essentials, the question of territory and the question of an indemnity, opinions in both countries must have been formed.

I replied that preliminaries, however abbreviated they might be, demanded time; that I declared it impossible to conclude them in forty-eight hours, and that I would not have any share in such violent procedure. That I could understand it if our good faith were under suspicion, and we were supposed to have any idea of war in the background; but that no one could doubt my desire to make peace, if it was not made unacceptable for us; that the work of summoning the new Assembly, its meeting, its constitution had been carried out with unprecedented celerity; that everything had been hurried over; that I had myself done everything to avoid losing a single minute; that forming a Cabinet, especially in a situation so grave as ours, with so many different parties, was a most difficult task; that I had accomplished it in two days; that I had introduced the new Cabinet to the Assembly and an hour after I was on my way, travelling by night so as to get to Paris sooner; and scarcely had I arrived when I wrote to Versailles to ask for an appointment to which I was exactly punctual, although I had charge of all internal affairs (a heavy charge in the present state of our country); and that if I was thirty years of age instead of seventy-two I could not do more; that in face of conduct so clearly loyal, and I would even dare to say, devoted, to shut us within so narrow a ring of hours was an intolerable oppression to which I would not submit, let the consequences be what they might.

I had spoken with so much fire that Count Bismarck, much affected, embarrassed rather than vanquished, said to me:

"I am not the master. I am reproached with being too weak; the campaign against me that injured me so much at Prague is begun afresh; they say I am not capable of the task of reducing you to terms. In a word, I have a formal command from the King not to prolong the armistice and to fix the preliminaries between now and Thursday."

I replied that it was surprising that he, the author of Prussia's greatness, should not be the master.

"It is none the less as I tell you," he answered. "I must therefore leave you to go and take the King's commands."

Although I preserve a definite order, as much as I can, in my discussions, we were led at this point to speak of the entry of the Prussians into Paris.

"What!" I asked. "To satisfy your pride you would lay yourselves open to a catastrophe? I say catastrophe, for if Paris were sacked we should without doubt be the sufferers, but you would be dishonoured, and after such a tragedy no peace would be possible.

"But you will never take any but your own point of view," went on Count Bismarck. "If you have to reckon with the dignity of the people of Paris, I, too, on my part have to reckon with the honour and glory of the Prussian army, and to see that no one will be able to say, as your newspapers do every day, that this army, having come to the gates of Paris, did not dare to enter the city."

Then attending to the letters published by General Trochu, he added that the King was deeply offended that he, a soldier king, should have been warned against the danger of a pistol shot.

I tried to eliminate the King's pride from the affair by saying that there was no personal danger to him, and that, on the contrary, we should make it in a fashion a point of honour not to avenge ourselves by assassination; but that some fanatical persons might fling themselves on the Prussian soldiers, and that then there would be a chaos in which they would lose many men, and Paris might perish.

"We should know how to repel them without sacking the city," said Count Bismarck.

However, realizing the weak side of his pretensions, he suggested to me as an expedient capable of reconciling all claims, to allow them, by way of a guarantee for the settlement of the treaty of peace, to occupy a quarter in the heart of Paris—the Champs Elysées, for instance.

I pointed out that such an occupation, by reason of its duration, might be still more dangerous than a brief appearance of the Prussian army in Paris.

Count Bismarck did not insist, and as I felt where his difficulty lay, I said that if he wished I would speak to the King about it (for I desired to see him to present my respects to him), and that I would try to address myself to his heart and make him understand how little his honour was involved in this entry into Paris.

Somewhat anxious, Count Bismarck said to me:

"Without doubt you must see him, but do not press him too much. Kings, you see, are not accustomed to lives as toilsome as ours. At his age we must be careful of his strength. Besides, he does not like talking of affairs unless his Ministers are present."

I trembled to broach the question of the conditions of peace; however, it must be done.

"Let us come now to the great question," said I to the Count.

"I have already told you my mind on the matter," he replied. (At these words I hoped he would not ask much more than in November.) "I do not wish

THE PEACE PRELIMINARIES

to jockey you, it would be unbecoming. I might speak of Europe, as they do on your side, and demand in her name that you should give back Savoy and Nice to their rightful owners. I will do nothing of this kind, and will only speak to you of Germany and France. I already asked you for Alsace and certain parts of Lorraine. I will give you back Nancy, though the Minister for War wants to keep it; but we shall keep Metz for our own security. All the rest of French Lorraine will remain yours."

Count Bismarck looked at me to guess what I was thinking. Mastering my emotion, I answered coldly:

"You had only spoken of the German portion of Lorraine."

"Certainly, but we must have Metz; we must have it for our own safety."

"Go on," I said, waiting to know the whole extent of his exactions before I should answer.

Count Bismarck then opened the question of money.

"When I saw you in November," he said, "I mentioned a sum to you. That cannot now be the same figure, for since then we have suffered and spent enormously. I had asked you for four milliards: to-day we must have six."

"Six milliards!" I exclaimed. "But no one in the whole world could find them. It was the soldiers who suggested these figures to you; it was no financier."

The cold, determined, even scornful tone of my reply put Bismarck out of countenance.

"I listened without saying a word," I said, "but you are not to think I admit your demands: Alsace, Metz, a French city, six milliards, all that—it is out of the question! We will discuss these terms, and to discuss we must have time; let us extend the armistice."

If I had uttered a word implying an absolute refusal of any cession of territory, it was immediate rupture, war, disaster on disaster. I confined myself therefore to refraining from accepting the claims put forward, at the same time without giving the idea that I rejected them.

"I will not jockey any more than you," I said finally, "but I shall let you know my terms . . . and then, if you demand impossibilities, I shall withdraw and leave you to govern France."

With these words in his ears Count Bismarck left me to go to the King to ask for an extension of the armistice. It was granted until midnight on Sunday, and Count Bismarck informed me that the King would receive me next day.

Wednesday, February 22nd.—I went on Wednesday, the 22nd, to pay another visit at Versailles.

Arriving at one o'clock precisely, I went to the King's quarters, at the Prefecture. He received me at once. I had not seen him for more than twenty years. Our interview lasted a considerable time. He laid special stress on the entry of his army into Paris.

I gave the King all the arguments against this idea. I was careful to avoid the suggestion of an attempt on his life; but I insisted on the possibility of a collision that might bring about the sacking of Paris, from which Prussian honour would have to suffer grievously.

He answered for the discipline of his army, but made no promise, saying that this army, so devoted to its King and to Germany, must be considered, and that to forbid it the right of entry into a capital it was proud to have reduced to surrender, was very hard.

From the King's quarters I went to those of the Crown Prince. He touched with me on the conditions

THE PEACE PRELIMINARIES

of peace to which we would be resigned to submit, with a delicacy and kindliness, at least in appearance, that gave me some hope.

I spoke to him of the entry into Paris.

He replied in a strain little differing from the King's, and I left him to go to Count Bismarck.

The day was stormy. We left generalities; and the necessity of arriving precisely at facts gave rise to hot discussions.

Knowing that it would be useless to try to recover what was already lost, I reserved my efforts to save what perhaps could still be saved, and I declared that we would not give up any part of Lorraine. Metz especially, which François de Guise disputed from Charles V, was the subject of a lengthy discussion on my part. I reminded Count Bismarck that in November he had promised to have it given back to us.

"What was possible in November," he replied, "is no longer possible to-day, after three months' bloodshed."

And he added that if we were resolved not to consent to surrender Metz, it would be useless to continue the negotiation, and we must break off at once.

"We shall see," I replied, "whether we shall have to break off; but let us go on to the other points."

Count Bismarck then, with some signs of embarrassment, began to remind me of the sum of six milliards mentioned the previous day, and described it as very modest, since, he said, the mere cost of the war came to four milliards.

I showed him that this was utterly impossible; that in France, where expenditure was all the time heavier than in Prussia, the cost of the war in itself only came to about two milliards, which we found enormous; and that if this year we were faced with a deficit of three milliards, it was because to the two milliards cost of the war there must be added at least a milliard for bridges, broken-down tunnels, roads to be repaired, necessary indemnities, railway transport, and finally, the loss of at least one-third of the year's taxes; that in no case could it be brought up to four milliards; with six milliards there would be at least three milliards of profit for Prussia, which would turn the war indemnity into a mere financial speculation.

Count Bismarck replied that the war had cost more in Prussia than in France, because they had had to bring everything from Germany.

I replied that we also had immense transport operations, and that besides, the Prussians had seized on all the resources of our soil, and what they had taken possession of on the spot was ample equivalent for all the cost of their transport.

The Count seemed to set particular store by the money. He declared, with some temper, that the figures on which the indemnity had been calculated came to him from Prussia; that on this occasion he was only a mouthpiece, etc.; and that he could not settle anything before telegraphing to Berlin.

It was agreed then that he should telegraph, and that when he received the answer from Berlin, he would send special envoys to treat with me on this point.

This incident terminated our interview.

Thursday, February 23*rd.*—We have been visited by MM. Henckel and Bleischröder, Count Bismarck's financial representatives, who repeated to us all he had said. The discussion only dealt with the means of procuring the six milliards demanded by Prussia.

We have proved to them that this financial operation

THE PEACE PRELIMINARIES

was impossible; that so huge a sum could never be obtained from European capitalists.

M. Bleischröder, more straightforward than M. Henckel, understood this and almost agreed.

The same evening.—First meeting of the Commission. The fifteen members being all present, I gave them a full account of the negotiations. I was greatly affected, and the Commission with me. It is true we were to keep the greater part of Lorraine, but Metz was lost!

I left them in my own uneasiness with regard to the eastern frontier, and especially with regard to Belfort, the most important point of this frontier.

As for the financial question, I said that six milliards had been demanded of us, and that I would not give this sum. All agreed that it was excessive; all with one accord thought and said that while resisting we must none the less sign the peace, for nothing could be more disastrous than to start the war again; and the Commission expressed the greatest confidence in us.

Friday, February 24*th.*—This has been, assuredly, the most animated and most dramatic day of this grievous negotiation.

M. Kern, the minister of the Helvetian Confederation, a most worthy man, and of the best intentions towards France, came to talk to us of our communications with Switzerland and the need of preserving them. He exaggerated our interests in the matter, for on this side the great interest lies in the military frontier and Belfort above all. I advised him to go without delay to Count Bismarck, and speak to him of what was on his mind. He did go, and as soon as he returned to Paris he came to tell us that he had been very badly received and even rudely.

"What are you coming here for?" Count Bismarck

had said. "What are you trying to meddle in? This is a question that is to be settled between France and us; and you neutrals are not to meddle at all with it. We have laid down our conditions; they are irrevocably fixed, and we shall not alter them. If they are not accepted, the war will begin again."

M. Kern was completely dismayed, and he told us there was no hope, and that we must make haste to draw France from the pit into which she had fallen.

This report was hardly encouraging, and we set out, M. Jules Favre and myself, in a very uneasy mind. We were determined to present a kind of ultimatum, to hold fast to it, and to make an end, since the armistice expired at midnight on Sunday.

We found Count Bismarck very ill, but sufficiently calm, to all appearance.

Coming back to the question of territory, we spoke of Metz before everything else, Metz, the city that was French *par excellence.*

Count Bismarck told us that he considered it highly impolitic to drive France to despair, and that he had opposed Count Roon's project of seizing two-thirds of Lorraine, that we were to lose only a very small fraction of it, but that there was no possibility of leaving Metz to us.

"In Germany," said he, "they accuse me of losing the battles Count Moltke has won. Do not ask me for impossibilities."

It was evident that the decision on this head was irrevocably fixed, and that we must reserve our energies to save the eastern frontier.

We next went on to the question of the money.

THE PEACE PRELIMINARIES

I feared that Count Bismarck might take his stand upon his sum total of six milliards, and refuse to abandon it. He told us, calmly enough, that he had telegraphed to Berlin, that they had again insisted afresh on the amount of expenditure incurred, on the widows and orphans whose pensions we were intended to pay, on the maintenance of the prisoners, on the necessity of giving the southern states their share; but in the end that they had stopped at a total of five milliards, from which they would make no deduction.

I perceived that on this point a rupture would probably be the result of discussion. Count Bismarck was inflexible. I promised myself that later I would cause all the requisitions in money levied by the Germans up to that moment to be entered in this total.

And then, upon the question of Belfort, I entered upon a struggle that I shall remember as long as I live. Belfort, Belfort is the eastern frontier; in fact, if the Prussian troops can come by Verdun and Metz, the South German troops will always come by Belfort, especially if the neutrality of Switzerland is violated. I spoke, then, of Belfort.

Count Bismarck said at once that this fortress was in Alsace, and that it was decided that the whole of Alsace should be transferred to Germany. Throughout two hours, now with menaces, now with entreaties, I declared that I would never let Belfort go.

"No," I cried, "I will never surrender both Metz and Belfort. You mean to ruin France in her finances, ruin her on her frontiers! Well, take her, administer the country, levy the taxes! We shall retire, and you will have to govern her in the eyes of the whole of Europe, if Europe permits."

I was desperate. Count Bismarck, taking my hands, said to me:

"Believe me, I have done all I could; but as for leaving you part of Alsace, it is quite impossible."

"I sign this very instant," I rejoined, "if you give me Belfort. If not, nothing; nothing but the last extremities, whatever they may be."

Beaten, exhausted, Count Bismarck then said to me:

"If you will, I shall make an effort with the King; but I do not believe it will succeed."

Immediately he wrote two letters, which he dispatched, one to the King, the other to Count Moltke.

"I ask Moltke," said he, "for we must get him on our side; without him we shall obtain nothing."

Half an hour passed. Every sound of footsteps in the antechamber made our hearts leap. At length the door opens. We are told that the King is out of doors, and that Count Moltke also is not at his house. The King will not come back until four o'clock: no one knows when Count Moltke will return. We decide to wait, for to go away without having settled the question would be to lose.

Count Bismarck leaves us to go to dinner, and we pass an hour, M. Jules Favre and I, in inexpressible anxiety. Count Bismarck appears again. The King has come back, but does not wish to decide without having seen Count Moltke. Count Moltke arrives. Count Bismarck leaves us to go and talk with him. Their conversation seems very long to us. Count Bismarck returns, satisfaction in his face.

"Moltke is on our side," said he; "he will turn the King."

A fresh wait of three-quarters of an hour. Count

Bismarck is sent for, who goes to find out what Count Moltke reports. After a long talk with him he at length comes back, and, his hand on the key of the door, he says to us:

"I have an alternative to propose to you. Which will you have, Belfort or the abandonment of our entry into Paris?"

I do not hesitate for a moment, and with a look to M. Jules Favre, who divines my feeling and shares it:

"Belfort, Belfort!" I cried.

The entry of the Germans into Paris must needs be a cruel blow to our pride, a danger to us who held the reins of government; but—our country before everything!

Count Bismarck rejoins Count Moltke, and at length brings us the definite concession of Belfort, on condition that we will give up four little villages on the confines of Lorraine, where eight or ten thousand Prussians are buried. We respect this religious regard of the monarch for his soldiers.

We had left Paris at eleven in the forenoon; we leave Versailles at half-past nine at night, having saved Belfort for France.

From ten o'clock until midnight we hold a sitting of the Commission. We relate everything to them, and receive their thanks for our efforts.

Saturday, February 25th.—The bitterest day of my life! The preliminaries of peace were to be signed.

These preliminaries had been badly drafted by the Germans; but had they even been drafted more clearly, they would still have given rise to difficulties of interpretation; for it is when one is obliged to come to an exact understanding of a clause in order to execute it that unforeseen and unavoidable disagreements occur. Count Bismarck was in a hurry, because the King was himself in a hurry to leave; he wanted to rush everything, little caring about a wording he was certain he could turn to his own advantage, ill besides, and mastered by his temper worthy of a savage.

PRESIDENCY OF THE REPUBLIC

ON February 17, 1871, at Bordeaux, the National Assembly, by an almost unanimous vote, had invested me with the executive power of the French Republic. On May 24, 1873, at Versailles, this same Assembly having given a majority in favour of a measure that I could not accept, I resigned the power I had received from it.

I am about to recount the principal acts in which I took part, in the government of France, between these two dates.

At the moment when I accepted the burden of power, at Bordeaux, I was far from thinking that we ought to renounce all hope of one day re-establishing Monarchy in France; but such an enterprise seemed to me doomed to certain failure if it were attempted in the position in which we then found ourselves. The three sovereigns who had followed one another—Charles X, Louis Philippe, Napoleon III (especially this last, not having been willing to accept the strictly constitutional system of England)—had alienated independent minds and shaken the royal power.

For a long time I had said to myself, "If Royalty refuses to cross the Channel with us, it will drive France to cross the Atlantic." And so, while regretting that our princes had not fully carried out, as it is in England, the constitutional form of monarchy adopted by France, I was not surprised that the march of events had made a new trial of a Republic inevitable.

This result, which I had foreseen, from the mistakes of the preceding Governments, was when we met at Bordeaux an indisputable fact that could not be escaped; for, even supposing that the various monarchical parties had been able to agree among themselves on one of the three pretenders to the crown, the greatest cities in the South were in revolt and Paris in the hands of two hundred thousand fanatics,. and these towns would never have opened their gates to a king chosen at Bordeaux.

Even in Bordeaux, where at that time we only had two regiments, incomplete in numbers and not very reliable, to oppose to twenty thousand Republican National Guards, all tinged with fanaticism, the Assembly was so far from being able to attempt to restore the Monarchy, that it could not have managed to take the power from the grasp of M. Gambetta without the energetic intervention of M. Jules Simon and the other delegates of the Government of National Defence, expressly sent from Paris to ensure the regularity of the elections.

Besides, the Assembly so clearly recognized the necessity of acknowledging the Republic *de facto*, that it entrusted me with the supreme power, with the title of Head of the Executive of the French Republic—a title which provoked no protests from the Royalists. Neither did they protest against my language when, at the sitting of February 19, 1871, I declared from the tribune in set terms that I accepted power to exercise it in the name of the Republic until the day when, the task of restoring the nation having been accomplished, France would be called upon to pronounce on her future destiny.

The Monarchist parties then looked for nothing from me but the re-establishing of peace and order. France and Europe also counted on the same thing. And so, less than an hour after the vote that placed me in power, the ambassadors of England, Austria, and Italy came to inform me of the official recognition of the new Government by their Cabinets, which had acted in concert to give me this sign of their confidence. Their example was followed, a few days after, by Russia, Switzerland, Portugal, Belgium, and Turkey.

On the 18th of February, 1871, I presented to the Assembly the Ministry I had just formed, which was made up as follows: M. Jules Favre, for Foreign Affairs; M. Picard, Minister for the Interior; M. Dufaure, for Justice; General Le Flô, for War; Vice-Admiral Pothuau, of Marine; M. Lambrecht, for Commerce; M. de Larcy, for Public Works; M. Jules Simon, for Education. Finance was reserved for M. Ponyer-Quertier, not then in Bordeaux, whose acceptance was only known later.

The armistice concluded on the 28th of January, 1871, between the King of Prussia and the Government of National Defence, in order to allow France to elect an Assembly to pronounce on the question of peace or war, terminated on the 21st of February.

On the 19th, after accepting from the Assembly the mission of going to discuss the preliminaries of peace with the Chancellor of the German Empire, I left Bordeaux for Paris, whence I proceeded to Versailles on the 20th of February.

I have preserved, in notes taken after each of my

conferences with Count Bismarck the memory of this negotiation in which Belfort was all I could save from the demands of the conqueror. On the 26th of February, the interests of France obliged me to sign the preliminaries of peace.

I took advantage of this journey to come to an arrangement with the Bank of France and to obtain fresh advances from it; for there was no longer anything coming into the Treasury, as the Prussians were collecting the taxes of the North as far as the Loire, while the local administrations in the South were disposing almost at their own pleasure of the resources brought in by the collectors-general.

After this I went to Bordeaux, where the Assembly perceived the necessity of approving the preliminaries of peace I had just signed, without giving themselves up to discussion and imprudent speeches.

I had left Paris in an alarming state.

M. Jules Favre wrote to me immediately after my departure, saying that if I did not bring back the Government to the city he would resign, and all his colleagues with him; for the revolutionary party in Paris was becoming more and more difficult to control, and pretended that we were staying in Bordeaux so as to proclaim a monarchy there. It was daily becoming more difficult to exercise the power of the State from so far off, and a prompt decision on the point was essential.

It was on this occasion that differences of opinion began to display themselves among the various parties in the Assembly. The Right, troubled over the disquieting state of Paris, would have wished not to leave Bordeaux, where they also hoped to have greater freedom to follow their real inclinations. At the very most they consented to go as far as Orléans. The Left, inspired by the opposite motives, would gladly have gone to Paris.

By way of compromise, I thought for a moment of proposing Fontainebleau as a temporary seat for the Assembly; but reasons relating to military order changed my intention, and fortunately so. I saw that if Paris should rise, as we could not but fear, the troops detached to guard the Assembly would be missing from the army that would march to quell the insurrection. This consideration led me to prefer Versailles to Fontainebleau, as it was only four leagues from the capital, and dominated it completely by means of Mont-Valérien.

From Versailles, it was an easy matter to go to the help of the army; if the latter were forced to give way, it would find a *point d'appui* close at hand and very solid. I proposed Versailles, therefore, though naturally without giving the reasons for my preferring it. I was obliged to intervene strongly between the Right and the Left to make them adopt this solution of the difficulty.

To the Right I explained the absolute necessity of governing Paris from the nearest possible point, and to the Left I said very sharply that honesty would not allow me to promise the Assembly complete safety in Paris. In the end I convinced both, and obtained that the Assembly and the Government should transfer to Versailles on the 20th of March.

I have already, in my deposition on the insurrection of the 18th of March, made before the Parliamentary Commission of Inquiry, related the principal events of this period. To-day I shall complete that account by certain details which will display the difficulties of every kind I had to surmount in re-establishing order in the capital.

The first and greatest of these difficulties was to disarm the populace, which was holding four hundred and fifty thousand muskets (this was the total number given up), and had taken possession of an immense quantity of both siege and field artillery. To carry out this perilous operation we had barely eighteen thousand dispirited troops, partly demoralized by the revolutionary ferment in the midst of which they had lived during the siege. General Vinoy, a cool and intelligent officer, was in command.

We settled with him, after having discussed the matter in Council, that he should try, on the 18th of March, in the morning, to get hold of the field artillery parked by the Parisians on the heights of Belleville and Montmartre.

On that date, by five o'clock in the morning, General Vinoy had occupied these positions and had made himself master of the artillery without striking a blow. But on this occasion he failed in that keen vigilance that brings success in war. The guns once taken, he should have put to the teams at once and brought them away, drawing up his troops in the rear so as to assure the success of his operations.

Hurrying up during the night from Versailles, I reached the Staff Office, in the Louvre, where I found the general. He was, he told me, absolutely free from anxiety. I did not share his feeling of security. As long as our guns were not taken away, and the troops stayed idly round them, there was always the fear of having them surrounded by a hostile crowd. Before long, as a matter of fact, aides-de-camp came to warn us that there were very ominous groups forming about

PRESIDENCY OF THE REPUBLIC 123

the guns, and that it would be most difficult to advance in Paris, with a thousand or twelve hundred horses dragging artillery, through a mass of the populace, packed and irritated.

I urged General Vinoy to go at once to the threatened place, and I went to the Foreign Ministry, where I had summoned the members of the Government.

There I learned that my fears were being realized; our troops, masters of the guns, could not fetch them off, drowned as they were in the floods of an excited multitude. At this news, trouble of mind and confusion of opinions were speedily at the highest pitch, even in the Council. General Vinoy, having sought in vain to get to the central scene of insurrection, had lost his usual coolness. It seemed to me then that the wisest step to take was not to attempt, for the moment, to bring away the guns, but to withdraw our troops in good order, without a conflict, and to rally them on the left bank of the Seine. General Vinoy at once issued orders to that effect.

While awaiting the execution of this manœuvre, and at the advice of the Council, who thought the National Guards might be of some assistance to us, the drums were bidden sound the *générale* to bring them together. If by this means we could collect twenty or even fifteen thousand men prepared to act with us, we could add them to the regulars, and thus having thirty thousand men at our disposal, we would give battle.

While the drums went out through the Paris streets, a continually increasing seditious crowd, armed with muskets that had imprudently been entrusted to them during the siege, swept into the Champs Elysées and the Place de la Concorde.

At two in the afternoon we were still awaiting the

return of the troops General Vinoy had recalled. At last they appeared. I went to meet them, towards the head of the Pont de la Chambre des Députés, emerging from which I saw, on horseback, General Faron, who had brought his division off safely. Modest, gentle, heroic, he had opened a passage through the insurgents, even carrying off several guns in spite of them. The other divisions, less deeply engaged than General Faron's had been, came one after the other to rally along the Seine, with their divisional artillery, and our stout Vinoy, having speedily recovered his coolness, was ready to carry out any orders he might receive. By that time it must have been four o'clock. All the vigorous and trustworthy element in the National Guard having already left Paris to go and rest after the fatigues of the siege, barely six hundred men had responded to the *générale*. We could, therefore, use only the army for any action, and the army was eighteen thousand strong no longer, for two or three thousand men at least, set to guard distant posts, had not been able to rejoin us. In these conditions, to attack the insurrection would have laid us open to a certain check; the insurgents would throw up barricades, and we would never be able to reduce them.

On the other hand, were we to stay in Paris and do nothing, the moral infection would lay hold of the army, which would not be long before abandoning us. Retreat on Versailles was, therefore, forced upon us. At Versailles we could encamp the army, reinforce it, raise its spirits, and in this way presently bring it back a hundred to a hundred and fifty thousand strong.

I made up my mind at once to this course; but in the Ministry there were three men of the Fourth of September—MM. Jules Favre, Jules Simon, and Picard

—whom it was hard to convince that this retreat was necessary. Accordingly I decided the matter myself, and had orders sent to General Vinoy, about six in the evening, to recross the bridges, under cover of his artillery, and to retire on Versailles by way of Sèvres on the one side, and by Saint-Cloud on the other. I left MM. Jules Favre, Jules Simon, and Picard hesitating whether to follow me or no, and, escorted by some light cavalry, I bade adieu to Paris.

Reaching Versailles about the end of the day, I sent for the mayor, M. Rameau, and asked him for bread, meat, and straw, to feed and lodge the troops, and thanks to his intelligent and patriotic energy, all was speedily got ready.

It was in this wretched night that news was brought to me of the assassination of General Clément Thomas and General Lecomte, the two earliest victims of the Paris insurrection.

Our soldiers arrived on March 19th, in good order, without having been disturbed by the insurgents. I had them settled, well provided with victuals, under canvas in the camp of Satory.

In a week, through the recuperating influence of camp life, upon which I counted, these troops recovered the smartness and military spirit they had lost during their stay in Paris. Presently, rallying stragglers, and a regiment that had remained shut up in the Luxembourg Gardens, calling up all the troops that remained from the North to the South of France, I managed in a fortnight to bring the strength of our forces up to nearly fifty thousand men, mustered at Versailles.

I have not always obtained justice from the National Assembly; but this time the fortunate retreat from

Paris, and the swift and solid concentration of the remains of our army won me unanimous praise, and MM. Jules Favre, Jules Simon, and Picard, who had rejoined us, themselves proclaimed that I had taken the wisest course. The Government then was rallied like the army.

At the same time, in spite of this general approval, the Assembly had nominated a Commission of fifteen members, ostensibly to help me with its counsels, but in reality to keep watch over my actions. Agitated, uneasy, devising scheme upon scheme, they would perhaps have prevented me from retaking Paris if I had allowed myself to be guided by them.

During the fortnight that I spent in restoring the soldiers' spirits and increasing their numbers, the insurgents, in possession of Paris, had on their side taken the forts on the left bank of the Seine, which were not occupied by the Prussians: we had been obliged by the necessity of concentrating the garrisons at Versailles, with the exception of Mont-Valérien. We could then foresee that the insurgents would make an attempt on the position of Châtillon on our right, and another towards Neuilly, which would give us the opportunity of inflicting a check upon them, and to make the army definitely take sides with us, since, according to the malcontents of the Assembly, their disposition was doubtful.

We arranged with General Vinoy, who summed up the situation very accurately, to post one division about Châtillon, another at Neuilly, keeping the bulk of our forces between Versailles and Neuilly, to direct it to whatever point was most seriously threatened.

In the morning of the 2nd of April, Mont-Valérien having observed a troop moving on Châtillon, and a much greater crowd upon Neuilly, everything was on foot. General Pellé, a brave man if ever was one, seized Châtillon, which at first had been occupied, and though seriously wounded, put the attackers to the rout.

Reassured by telegraph as to this side, I hastened to send to General Vinoy's help the troops kept as reserve at Versailles and at La Bergerie, in the direction of Villeneuve-l'Étang; an imposing force was thus mustered on the slopes of Mont-Valérien. The insurgents were allowed to clear the bridge of Neuilly, and deploy in the plain. The cavalry, at once hurling itself on them with the utmost determination, forced them to re-enter Paris.

All this was carried out with rare presence of mind and vigour by General Vinoy, who in these days of the 2nd, 3rd, and 4th of April decided the future behaviour of the army by engaging it irrevocably against the insurrection, and by making it at all points victorious. From that time it was no longer the object of doubt; but it still remained to bring it to break into Paris. All my efforts were directed to bring about this great result as quickly as possible.

The forces at our disposal at this moment were insufficient to undertake the siege of Paris. For that it was necessary that they should be brought up to a hundred and fifty thousand men, at the least. With no little trouble I got Count Bismarck to give us back some hundred thousand prisoners, and as he could not send them to us by the railways, which were already choked up by the German troops returning to their homes, he sent them to the Hanoverian ports, where I had them fetched by all the ships procurable at Brest and Cherbourg.

The Bank of France advanced the Treasury the necessary money to furnish arms and equipment for them. Hastily I collected rifles, uniforms, and provisions at Cherbourg, at Cambrai, at Dijon, three points upon which our soldiers, as they turned into France, were directed, there to be incorporated under the command of Generals Ducrot and Clinchant. At the same time, thanks to the activity of Captain Krantz of the navy, the ports of Brest and Cherbourg sent us a powerful siege artillery, with a considerable stock of ammunition.

In thus making ready for the struggle with the Commune, I was the real champion of order, and I showed the army it could depend on me, its oldest friend and most constant upholder. And so all the generals had come to offer their assistance : Douay, Frossard, Montaudon, de Ladmirault, Bataille, du Barail, Marshal Canrobert, and finally Marshal MacMahon. This last general, healed of the wound he had taken at Sedan, had settled at Saint-Germain. He had a private reason for showing trust in me. At the moment of the Fourth of September, when a rumour was widely spread that he had just been wounded, perhaps mortally, seized with patriotic emotion, I sent him my card with a brief message written upon it. He had thought himself ruined in the public regard after Reichshoffen and Sedan. This sign of sympathy from a statesman with whom he had no relations had comforted and encouraged him.

He had come then to visit me at Versailles, and had displayed a modesty and simplicity that greatly impressed me. At this moment, he said, all honest folk, especially the heads of the army, owed me their help;

and without actually offering his, he added that of all those whom I might ask to serve nobody could refuse. My welcome encouraged him to come again, and he did actually come again, and made the journey from Saint-Germain to Versailles several times to come to the Présidence.

As I have said before, everything was being got ready for the siege of Paris. Every morning at the Présidence we held a kind of council, made up of Captain Krantz, chief of staff to Vice-Admiral Pothuau, the Naval Minister, General Valazé, Under-Secretary for War, M. Sanson, Divisional Inspector, with General Borel, the head of the General Staff, M. de Franqueville, the Director-General of Railways, and lastly General Appert, who was in command of the military district of Versailles.

In this council a report was made to me of what had been done during the previous twenty-four hours, and we decided on what was to be done during the day. Thanks to the help of these intelligent, energetic, and loyal men, I was able, within six weeks, to muster at Versailles a solid army of a hundred and forty thousand men or thereabouts, and to bring up beneath the walls of Paris a numerous siege artillery with a thousand rounds for each gun, an unprecedented supply for attacking a fortified place.

As a result of their increase in strength I was obliged to divide our forces into two armies: an active army and a reserve. The reserve army, formed of three divisions, had for special duty to guard the seat of the Assembly and the Government, and to watch over the safety of both. The active army, divided into five corps, was more particularly intended for the operations to restore order.

Generals de Ladmirault and de Cissey, whom I had received with every consideration when they had come to offer us their services, had been each given command of an army corps. So with General Clinchant, who had organized the troops mustered at Cambrai, and who had distinguished himself with the army of the East, under General Bourbaki, for smartness, coolness, and common sense. I very soon had cause to congratulate myself upon choosing him. Another corps was assigned to General Douay, a former aide-de-camp to the Emperor, a spirited officer and most assiduous in his duties. Lastly I set General du Barail at the head of the cavalry corps.

General Vinoy had up to this time shown himself a vigorous commander at the head of the army of Paris; but his rank was not high enough to make it possible to put both the active army and the reserve army under his authority. Even supposing in capacity he was equal to the Marshals at our disposal, he would not have had the necessary prestige to dominate so many different characters and deserts. I invested him therefore with the functions of the Grand Chancellor of the Legion of Honour, still leaving him at the head of the army of reserve, in which post, when all the corps would be acting together, he would be under the orders of whatever commander-in-chief I might appoint.

Marshal MacMahon, who had not ceased to come to see me, but always without voicing any wish, seemed to me indicated by his rank for this supreme command. I offered it to him, but he replied to my proposal that he was a beaten man, and his nomination could only give rise to criticism.

"Beaten?" said I. "Everybody has been beaten,

unfortunately! And as for criticisms, it is for me to answer them."

The Marshal did not persist. His consent was instant. He asked for General Borel as his chief of staff, an officer long accustomed to serve under him. I had agreed to this, when next day General Borel came to see me, and whether sent by his chief or of his own accord he told me he thought it would be difficult to get the Marshal and General Vinoy to work in harmony, because they detested each other ever since the taking of the Malakoff, each thinking that on that occasion they had not been treated according to their deserts.

"I must cut you short," I replied. "General Vinoy has commanded the army most ably, and I will not sacrifice him to any one. By treating both the Marshal and the General well, by bringing them together, by making them feel the interest of the State, and, if necessary, the authority of the Government, I shall bring them to render most useful service."

And I succeeded in this with an ease that surprised me, and led me to think that General Borel had exaggerated the difficulty.

In this distribution of the strength of the army among chiefs of approved worth, I should have liked to be able to find a command for General Changarnier; but his age, his feeble health, and above all, his pretensions, had not allowed it, for he looked for nothing less than a marshal's baton.

As I could not promote to this supreme rank the generals who had just distinguished themselves pre-eminently in the bloody battles of the recent war against the foreigner, how could I have raised an officer, meritorious without doubt, but who had not served for twenty-five years, and who had never held any high command before an enemy? I could only, as a token of my esteem and my personal friendship, send him the grand cordon of the Legion of Honour, which I did with expressions which ought to have touched him. He considered this distinction below his deserts, and refused it in an impertinent letter. All parties were agreed in recognizing the absurdity of his behaviour.

After the concentration of our forces and their subsequent division into various army corps, it remained for us to devise, with the commanders of these corps, a plan of attack.

The Prussians occupied the north and the east of the perimeter of Paris, from the bridge of Asnières up to Aubervilliers, in the plain, and up to Romainville and Rosny on the eastern heights. As possible points of attack, then, we had only the southern forts: Montrouge, Vanves, Issy, and the edge of the Bois de Boulogne.

While I was on the Council of Defence, which was formed in the later days of the Empire, I had been very much exercised by the danger to which Paris was exposed through her insufficient fortifications on the side of Saint-Cloud and Meudon.

I pointed out this weak quarter to the generals. They recognized that from Saint-Cloud and Meudon considerable results could be obtained against the stronghold. It was proposed to arm these positions with twenty cannon. I demanded a hundred. To construct a battery of importance it was reckoned a month would be needed. This was too long a delay. I had heard the wealth and intelligence of M. Jules Hunebelle, a contractor for public works, very highly spoken of. I had him sent for. He got a thousand workmen together and the famous battery known as the Montretout was finished in a week. This honest man did not force us to pay for the work like a usurer, but like a true patriot.

The point upon which the efforts of the attack were to be concentrated being thus settled, the different corps were disposed around the precincts as follows: the first corps, under General de Ladmirault, a little to the left of the Point-du-Jour, at Courbevoic and at the Pont de Neuilly; the fourth corps, under General Douay, in the Bois de Boulogne, opposite the Point-du-Jour; the second corps, under General de Cissey, took up its position on the left bank of the Seine, before the forts of Issy and Vanves; General du Barail, with all the cavalry forming the third corps, had for his task to beat up the plain from the south and drive back the insurgents if they tried to come out by Montrouge, as they had done at the time of their attack on Châtillon repulsed on the 2nd of May; finally, behind, in the camp of Satory, General Clinchant with the fifth corps, and General Vinoy with the old army of Paris, acted as reserve for big occasions. The whole made up, as I have said, a hundred and forty thousand men actually under arms, with a very numerous field and siege artillery.

The attack on the enclosure from the side of the Bois de Boulogne was only possible after the reduction of the fort of Issy, whose fire would have enfiladed our trenches and been excessively troublesome. I proposed to batter it with sixty and even eighty heavy guns.

Except General de Berckheim, every one was doubtful whether this unusual concentration of means of attack could bring the advantages upon which I reckoned—that is to say, silence the fire of the besieged garrison, make their position untenable, open a breach without the assistance of a breaching battery, and allow the besiegers to break into the fort without undergoing the dangers of an assault.

On the 26th of April the attack opened with forty and afterwards sixty pieces. Towards the sixth day, every piece (only two of which had been put out of action) had fired three to four hundred rounds, which proved that our provision had by no means been excessive, as had been pretended at first. During this unceasing cannonade General de Cissey, without losing any time, had boldly opened his trenches, which, under cover of the guns, were driven with astonishing speed up to the very foot of the walls. At length on Tuesday, the 9th of May, our soldiers, seeing the fort was absolutely silent, turned it, and finding the gate open, perceived that it was abandoned.

Thus, in accordance with my expectation, by dint of artillery alone, our soldiers had succeeded in getting hold of the fort, without having had either to open a breach or to expose their lives in an assault. The news of this put an end to the rumours which evil-wishers were spreading about our supposed daily defeats, and the impossibility of the final success of our enterprise.

While I was devoting my days, and my nights very frequently, to preparing the means of subduing Paris by force, without neglecting those that might occur of penetrating into the city without violence, I was not spared parliamentary embroilments. One day in particular M. Mortimer-Ternaux, one of the most restless of the Orléanists in the Assembly, questioned me on the communications I had held with the Paris Commune.

Now these communications were as follows:

Many persons, sometimes very excellent people too (the courageous and honourable Schœlcher was one of them), would have liked to obviate the punishment that awaited the members of the Commune, among whom they counted misguided friends of their own; others were afraid lest the Republic should be carried away into a civil war. Both these parties, seeking for a way to put an end to the struggle with the insurrection, came to tell me they hoped to persuade the heads of that insurrection to yield, if I did not make conditions too severe for them. I made the same reply to all.

"Do you come in the name of the Commune? I have no ears for you; I do not recognize belligerents."

"No," they would answer, "we come in our own names, to prevent the shedding of blood. Assure the heads of the Commune that their lives will be spared, and promise us that the army will not enter Paris; on these conditions we promise to have the struggle brought to an end."

"I have no conditions to accept and no engagements to make. The reign of law will be established in Paris absolutely, and the guilty, whoever they may be, shall be submitted to that law. As for the army, in France it is everywhere at home; it will enter Paris in a body and will plant the tricolour where the red flag has flown. Paris will be as much obedient and submissive to the power of the State as a hamlet of a hundred inhabitants."

Such invariably was my reply.

To these well-wishers who came and went were added the representatives from the large towns:

mayors or municipal councillors from Lyons, Marseilles, Grenoble, Toulouse, Bordeaux, Nantes, etc., etc. They held Paris to blame, they said, and would give up all idea of joining her if I would assure them that I was not the instrument of a plot hatched in the Assembly to do away with the Republic.

For these my reply was as plain and outspoken as for the former. I told them that doubtless there were in the Assembly members who favoured the restoration of the Monarchy; but there was no plot to overthrow the existing Constitution, that in any case if there were such a plot I would not lend myself to carry it out.

They withdrew fully persuaded of my good faith; to that conviction I owed the inaction of the great towns—that is to say, the safety of France and society; for if we had been forced to detach fifteen or twenty thousand men from the army of Versailles in order to restrain Lyons, Marseilles, Toulouse, Bordeaux, we should never have got into Paris.

It was in these circumstances that on the 11th of May M. Mortimer-Ternaux questioned me as if I had betrayed the cause of order, while I was wearing myself out in efforts to defend it.

Indignant at so much ingratitude, I answered the question harshly, and demanded an immediate vote of confidence, which I obtained by five hundred votes, even though my heat had provoked the Assembly to some displeasure.

The taking of the fort of Issy by General de Cissey, which happened on the 9th of May, having delivered us from the fire that would have spoiled our principal attack from the side of the Bois de Boulogne, it had become possible to begin this attack. A council of war was held on this subject on the 12th of May at the Présidence. There were present: Marshal MacMahon, Generals de Ladmirault, de Cissey, Vinoy, Le Brettevillois, Clinchant, du Barail, Douay, de Courville (of the Engineers), Princeteau (of the Artillery).

There were no two sides to take as to the manner of attacking. The regular and classic methods of a siege were to be used; that is to say, we should open a trench in the Bois de Boulogne, before the gates of Auteuil, Saint-Cloud, the Point-du-Jour, which was to fall to General Douay on the right. At the same time General de Ladmirault would on his left bombard Neuilly and l'Étoile, and General de Cissey, seizing the fort of Vanves as he had the fort of Issy, would begin his approach works against the part of the circuit that fell to his charge. It was fully understood that the great battery of Montretout would continue its fire against the circuit, as much to protect General Douay's approach works as to destroy the means of defence.

Unfortunately, a regular attack by trenches must be slow, too slow to please the Assembly, and specially Prince Bismarck, who threatened to take action himself if we did not move more rapidly. For that reason we had thought of buying entrance through one of the gates of Paris. Every day somebody came to offer us a gate for one or two millions. The go-betweens of these bargains always said they were sent by the principal leaders of the Commune. Greed brought them, but the fear of being shot by the insurgents prevented their ever coming to a definite proposal, which could not prevent some members of the Assembly from pretending that with five hundred thousand francs I could enter Paris without striking a blow, but that I wanted the glory of taking it by force of arms, were I to sacrifice never so much precious life.

Once only was a plan that seemed feasible suggested to me by a very bold fellow who went in and out of Paris every day. I promised the reward after the service was done, and everything was arranged for, I think, the night of the 13th of May.

At midnight, General de Ladmirault stole down into the Bois de Boulogne by Courbevoie and noiselessly took up a position close to the gates of la Muette and Auteuil. General Douay at the same hour left his trenches and posted himself near the Passy gate. Carefully selected troops of police, followed by engineers, were to come up to the gate that had been indicated and promised to us, and the moment it was opened they were to fling themselves through it, overpower the post, then divide half to the right, half to the left, to go and seize the two neighbouring gates and open them to the army.

The whole of Vinoy's reserves were put in motion. There were eighty thousand men hidden in the Bois without any one having heard the slightest sound. The weather was clear, but cold. I spent the night in the Bois with General Douay, waiting for the signal. We waited in vain.

At four o'clock the Marshal, who was at the cedar between the two lakes, sent word to me that as the day was drawing near, he thought he ought to order the retreat, fearing lest his troops might be riddled with grapeshot as they withdrew. I approved, and the retreat was achieved in good order ; we did not even have a man wounded, though before daybreak some volleys of grape had been fired at us.

I went back to Versailles, arriving at seven in the morning. Very little was known of this adventure. None the less, a report went about that we had lost heavily in a night attack.

As for those who were to sell the gate that was not delivered, they pretended that one of them had been shot, that all of them narrowly escaped the same fate, and that it was no fault of theirs if the siege of Paris had not ended that night.

There was another way to penetrate into Paris by surprise, which we went into carefully with the Marshal, so great was our desire to avoid bloodshed. The Prussians were witnesses to our efforts, and showed themselves disposed to further them. Established at Saint-Denis, they held the railway that ended at this part of the circuit of Paris, and offered to hand it over to us. But as we could not consent to accept the help of the foreigner to reestablish order at home, we had to keep to the plan of attack by main force agreed upon in our council of war on the 12th of May.

The very day of our bootless vigil in the Bois de Boulogne, General Cissey informed me that he had just made himself master of the fort of Vanves, and that, delivered now from the fire of Vanves and of Issy, he was about to attack the circumvallation immediately so as to make a breach in it. This new success won us an increase of confidence from the Assembly.

Every day of this week, from the 14th to the 21st of May, I passed my time now in the batteries of Montretout, now with those of General de Cissey, where the danger, thanks to the superiority of our guns, was not very great. We could see, at the end of the week, that the walls would shortly be accessible, and it was agreed that on Sunday, the 21st of May, we should assemble in council of war at Mont-Valérien to fix the day for a general assault.

I left Versailles, then, on Sunday, the 21st of May, at three in the afternoon, to go to Mont-Valérien. Already I was at the base of the slope leading to the fort, when an officer, coming up at the gallop, told me that General Douay would not be with us, as he was engaged in entering Paris.

Filled with this unexpected news, I made my horses go quicker, and reaching the fort, I found the Marshal and General de Ladmirault already informed of it, the latter seeming at ease, though perhaps a little vexed not to be the first to enter Paris. As for the Marshal, who never left the telescope directed upon the Point-du-Jour, he suddenly exclaimed:

"We are repulsed!"

His words moved me extremely, and I ran to one of the telescopes to see with my own eyes what was going on. I did actually see, at the gate of the Point-du-Jour, soldiers coming out, but calmly, in no hurry, with nothing that seemed like flight. Captain Krantz, who had a very sure eye, and who also had a telescope, answered:

"Those fellows are not in flight. We are not repulsed; but they are carrying out some manœuvre that we cannot understand from here."

These words, which tallied with my own impression, were speedily confirmed by the movements of other soldiers obviously proceeding towards the door; it was impossible then to believe in a check. Joy came back to my heart and all our hearts, including General de Ladmirault's.

A quarter of an hour after all doubts were at an end. We saw what might have been two long black snakes winding along in the folds of the ground, present their heads at the gate of the Point-du-Jour, through which they entered. It was a division from General Douay's corps, which, master of the circumvallation, was entering in two columns.

The fire from Montretout had demolished the Point-du-Jour gate, the debris of which and of the drawbridge had filled the ditch in a way that made a practicable passage. All firing from the fortress had ceased: our soldiers, always daring and inquisitive, jumping up on the breastwork of the trenches, had seen a man on the abandoned rampart waving a handkerchief.

This was the famous Ducatel who, animated by an honest and courageous zeal, had gone forward thus far and was signalling to our soldiers the possibility of entering. The men had run to the broken gate and had penetrated within the fortifications, passing over the broken timbers of the drawbridge. The General had entered with them, and finding some deserted field-guns, he had sent to fetch shells for them. This was the explanation of the movements to and fro of the soldiers going in and out, which had made us so uneasy for a moment.

It was time to leave Mont-Valérien in order to dispatch the whole army through the gate General Douay had just opened. This was a matter for the Commander-in-Chief. We arranged with the Marshal then that he should go without delay and put himself at the head of De Ladmirault's corps and Douay's, while I should go to Versailles to send him all Vinoy's and Clinchant's troops and to pass General de Cissey, who also had made a practicable breach in the fortifications, the order to enter Paris and occupy the quarters on the left bank.

Arriving at Versailles, where I had been preceded by the news of our success, I informed General de Cissey of the events of the day and the orders of Marshal MacMahon. At the same time, with the commissary Sanson and Captain Krantz, I gave and superintended the carrying out of the order to transport sufficient provisions and straw for the soldiers' temporary camp. After dining with my family and a few friends who shared my joy, I slept a little. At two in the morning of Monday, the 22nd of May, I set out once more for Paris, where I entered at three o'clock by the Point-du-Jour gate. On the way I had passed lines of wagons full of stores for the army.

Moving off to the left, I met the columns of our troops entering by the Auteuil and the Passy gates, and I saw the Marshal preparing to establish his headquarters on the heights of the Trocadéro, from which he could easily send help towards any point that might be threatened.

We were a little afraid of falling into a trap at the Trocadéro : the immense stock of powder stored in the cellars of Passy, they said, might blow up the whole advanced division of the army. Ducatel declared that nothing of the kind need be feared, and to prove his sincerity he marched some paces in front of General Douay. Our uneasiness only came to an end when we learned that General Douay was safe and sound, and had seized the Trocadéro without striking a blow. We heard also that General de Ladmirault, having reached the Arc de Triomphe in the Etoile, was engaged in the Champs Elysées. His difficulties were to begin in the Place de la Concorde, all the exits to which were barricaded with masonry. On his side, General de Cissey, operating on the left bank, was penetrating into the Faubourg Saint-Germain.

From this moment there only remained a barricade war throughout the whole of Paris, during which I had little to do but watch over the comfort of the army while it was shedding its blood for France. I decided therefore to return to Versailles.

It was still night when I had entered Paris. As I left the city day was breaking. I was passing through the Bois de Boulogne, now a mere heap of broken rubbish, when I saw coming towards me a confused crowd of men and women of every age, in the strangest costumes; they were held in check by soldiers, who were driving them before them. These were insurgents who had been taken prisoner and were being brought to Versailles. Their faces still displayed the fury of the fight, the despair of defeat. Ruin and hate!—that is all that civil discords leave behind them.

As soon as I arrived at Versailles I went to inform the Assembly of the army's entry into Paris. During the sitting of May 22, 1871, they unanimously testified their satisfaction and gratitude in the following resolution:

"The Assembly declares that the land and sea forces, and the Head of the Executive Power of the Republic have deserved well of their country."

The anxieties of the siege were followed by those of guarding and maintaining the prisoners, whom it was urgently necessary to place at a distance from the scene of the struggle. We expected from forty to fifty thousand of them, criminal for the most part, but even so to be humanely treated. I had enclosures got ready in the dépôt at Satory, in the barracks, in the orangery of the Château de Versailles, covered as far as possible, and straw, bread, and water were brought into them; there we shut in these poor people, surrounded with guns to keep them in order; for there was not a soldier left in Versailles, all having been sent to Paris except about a thousand gardiens de la paix and a battalion of picked gendarmes charged with the safety of the Assembly.

When I think of the almost superhuman efforts demanded of me by the struggle against the insurrection and its consequences, when I compare my devotion to the task of restoring order with the scanty gratitude since shown me, I find once more confirmed the philosophic precept that the satisfaction of doing well is, in this world, the only certain reward for duty done.

The struggle against the Commune, from the entry of the army into Paris, resolved itself into a succession of street fights, in which the army, continually undergoing point-blank fire without any chance to return it before clearing the barricades, took furious vengeance on the vanquished, as soon as they were in its grasp. I issued most severe orders in the endeavour to restrain the soldiers' wrath, and the Marshal on his part did all he could to prevent bloodshed. Unhappily, this street battle lasted a whole week, from the 21st to the 28th of May!

On the first date we occupied the Faubourg Saint-Honoré, the Place Vendôme, and the Place de la Concorde; the barricades here being taken in the rear. Ladmirault's corps, on the left, rolled along the ramparts up to Montmartre, which, also taken in the rear, offered hardly any resistance. On the right, de Cissey's corps swept over the Faubourg Saint-Germain as far as the Panthéon: in this quarter the struggle was heavy, and cost several heads of the insurrection their lives.

Suddenly a terrible sight struck the whole army, and all the honest and peaceable population left in Paris, with blank amazement and horror. Tremendous flames shot up from the Tuileries, the Palais-Royal, the offices of the Légion of Honour, the Cour des Comptes, the Hôtel de Ville, the Ministry of Finance. The insurgents, in their criminal rage, seeing Paris falling through their hands, wished to leave us nothing but ruins. They had dashed paraffin over the walls and on the inside of all these public monuments, and set them on fire as they were forced to withdraw before the army. The Louvre and its priceless collection only escaped destruction through the devotion and courage of their keeper, M. Barbet de Jouy, aided by a few of the attendants who stood manfully by their post. Barely another hour and many of the greatest works of human genius would have been lost for ever.

In the midst of these dramatic scenes every day increased our cruel anxiety as to the fate of the hostages. The Archbishop of Paris, Monsignor Darboy, M. Deguerry, the Curé of the Madeleine and the best of men, President Bonjean and Gustave Chaudey, Republican guards and gendarmes, a great number of priests, Jesuit fathers and Dominican fathers, had been seized by the insurgents, put behind lock and key and proclaimed hostages.

We had often been approached with the proposal to exchange the notorious Blanqui, legally held in a State prison, against some of these hostages, if we wished to save them from certain death. The proposal and the threat were so monstrous that I could neither accept the one nor believe in the other. One day, however, among the letters addressed to the Government, there was one which Monsignor Darboy had written in the agitation of the most cruel anguish to implore me to consent to this exchange. I was deeply moved, shaken by this letter. The Ministerial Council, to which I communicated it, nevertheless remained inflexible; for, said they, besides the scandal that would arise from the bargain, the creation of such a precedent would entail one of the gravest dangers. If we were to embark upon this course, the most infuriated of the Communards would lift their hands against all the most distinguished people left in Paris to effect an exchange for the worst malefactors.

In these painful circumstances I thought it my duty to have recourse to the Committee of Fifteen, which, as is already known, had been instituted by the Assembly to help the Government, at need, in the business of the insurrection, and I asked its advice, after laying before it a full account of the situation, and reading it the letter from the Archbishop of Paris as well as letters from other unfortunates who had fallen into the hands of the most implacable partisans.

The Committee was greatly affected by the reading of these letters, especially that of Monsignor Darboy. Nevertheless, they were unanimous in declaring that it was impossible to accept the proposed bargain, and their reasons were the same that had decided the Council as a whole.

This double unanimity put an end to my hesitation, but not to my anxiety. I was still buoyed up by the hope that the gaolers of the unfortunate hostages would shrink from the execution of so great a crime, or that we might perhaps arrive in time to prevent it.

In the meanwhile I gave back threat for threat, and declared that the heads of the murderers would answer for those of their victims. It is easy to understand, when such pledges remained in such hands, with what dolorous interest I watched the prolonging of this struggle, which followed from day to day, going to the different posts of the army and marshals' staff quarters.

On Friday, the 26th of May, we were very close upon the final deliverance of Paris from her oppressors, so rapid had been the army's progress. Unhappily, as the insurgents retired before us they always took the hostages with them and shut them up in prisons farthest away from our sphere of action—that is to say, near Belleville and Charonne.

On Saturday evening, May 27, we were at the foot of these heights, and on Sunday morning the naval brigade at the head of the attack carried the last barricades with irresistible dash.

Alas! penetrating into the prison of la Roquette, they found the hostages there no longer! The insurgents had murdered them: Gustave Chaudey on the 23rd of May, at Sainte-Pelagie; Monsignor Darboy, President Bonjean, M. Deguerry, and three other priests, on the 24th of May, at la Roquette.

At the same time we learned that at another point in Paris, in the Rue Haxo, ten priests or members of religious orders, thirty-five gendarmes, and two other prisoners had been put to death. After the burning of Paris, the massacre of the hostages! The Commune had kept its word.

The struggle once over, we had to see about opening the city gates, which had been militarily shut as in the siege by the Prussians, re-establish communications by rail, bring in provisions, carry away the wounded, bury the dead outside the walls, facilitate the return of the various authorities, of all the heads of commerce and industry, in a word restore to its place everything that had been violently torn from its place, and bring back order and life to this great body overthrown from head to foot.

Under the orders of clever M. Alphand, who for twenty years had been in charge of the public works of Paris, thousands of workers swept away the barricades, restored the thoroughfares, and as far as possible effaced all the vestiges of insurrection. We took advantage of the overthrow of demagogy to order a general disarming of the people.

This order, carried out without resistance, brought 450,000 rifles into our hands! . . . I also had the cannons seized, and of these we found about two thousand, part of which were put back in the forts, another part on the square of the Château, at Versailles, and the rest returned to the arsenals. At the same time I was occupied with the question of the prisoners shut up at Versailles, where it was impossible to keep them any longer, in places that were both cramped and hard to watch over.

I formed the plan of sending them to different parts, and having them kept under guard in hulks, as the English had done already with prisoners of war.

Thanks to the diligent labours of Captain Krantz, in a few days the old warships at Cherbourg, Brest, Lorient, were anchored and arranged so as to accom-

modate nearly 40,000 prisoners. We sent down all
the clothing, of poor quality but clean and wholesome, which had been bought for the troops in the
recent war; with this we clad these ragged fellows.
We gave them the same rations as our sailors themselves, and on certain occasions, when we had fears
of typhus, they received wine and coffee. The English
Press, always very well informed, declared that greater
humanity had never been exercised towards greater
criminals.

All minds were tranquillized, and Paris, into which
foreigners were coming in great numbers, seemed
born again. However, bent as we were beneath the
weight of our misfortunes, we could not think of
giving fêtes. One only, for the army that had behaved so admirably, was natural and justified. I mean
a great review. Besides, the recent and extraordinary
success of the loan of two milliards, with which I
had just been occupied, and the reawakening of French
industry had brought back hope to every heart. This
review, then, could only confirm these happy omens.
Fixed for the 12th of June, and several times put off
on account of bad weather, it was held at length
on the 29th of June, precisely a month after the
taking of Paris.

The army that took part in this review counted a
hundred and twenty thousand men, not yet in new
uniforms, but in real war equipment, their bearing
confident and proud from having forced the walls of
Paris that had defied the Prussians. Never had a
hundred and twenty thousand men been seen
assembled for a military fête. They were drawn up
in the Longchamps racecourse, in the Bois de Boulogne,
in a fashion terraced on the huge slope that rises, in

front of the race stands, right up to the edge of the wood. The infantry were massed in the centre, and a numerous artillery and something like fifteen thousand horse were placed along the front and supported the wings.

I took my place with the ministers in the central pavilion of the racecourse, with the President of the National Assembly on my right. The seats on the right were occupied by the deputies, and on the left by the Diplomatic Corps and the chief functionaries of the State. Satisfaction beamed on every face, like the joy of a convalescent in a sunny day. And I myself at that moment found the burden I carried not so heavy as usual.

Marshal de MacMahon galloped down the front of the troops; then, surrounded by a large staff in campaigning array, he came and took up his position before the central pavilion. The march past then began. That army, which had been called undisciplined, that was thought incapable of manœuvring, marched by with admirable precision and in perfect step. At every moment the spectators, carried away by enthusiasm, broke into wild cheering, especially when there passed a regiment that had won special mention in the war.

The hour advanced, for a march past of a hundred and twenty thousand men is a lengthy operation, and we must make haste. The guns then went off in close order at the trot, the cavalry at the gallop, with General du Barail at their head, and all these rapid movements, carried out in concert, presented a magnificent spectacle. The Marshal then came to salute the benches of the Assembly and the Presidential party; I descended to shake him by the hand, and the fête was over.

Returning to Versailles, I brought all the heads of the army together at a great dinner. The greater part of the Assembly, without distinction as to right or left, came to the reception that followed. Everything then went off in the best possible fashion on this good day for France.

Although order was restored and the demagogy reduced to impotence, we could not disband the army of Paris, and that for three important reasons: it was essential to remain strong at all times in face of the revolutionary party, as the only way of keeping it in awe; we had also to keep an imposing force before the Prussians, if we wished to escape from the position in which we had been recently, that of a nation reduced to yield on every occasion; finally this army of Paris was the beginning of the permanent formation with which I intended to lay the chief foundation of our military reorganization.

The army of Paris remaining intact, it was but just that the supreme command should still be in the hands of Marshal de MacMahon, as the reward of the services he had just rendered. It was this consideration of justice that prevented me for the moment from yielding to my desire to offer a command to General Canrobert, whose intelligence and loyalty I fully appreciated. General Borel, when I told him of my intention, appeared to doubt whether his chief would accept, which astonished me a little. The Marshal afterwards came to see me, doubtless having been apprised of my conversation with General Borel. Laying aside his extreme reserve, he opened the subject that was on his mind, and thanked me for my arrangements with regard to him; but the position I had made for him ceased, he thought, to be justified after the taking of Paris; it was a burden upon the State; it would be attacked; in a word it was better for him to retire. All this was said modestly and with the same attitude as the day on which I had made him the proposal to place him at the head of the army.

I gave the Marshal the reasons I have enumerated above, assuring him that they would be universally approved. He appeared touched at my insisting and did not persist in refusing.

It still remained to give the other chiefs of the army the rewards they had right to look for from the Government; then we should have to put the insurgents of the Commune on their trial, and above all to give the Prussians money so as to get them out of our territory as quickly as possible.

But before occupying myself with these various matters, I had to make a very necessary change in the composition of the Ministry. M. Picard could no longer hold the portfolio of the Interior. Continually complaining of the Press, which was very severe upon him, he made it a cause of quarrel with M. Dufaure, the Minister of Justice, who, he said, did not defend him simply to keep on good terms with the newspapers; and he had in the end exasperated his colleague to such a point that I had several times to intervene so as not to be exposed to receive the resignation of a man like M. Dufaure. General Le Flô could not be kept in the War Office either. This excellent officer would have commanded a division to perfection, but as an administrator he was less useful.

I have never been able, without regret, to sever myself from men who have worked with me, and

PRESIDENCY OF THE REPUBLIC 153

especially to sever myself from them without indemnifying them. I nominated M. Picard Governor of the Bank of France; but he preferred the less arduous post of French Minister in Brussels. General Le Flô was well satisfied to accept the Russian embassy. I must next think how to replace the two departing Ministers. M. Lambrecht passed from the Ministry of Commerce to that of the Interior. At Bordeaux I had entrusted him with the portfolio of Commerce, after an acquaintance that went back fifteen years and had taught me to appreciate him. He belonged to a wealthy and important family in the North. Grave and gentle in character, he was infinitely distinguished in every way, endowed with unusual powers of reason, and the greatest political tact, and he would have spared me many difficulties if he had lived. M. Victor Lefranc took his place at the Ministry of Commerce. A Republican of long standing, a witty and copious speaker, and knowing how to make friends, he was at this time much liked in the Assembly.

The vacancy at the War Office still had to be filled. I had to bear in mind very varying needs in matters concerning the highest places in the army. Generals de Ladmirault and de Cissey, after distinguishing themselves at Metz, had displayed high military qualities during the siege of Paris. Not being able in the present circumstances to make them marshals, I sought other means of rewarding their services. I summoned General de Cissey to the War Office, and General de Ladmirault was named Governor of Paris, the second post in the Army. General Montaudon received the command of the 1st Corps, a position he had deserved by his singular bravery. The 2nd Corps, now vacant, fell to General Bataille, an intelligent, energetic officer, a good man to employ in war. General Valazé, no less deserving, went back to Rouen at his own request, to command the division there; lastly, Captain Krantz, whose brains as well as his energy had proved most useful to us, was promoted to be rear-admiral.

After the reconstruction of the Ministry, the arrangements were made for the trial of the forty thousand insurgents guarded in the hulks at Brest and Cherbourg. It was said that, as the prisoners were taken *en masse*, many of them were the victims of mistakes; and there was no lack of deputies from all parties to bring forward claims that were sometimes well founded.

We sent then to Brest and Cherbourg sixty Commissioners and several members of the Military Bar, charged to examine all these claims and to let us know all cases of mistakes they might find proven. As a consequence of their report we were able to take out of the hulks and set at liberty some ten or twelve thousand prisoners, adjudged less deeply compromised than the rest.

There were still thirty and some odd thousands left. It was impossible to grant them an amnesty; that would have been against all human conscience, since beyond doubt those responsible for the massacre of the hostages were among this number. Failing an amnesty, there were only two courses to be taken— either to transport them in a body, without a trial, to some distant colony, or else to try them all one by one.

As for transporting them in a body, an extraordinary law would be needed; for it was a matter of inflicting punishment on accused persons without establishing their guilt. As for trying them individually, it involved the inconvenience of tossing back into the streets of Paris all—and they would be a great many—whose guilt might not, for lack of evidence, be proved. But this latter alternative had the immense advantage of being in accordance with the common law, and since we desired to restore respect for the law it was proper to begin by respecting it ourselves. And so the Council was unanimous in the opinion that all the prisoners should be sent before a military court, the only one competent to know all the truth of the insurrection. Twenty-two councils of war were therefore set up in the division of Paris, and many officers were selected from among the most capable to set on foot and maintain the criminal prosecutions.

This matter put in order, we had to think of that which was becoming the most urgent of all: I mean the question of finance. In the execution of the peace preliminaries signed at Versailles the Prussians had very urgently pressed us to conclude the final treaty without delay. It was their right, and our interest. If by the preliminaries of Versailles we had obtained the evacuation of Paris and all the left bank of the Seine from the forts to Alençon, le Mans, Tours, and the southern part of the Côte d'Or, the German army was still occupying the forts on the right bank of Seine, at Paris, as well as Normandy, Picardy, Flanders, Champagne, Franche-Comté, and Burgundy. We had, then, the greatest possible interest in determining and fulfilling, as quickly as possible, the conditions which would allow us to decrease this huge occupation. For this reason M. Jules Favre, Minister for Foreign Affairs, and the Minister of Finance, M. Pouyer-Quertier, were sent to Frankfort, where they signed the formal treaty of peace on the 10th of May, 1871, with Prince Bismarck and Count von Arnim.

In the treaty it was stipulated that of the five milliards of the indemnity three could not be demanded before the 2nd of March, 1874. The first two would be paid on the following conditions of maturity:

1. Thirty days after the defeat of the Commune: half a milliard, immediately followed by the evacuation of the Somme, Seine-Inférieure, and the right bank of the Eure.

2. On the 31st of December, 1871, a milliard, with the evacuation of the Oise, Seine-et-Oise, Seine-et-Marne, and the Paris forts on the right bank.

3. Finally, on the 1st of May, 1872, a fourth half milliard would free the departments of the Aisne, the Aube, the Côte d'Or, the Haute-Saône, the Jura, and Doubs.

The German army would continue to occupy the six departments of the Marne—Haute-Marne, Ardennes, Vosges, Meuse, Meurthe-et-Moselle, and the district of Belfort—as a pledge for the last three milliards still to pay.

Still five hundred thousand strong, this army was to refrain for the future from all requisitions, or levying of taxes, and would be maintained at the expense of the French Government at certain agreed rates. Its strength would be gradually reduced in proportion to the restoration of order and the fulfilment of our obligations.

To these stipulations were added all the customary ones regulating the lot of the inhabitants of the annexed territory. Furthermore, it was agreed that the section of the eastern railway that lay within the departments annexed to Germany should become the

PRESIDENCY OF THE REPUBLIC

property of the German Government against a sum of three hundred and twenty-five million francs, to be deducted from the second instalment of five hundred millions.

Lastly, by the terms of Article 6 in the peace preliminaries signed at Versailles on the 26th of February, 1871, our soldiers who were detained as prisoners in Germany should have been sent back at once and in full numbers immediately upon the ratification of that treaty. In spite of this express stipulation Count Bismarck had only sent them back little by little and with a deliberate slowness. Our negotiations at Frankfort obtained that this return of the soldiers should be more in conformity with our rights.

This treaty, which had been greatly discussed, was an immense relief to us: but it obliged us to pay fifteen hundred million francs in 1871—that is to say, within eight or nine months. It was necessary, then, to attempt without any delay a first trial of our credit by raising a loan without precedent in its dimensions, as well as by the difficulty of the circumstances in which it was undertaken.

To further its success, I resolved to ask the Assembly to decide to make it by public subscription and in 5 per cent. stocks. Public subscription was a method of borrowing whose popularity with capitalists had already been proved many times by experience; and it was matter of common knowledge that the rate of 5 per cent. would be the most suitable for the small investor. Besides, 5 per cent. offered the borrowing administration no distant opportunities of an advantageous repayment, while giving lenders a considerable remuneration between the price of this repayment and the price of issue. As for the issue price, it could only be fixed on the eve of the opening of the lists and in accordance with the state of the money market at that moment; but I calculated that it would mean not less than 6 per cent. interest on the money actually invested.

For these reasons, on the 6th of June, 1871, I laid before the National Assembly the draft of a law authorizing the Government to raise by public subscription a loan of two milliards five hundred million francs in 5 per cent. stocks.

The five hundred millions, added to the two milliards of war indemnity payable in 1871, were meant to pay the interest due or falling due on this indemnity, and to cover the expenses of the subscription as well as all other necessary expenses of the operation.

To enjoy so great a credit, and in the not very distant future a still greater credit, it was necessary to describe on what guarantees we thought ourselves justified in relying. When I subscribed at Versailles to the financial demands of Germany I knew that France was well able to carry the increased burdens laid on her by war and defeat; and before asking a credit of five milliards on her behalf I had studied and recognized as solid the bases upon which the equilibrium of her receipts and her expenditure could be established.

The Empire, before its last disasters that had become ours, had brought us to a financial state in which the receipts rose to about two milliards, to cope with more than two milliards of ordinary expenditure. That meant a deficit. To conceal this and give us an appearance of prosperity by showing an excess of receipts over expenditure no account was taken either of departmental expenditure, which should have figured in the ordinary budget, or of other charges that were wrongly carried on the so-called extraordinary budget. If these tricks, planned to create belief that the situation was better than it was in reality, were discarded, we might calculate the receipts and the normal expenditure of France before the war as about two milliards. I had taken these figures as the starting-point of our future budgets. From the declaration of war to the signing of peace the public debt had increased by about eight milliards, the interest on which must be added to the two milliards of normal expenditure before the war.

Here are the details of this increase in the public debt, both in capital and in interest:

WAR EXPENDITURE.

	Capital.	Interest.
1. Magne Loan raised under the Empire at the beginning of the war	800	30
2. The Tours Loan	210	15
3. Contribution of the Departments for the mobilized troops and stocks	200	10
4. Loan from the Bank of France at 1 per cent.	1,500	15
5. To be paid to the Railway of the East for the value of the part of the line ceded to Germany	325	16
6. War Indemnity at 6 per cent.	2,000	120
7. War Indemnity at 5 per cent.	3,000	150
Total	8,035	356

Millions of Francs.

It was proper to add to these three hundred and fifty-six millions of interest a strong sinking fund, if we did not wish our credit to be crushed by the vastness of the debt that would weigh upon us as a capital sum. I boldly determined to ask for two hundred millions for a sinking fund.

There were, then, five hundred and fifty-six millions

of taxes to strike in order to balance receipts with expenditure, except perhaps a reduction might be made under some heads in the budget, a reduction whose dimensions could not as yet be estimated.

Never before had such an increase of burden been imposed upon a nation at a single stroke; but as this increase was the condition of our resurrection, I hesitated the less in taking it as the basis of my future proposals to the Assembly, that I had assured myself by a very careful examination of all our taxation that it was not beyond the strength of France.

This examination had proved to me that the fees of registration and stamps could be doubled without any fear of exhausting this source of revenue. By imposing an increase of 30 to 50 per cent. on the duty on sugar, wines, coffee, alcohols, and 20 per cent. in the case of tobacco, there would be no danger of decreasing the great consumption of these articles. The postal service could endure without any inconvenience the same surcharge of 20 per cent.; a duty on railway transport would be most fruitful, and its collection very simple if it was made by the company's employees.

These various surcharges or creations of taxes had the advantage of producing no new inconvenience, in their shape, and no noticeable increase in the cost of collection. For this reason I preferred them to new taxes whose mere novelty would have made them vexatious and not very productive. I meant, then, to reject all innovations, except the tax on railway transport and on paper, which have been successful, and the tax on matches, which so far has hardly brought in as much as we expected.

These various resources, which might be valued at

PRESIDENCY OF THE REPUBLIC

three hundred and fifty millions, were still about two hundred millions less than the budget needed. The Left had its method all ready for establishing the balance of the budget—an income-tax.

This tax would be the fairest of all, if there were any sure way of calculating the means of each taxpayer, but for this valuation we have only the declaration of the taxpayer himself, too insecure a foundation to build a tax upon, or else an inquisition into private fortunes by Treasury officials, an odious and arbitrary method. An income-tax would be a tax full of discord, and the experience of England and Italy in the matter is not conclusive, as the conditions in which it is established in each country are very different from those in which it would be established in France. I was, then, resolved to resist it with all my energy, and the Council readily yielded to my views.

I looked upon it also as very imprudent to load the land with fresh burdens. Land is the eternal drudge: it pays for all local follies and those of Governments as well. A tax on salt, easy to collect it is true, would, like the land tax, have been endured by the country people. But it was wise not to exhaust in advance these last resources, for one can never be sure that fresh mistakes may not bring about new extremities.

Income-tax, any increase of the taxes on landed property and on salt, being removed from my forecast, there remained only raw materials to bring us in the two hundred millions still needed to balance our budget. This tax, which for a long time had yielded considerable sums without being burdensome, had only been abolished when M. Rouher, captivated by the theories of Free Trade, had tried to suppress all taxes on foreign goods. Without inconveniencing those on whom it fell, without increasing the costs of collection, it could bring in perhaps two hundred millions. Upon this head there was no element of the unknown to fear, since the experience of generations guaranteed the reality of the results on which we reckoned. We had only to fear the resistance of the great manufacturers, a resistance which I had resolved to combat with all my power so as to raise the fortunes of the State once more.

On these bases it was possible to strike the budget without too many fiscal innovations, without too heavy sacrifices, and with a strong sinking fund. There was still a burden to foresee and to set down outside the budget: expenditure which I made the foundation of what has been called, on my suggestion, the liquidation account. This account had nothing in common with the old budget extraordinary of the Empire. I need only carry under this head expenditure which once made would not be repeated, such as the repairing of our strongholds, the replacing of war material that had been lost or spent or grown obsolete, the maintenance of the army of occupation, and indemnities for certain localities that had been damaged by the war, such as Paris, for example. The debit side of this account might be calculated at four or five hundred millions, and the assets at two hundred, actually consisting of stocks held by the State, and the balance of the estimated expenses of the loans. We had at least three years to meet these expenditures; it was easy to leave them to the floating debt without calling upon our credit.

Our financial position for the future was therefore reassuring, if the Assembly was willing to take the path I would point out to it. It was reassuring also for the present; for the taxes, which after our defeats had been collected by the Germans, or abused by being spent uselessly, to-day were coming regularly and intact into the Treasury. Lastly, industry, which since the restoring of order had been springing up afresh, was bringing public prosperity back with it. But there was still a great uneasiness in many minds, for the day of meeting the war bills was much dreaded.

My speech before the Assembly on the 20th of June, 1871, on behalf of the law authorizing the loan of two milliards proposed by the Government, calmed these anxieties. It had a great effect upon the Assembly, and particularly on the world of finance. Relying on the calculations, the forecasts, and the considerations I have given above, I showed that supposing a reduction of a hundred and fifty to two hundred millions in expenditure feasible, our next budgets would carry four hundred and fifty millions (including, it is true, two hundred millions for the sinking fund) more than the two milliards of normal expenditure shown by the last budgets of the Empire. I would therefore have to ask the Assembly for nearly four hundred and fifty millions of new resources; we could certainly obtain this by increasing several existing taxes and taxing raw materials, for I absolutely rejected a tax on income.

Within the four corners of this budget, and in case of urgent need, we could have recourse to the floating debt now reduced to six hundred and fifty millions, the lowest figure it had reached for thirty years, or to the Bank of France, whose patriotic help in the critical circumstances through which we were passing I took some pains to signalize.

The clearness and straightforwardness of my explanations convinced the Assembly, who at the same sitting, and without a dissentient voice, voted for the law authorizing Government to contract a loan of two milliards by public subscription, in 5 per cent. funds, and two hundred and twenty-five millions over and above to defray the cost of the operation.

The time granted by the Treaty of Frankfort for paying the first five hundred millions of the indemnity was to expire on the 30th of June. The vote of the National Assembly authorizing the loan being given on the 20th, we had barely ten days left to enable us to meet our obligations. I did not doubt that the loan would be covered with a wide margin; but the Financial Minister, M. Pouyer-Quertier, a man of very uneven temper, by turns excessively confident or anxious without any reason, as the moment came near for the test, had hours of extraordinary agitation which sometimes, I confess, he infected me with. Without any fear of mistake, we could reckon on the public subscription rising to a milliard, for already it had covered, and more than covered, loans of eight hundred millions. But it had never been tried for two milliards, and if we failed, what a catastrophe! Our credit would be ruined, and with it our deliverance brought to naught. For this reason I accepted the proposal, made by the most powerful banking houses in Paris, to guarantee the second milliard for a commission of twenty odd millions. The rate at first appeared excessive; afterwards, on calculating what it would cost the bankers to procure the half milliard or whole milliard not subscribed, if the loan was not wholly covered, I found the claim less exaggerated. This combination had a still further advantage: it

PRESIDENCY OF THE REPUBLIC

gave the bankers a direct interest in our success. We were about to give battle with our allies well satisfied, and subscribers, encouraged by their example, would come boldly forward.

There was only one other point to settle, the price of the issue. When great companies issue capital, this price is determined by the demand. On the contrary, when a public subscription is opened, no bidding is possible, and it is the Government that fixes the issue price, from the current interest for capital in the money market at the moment of the operation. A close study of this market and the opinion of men most competent to judge led the Government to think that it would be proper to offer interest at about 6 per cent., which brought the issue price to eighty-two and a half.

Decided between M. Dutilleul, the Directeur du mouvement général des fonds, M. Pouyer-Quertier, and myself a few hours before the printing of the *Journal Officiel*, the figure was not known to any one before the distribution of this gazette, which at the same time, the 23rd of June, announced the opening of the subscription lists for June 27th. Everything had to be improvised. The Finance administration had not yet been transferred to Paris, on account of the burning of the official building by the Commune. Hastily the "direction de la mouvement des fonds" was installed in the house of the Minister of State under the Empire, that is to say, in the Louvre, and the wickets for the subscription were set up in the Palace of Industry. The Finance Ministry camped where it could.

On the 26th all was more or less ready, and from early morning on the 27th subscribers flocked to the wickets. Their eagerness was not to be compared with what they displayed the following year for the loan of three milliards; but already it was very great and showed perfect confidence in the general situation. From hour to hour we had most reassuring news, and though I had never entertained any serious doubts, I was profoundly satisfied at having a proof that France, if carefully governed, would find the necessary resources to raise herself again.

Before the end of the day the Paris subscription had overpassed the sum of two milliards five hundred thousand, and the wickets were then shut. Next day to this total was added one milliard two hundred and fifty millions subscribed in the provinces, and one milliard one hundred and three or four millions in foreign countries, which brought the sum offered by capitalists to France up to four milliards eight hundred and ninety-seven millions: more than two and a half times the amount asked for! An excellent beginning to reassure us for the appeals we should still have to make, and before very long, to both French and foreign capital.

The loan was to be paid in sixteen equal monthly payments, starting with July, and the first payment exacted as guarantee had yielded three hundred and twenty-three millions; anticipated payments from subscribers who wished to pay in advance, at a discount, raised the amount to eight hundred and forty-seven millions, in the month of July, and four weeks later, with the August payment, the Treasury had received a total sum of one milliard three hundred and fourteen millions. For the country it was a marked triumph of its wealth, its patriotism, and the proof of the high confidence it reposed in the Government.

Henceforth there was no uneasiness as to the payments to be made to the Prussians. The first of these, fixed at five hundred millions, having been made on the 15th of July, the departments of the Somme, Seine-Inférieure, and the Eure were on the 22nd of the same month freed from foreign occupation, and the towns of Rouen, Amiens, and Evreux sent me the most touching messages of gratitude.

Europe was struck with the marvellous rapidity with which we rose up again after our disasters. Here I should say a word as to the disposition of the Great Powers towards us.

Russia, though always held by the affection of the Emperor Alexander towards his uncle, now become Emperor of Germany, began to find a cause for disquiet in the developing power of her neighbours. Neither did she forget her old jealousy of England, kindled afresh every day by events in Central Asia. She therefore looked upon France as a useful and probable ally in the future.

As for Prussia, I was very excusably sinning in occupying myself in organizing the army; but as I was paying punctually, while keeping order and not encouraging rancour in France, the German Government was only exacting on the question of proper securities for the full payment of our debt.

As for Austria, the Emperor, his family, and the army applauded our efforts and wished the recovery of France, which might one day be a necessary counterpoise to Prussia. But we could not win the sympathy of the Hungarians, who reproached us with our friendly relations with Russia, nor that of the Austro-Germans, who naturally, through pride of kinship, ranged themselves with our conquerors

Besides, the ruling minister in Austria, Count Andrässy, was favourable to Prussia.

In England, the nation, just and friendly, would not have liked to see Prussia become so great, nor France so weakened: it watched our regeneration therefore with deep interest; and if Mr. Gladstone and Lord Granville had no great leanings towards us, they were none the less determined not to allow any fresh violence in Europe on the part of the Prussians.

Lastly, Italy, knowing that I had taken my own view, regretfully indeed, of Italian unity, was grateful to me for pursuing a firm and friendly policy towards her that alone perhaps could hold her back on the slope towards an alliance with Prussia. We were, then, looked upon as a Power to be reckoned with.

Not to interrupt my outline of the Government's financial schemes, schemes approved by the Assembly on the 20th of June, and sanctioned by the confidence of the subscribers to the loan on the 27th of the same month, I have said nothing of the sitting of the 8th of June, in which two questions of no little political interest had been settled: one with regard to the abrogation of the laws of 1832 and 1848, which had exiled the elder line of the Bourbons and the Orléans princes; and the other which concerned the ratifying of the elections at which the departments of la Manche, Haute-Marne, and the Oise had sent the Prince de Joinville and the Duc d'Aumale to the Assembly.

The Orléans princes, immediately upon the Fourth of September, had hastened back to France, inspired by patriotism certainly, but also to take advantage of the chances the fall of the Empire might offer for the return of their dynasty. I would have preferred this family to any other, if I had thought a monarchy possible at the moment. But Republicans and Legitimists, together a great majority in the Assembly, would have opposed it, and any attempt I might have made to assist this restoration would, on my part, have been not only a want of loyalty towards Legitimists and Republicans, but also the violation of my duty to France, for my mission was to bring peace to her by preventing party conflicts. I did not hesitate, therefore, as far as lay with me, to discourage the aspirations of the Orléans princes, aspirations they had manifested by asking for the abrogation of the laws condemning them to exile, and the ratification of their elections.

The avowed partisans of the princes in the Assembly were numerous. The monarchist Right Centre, which only accepted the conservative Republic for want of something better, was not sorry to have a chance of casting a monarchist vote; the Legitimists, thinking of a possible fusion of the two lines, did not wish to offend the Orléans princes by voting against them; lastly, the Moderate Left itself, out of respect for its principles, found that the title of Prince was no reason that could be allowed to invalidate the choice of universal suffrage. It was clear that with this disposition among the parties, the Assembly would vote for the abrogation of the exiling laws and the ratifying of the elections.

The sitting of the 8th of June, 1871, in which these questions were to be discussed, naturally attracted a great number of curious onlookers, and when the Commissioners had made their reports I asked leave to speak.

I declared that I could not share the favourable

disposition of a great number of the members of the Assembly towards the conclusions of these reports. The Republic, I said, charge of which I had accepted, was and must be in my eyes the public peace, which might well be compromised if at this juncture we allowed the representatives of dispossessed or broken Governments to reside in France, most of all if we allowed them to exercise political rights.

Under all the preceding forms of government, I had upheld this opinion, and to-day the members of the Constituent Assembly of 1848 knew the price France paid for refusing to listen to my advice on this point. At the same time, as the Orléans princes had assured me that they would not appear in that Assembly, and would not justify any of my apprehensions, I believed I might give up my opposition to the proposed law.

The findings of the reports being immediately put to the vote, by a great majority the Assembly abrogated the exiling laws of 1832 and validated the two elections.

After this vote, the Government had to concern itself with the numerous elections needed to complete the Assembly, in which one hundred and seventeen seats were vacant through deaths, resignations, and most of all, multiple elections. The troubles of civil war, now in one province, now in another, had not allowed these vacancies to be filled as they arose. But since these difficulties were past, the Government summoned the electors. At the same time it decided not to interpose in the elections: in the first place because it had no interest in so doing, its popularity in the country being still unimpaired; then because many members of the Cabinet, who in the days of the Empire had protested against official candidatures, feared lest they should be accused of inconsistency if they allowed a Government of which they formed part to interfere in electoral contests.

For myself, outside such procedures as those of the Empire during the time of official candidatures, I did not admit that a Government should remain indifferent, idle, dumb, in the midst of a crisis so grave for a free country as that of a general or even a partial election. At the same time, since there was no pressing need for us to play an active part, I issued orders to the prefects at the opening of the period of the elections, not to interfere with the canvassing of the candidates. They obeyed the order whole-heartedly.

The voting took place on the 2nd of July, and the chosen candidates, almost without exception Moderate but still Republican, gave the impression that France accepted the Republic if order was assured. This tendency of public opinion met with apparent resignation among the Monarchists in the Assembly, and filled the Republicans with hope.

The latter, after the abrogation of the exiling laws, also wished to have their success; and as the last elections had reinforced them with a round hundred votes, they dreamed of having the Republic formally proclaimed.

Already before the taking of Paris they had asked me to insist on this proclamation.

"I cannot," I had replied, "submit a proposal of such importance to the Assembly, at a moment when the menace of the insurrection might hamper the freedom of its deliberations. Besides, the present condition of things, though it bears the name of a Republic, is still merely a Government of order and security, to which every party can give its adherence without sacrificing its own opinions. On the eve of an assault that must be desperate and bloody, we must not tell our generals and officers, who are not all Republicans, that they are mounting the breach to lay the foundations of the Republic. Leave them the satisfaction of the thought that if they expose themselves to death, it is for the welfare of society, and not to ensure the triumph of a party."

The failure of this attempt on the part of the Left was known, and the Moderate section of the majority was grateful to me for it. But after the last election and its manifestations, it had become difficult wholly to turn a deaf ear to these fresh solicitations of the Republicans. Without going so far as the proclamation of the Republic, many Moderate members of the Assembly recognized the necessity of giving the executive power certain guarantees of duration and stability, which it needed in order to undertake or to finish the great matters it had in charge. With this thought they laid before the Assembly, on the 12th of August, 1871, a proposal which took the name of its promoter, M. Rivet.

This proposal, without binding the future by an untimely proclamation of the Republic, without impairing the sovereignty of the Assembly, tended simply to strengthen the executive power and give the country more security. But the Assembly insisted on seeing in it an intention of encroaching on their rights, and it was under the sway of this notion, whether pretended or sincere, that they nominated the committee that was to report upon the Rivet proposal.

This report was entrusted to M. Vitet. He drew it up in terms excellent for me; but his findings could only be inspired by the feeling of the majority of the committee. At the same time, he cleverly held out against their uncompromising attitude, and did not absolutely reject the proposal.

The two great divisions of the Assembly, the Left and the Right, the party of the Republic and the Monarchical party, in a long and heated discussion all but came to a decisive conflict, as though it were a matter of solving immediately and for ever the great question of the government to be given to France. Happily, MM. Léon de Malleville, Ricard, Rivet, Picard, and myself on the one side, and MM. Casimir Perier and Vitet on the other, succeeded in soothing these ardours of the Left and the Right.

To begin with, the proposal to give me the title of President of the Republic was adopted. The problem of how long my powers were to continue was a delicate one to solve. A very happy solution was arrived at, which was that their duration was to be the same as that of the Assembly itself. If it had been less, they would have seemed to fix a date to be rid of me; if longer, the Assembly would have been acting *ultra vires* in legislating for a time when it would no longer be in existence.

The Orléanists on the Committee would have wished to paralyse my influence on the Government by hindering my access to the tribune; but the Assembly sanctioned my right to take part in all parliamentary debates, on the sole condition that I should inform the President, by a message, of my intention to avail myself of this right, and in a word affirmed anew my responsibility to itself.

These decisions were made at the sitting of the 9th of August, 1871, at which I was present. After two speeches from the Right, M. Picard had made it felt that in the face of services rendered and still to be rendered, the duty of all was to rally to my augmented powers; and it was with this in mind that a majority of four hundred and ninety-one voices to ninety-four accepted the Rivet proposal, modified in the way I have described.

To sum up, this form of Constitution would confer on the head of the State the title of President of the Republic; it fixed the term of his power by making it coeval with that of the Assembly; lastly, by a new arrangement it made the President's participation in parliamentary debates more formally authenticated than ever in the past.

Immediately after this vote I established, by a decree, a Vice-President of the Ministerial Council, to satisfy those who believed it would be a useful measure. He would preside over the Council if the President of the Republic should be prevented from attending, and if by the latter's death the supreme power should be vacant, he would inform the Assembly what steps to take under the circumstances.

Shortly before the voting upon the Rivet Constitution, a change had come about in the Ministry. M. Jules Favre, an acrid speaker, but excellent at heart, in whom, by some strange phenomenon, violent speech was joined to the greatest sweetness of nature, wished to leave us, and to my great regret had left us on the 22nd of July, 1871. For some time he had been affected by the attacks of which the men of the Fourth of September were the object. They came from Bonapartists and Orléanists and Legitimists alike, who never forgave them, the one party for having opposed the Empire, the others for opposing

PRESIDENCY OF THE REPUBLIC

the restoration of royalty. And yet M. Jules Favre's character, so kind, so lofty, his generous devotedness when he signed the capitulation of Paris and the Peace itself, without hesitating over his inconsistency in adding his name to mine at the foot of the Treaty of Versailles—all these considerations might well have imposed silence upon the parties. It was not so, and before a last attack, which struck against what was dearest of all to him, his children, he resigned, in order to be unhampered in the prosecution he meant to bring against his slanderer.

Of three men of the Fourth of September who were part of the Ministry, two, MM. E. Picard and Jules Favre, had resigned of their own accord before the attacks of their political opponents. M. Jules Simon alone remained, and all the efforts of the Monarchists were now united against him. However, he was strong enough to defend himself, thanks to his profound cleverness and his singular capacity, and I was determined not to abandon him. For the present I had only to find a successor to M. Jules Favre.

Having conceived some hopes of persuading M. de Rémusat to emerge from the retirement in which he had lived for the past twenty years, I sent his son to find him at the Château de Lafitte, his family seat, a modest and delightful house within sight of the Pyrenees, which was a kind of harbour of refuge for the tranquil, pensive philosophy of its owner. M. Paul de Rémusat brought back his father, who at our urgent request consented, on the 2nd of August, 1871, to become Minister for Foreign Affairs. Then, as now, France could have no more worthy representative to act with foreign Powers. Grand-nephew of M. de Vergennes, grandson of M. de la Fayette, of noble manners, noble in mind and heart, living with perfect content and comfort on a moderate fortune, endowed with an intellect of the widest scope and freest play, a man of prodigious culture, often subtle to profundity, M. de Rémusat, a little sceptical by dint of seeing things under all their aspects, but not to be shaken in his good and great principles of thought and action, an unflinching Liberal, an ardent patriot, a wise politician, sometimes rather mocking, but with a gentle and amiable mockery, was precisely the right person to win favour from the aristocratic society of foreign Courts for a well-ordered Republic.

Every one approved this choice, and after a few conversations with M. de Rémusat, the diplomatists loved him as a man and appreciated his talents. He was a real increase of strength to the Cabinet.

The end of September was approaching. The Assembly had now been sitting for eight months without a break in the midst of continual agitations. It was worn out, and the heat of the season added still further to its mental fatigue. After passing most urgent taxes, those that gave grounds for no objection, and represented nearly three hundred and sixty millions, the Assembly had no reason to deny itself a few days' vacation. It prorogued itself then from the 17th of September to the 4th of December, 1871, leaving the country in a better situation than any one would have dared to hope for at the outset of its career, and full of confidence in the future, which only the extremists of the parties failed to share.

This was the first time the Government found itself deprived of the imposing entourage of the representatives of the nation. It might seem a good opportunity to try some seditious enterprise, and the Bonapartists were, it was rumoured, about to take the stage.

The Empire, painfully endeavouring to rebuild its reputation, had just had unlooked-for assistance from Marshal de MacMahon. In his evidence before the commission appointed by the Assembly to inquire into the acts of the Government of the Fourth of September, the Marshal, interrogated upon the capitulation of Sedan, had taken particular pains to defend the Emperor and to declare himself solely responsible for the events of that day.

The Bonapartist publicists at once laid hold of this testimony to exculpate the Emperor, and from this moment their language became very audacious. Doubtless, they said, it was wrong to make war without sufficient preparation; but who never made a mistake? According to them, the greatest part of our misfortunes were to be blamed upon the persons responsible for the Fourth of September; and those who, like myself for example, had been strangers to the Empire and the Fourth of September, and only occupied themselves in remedying the mistakes of both, would share all this responsibility, unless they immediately recalled the Emperor, or at least the Prince Imperial.

While talking in this way, the Bonapartists multiplied their comings and goings from Paris to Chislehurst, peddled the sayings, true or false, of the exiled family, and thanks to these tricks, had spread the belief that the Emperor would presently attempt a descent on some point on the coast, and try, like his uncle at Grenoble, to gain over the army.

I had no fear of such a danger, neither as far as the army was concerned nor the Emperor, whom I knew by sure report to be quite incapable of attempting this adventure, as much on account of his health as through lack of means; he even disapproved, I had been assured, of all this agitation of his party, which was hindering my efforts to restore the army and the finances of France. At the same time, since a Government can be the dupe of incredulity as well as of credulity, I recommended all the maritime, military, and civil authorities of the coastal departments to redouble their vigilance. This precaution was unnecessary, thanks to the prudence or rather the impotence of the Court of Chislehurst.

But the Prince Napoleon, who lived in Switzerland, whence he radiated towards Belgium, and especially towards Italy, was much less circumspect. Everywhere he showed himself, by his speeches, what he had always been: a witty, uncurbed individual, but erratic, acting always for himself, never for his party, which indeed never depended on him. Nevertheless, the Bonapartists secured his election as a member of the Council-General of Corsica, and wanted to make him President, and relying on the example of the validated election of the two Princes of Orléans, Prince Napoleon addressed himself to our consul at Geneva, to ask permission to go to Corsica in the exercise of his rights as Councillor-General. I sent word that he might go, but only to be present at the session of the Council-General; that the slightest disturbance, whoever caused it, would be put down at once with the utmost severity.

Everything happened as I had foreseen. The rowdy fellows who had flocked to Ajaccio, Corsicans and others, did not dare to make the demonstration they had planned; Prince Napoleon was not even elected as President of the Council-General, and soon after this check he started for the Continent again.

If I have recounted at some length this return of audacity on the part of the Bonapartists, it is to make certain later events more readily understood.

At this time something happened as grievous as unforeseen. On the 8th of October, 1871, M. Lambrecht, whom I had left the previous evening with every appearance of health, succumbed to an affection of the heart which had given no reason to expect so rapid a development. In him I lost a friend, a colleague gifted with uncommon political judgment, and that exquisite tact which is the first indispensable qualification for a Minister of the Interior. Firm in good sense, courageous at need, and always honourable and upright, like myself he only attached himself to his country's interests. A tinge of melancholy, arising from the malady with which he knew he was stricken, added still more to his natural distinction. He was universally regretted.

The whole Council shared my grief and my perplexity, for it was by no means easy to replace such a co-worker. I thought of my friend M. Casimir Perier. Already at Bordeaux I had wished to bring him into the Cabinet; but regarding the situation as too confused, and the right paths hard to discern, he had not accepted my proposal. Now the moment had come for him to take up public business. As he had the taste for it, I renewed my offers. I appreciated his courage, his absolute integrity, his lively, open mind, a real talent in writing, and wide practical knowledge of affairs. I proposed him to the Council, which unanimously approved, expressing the hope that my offer would be accepted. It was accepted after many explanations, which M. Casimir Perier, always most careful when it was a question of pledging his name, insisted upon. The choice met with general approbation, for M. Casimir Perier was justly regarded as a Liberal by the Liberals, as a Conservative by the Conservatives, and had not yet incurred the displeasure of the Right for having loyally followed a policy independent of any party, a policy with which my honour was involved.

The Cabinet, uniting at the same time MM. Dufaure, de Rémusat, Casimir Perier, Jules Simon, contained the best political names in the country, and formed, with General de Cissey, Vice-Admiral Pothuau, M. de Larcy, and M. Victor Lefranc, the greatest Ministry that could be composed under existing circumstances.

The prorogation of the Assembly had naturally inspired ministers also with a desire to have a vacation. I alone could not take any, having to devote every moment to a pressing and very difficult experiment, the camping of the army.

The corps I had kept, after the taking of Paris, as types of our coming military organisation, were five in number, some in barracks in Paris, the others under canvas and in the open at Vincennes, Courbevoie, Saint-Germain, Versailles, Satory, Meudon. At the approach of winter it was becoming urgent to replace this camping out by warm and healthy barracks for at least eighty thousand men.

Those who have not administered a great state in all its departments cannot know all that an army needs in time and care of every kind, especially when it is to be put in a winter camp. It is not merely a matter of providing dwellings that will be healthy, clean, and keep the men from heat or cold, according to the time of year; these dwellings must yet be laid out in a certain order, must form cities in which traffic must be easy, in streets passable not only to individuals, but to artillery wagons and commissariat carts. They must be provided with light, abundant water distributed, kitchens set up, many fireplaces, with extreme precautions against outbreak of fires, cleanliness and hygiene must be carefully watched over, schools are to be installed, recreation-rooms and churches opened, and for the officers quarters must be arranged with enough conveniences to ensure that camp life does not entail needless expense for them. I might go on for ever if I were to mention the innumerable details to which even the head of a state is sometimes obliged to descend if he intends that nothing is to be neglected or forgotten.

Every day in the afternoon I drove out, now to Satory, now to Meudon or Vincennes, in short to all the places occupied by the troops, and, accompanied by the officers in command, I examined the construction works on the barracks, and assured myself that the orders given had been carried out: for an order over which a strict eye is not kept is an order given in vain. In this way I reached the desired result. The officers and the soldiers, seeing how deeply I was occupied with them, were full of confidence in my care of them.

Barely had the cold season set in when all were already at home in the camps. There were advantages for military instruction and the military spirit, and beyond all for their health. The soldiers, well fed, well clothed, country lads for the most part, enjoyed this way of living, and the permanent camp, which in principle had been greatly criticized, met with no further objections or opposition. After this experiment, I began to see the modifications which would have to be made in this system, the extent to which it should be employed, the way in which anything burdensome in it should be distributed over the different sections of the army, and I believe that before long I should have made it simple and fruitful of excellent results.

These very diverse affairs had not turned me aside from the most essential of all, which was to pay off the Prussians so as gradually to push back to the frontier the area of occupation.

From the 1st of June to the end of September the Germans had received fifteen hundred millions, and in accordance with the Treaty of Frankfort, the area of occupation was reduced to twelve departments. Six of these, the Aisne, the Aube, the Côte d'Or, Haute-Saône, Doubs, and Jura, would be evacuated at latest on the 1st of May, 1872, after the payment of the fourth half milliard; the other six, the Ardennes, Marne, Haute-Marne, Meuse, Meurthe-et-Moselle, the Vosges and the district of Belfort, were to remain in the hands of the Germans until the final payment of our ransom.

From the month of August 1871 I had begun to dream of forestalling the payment due on the 1st of May, 1872; for, thanks to the payments in advance on the loan, the Treasury was already in a position to pay the fourth half milliard. But from a financial point of view there would have been a grave danger in attempting this operation so close to the moment when we had just transferred to Germany fifteen hundred million francs within four months.

A wise scheme had enabled us to procure two milliards, but the transferring of so great a sum out of France depended upon very delicate operations, and so much the more difficult as being without precedent. If we had wanted to pay only in gold, the country would have been despoiled of its coinage and a dangerous monetary situation would have been provoked.

We had accordingly applied ourselves to giving the Germans only as little of our specie as possible, and the greater part of the fifteen hundred millions we had just paid over to them was made up of bills payable in Germany, which we had obtained by purchase in the principal European markets. But these continual purchases having forced up the foreign exchange, the precious metals, which we had avoided sending directly to the German Treasury, none the less were leaving France, and a money crisis was always to be feared. In order to prevent it, I decreased the purchases of foreign bills, thus it is true depriving myself of the principal means of meeting the fourth half milliard, and in consequence of reducing the area of occupation by six new departments before the 1st of May, 1872. However, I had hopes that very keen and active interests that were acting for several months both at Berlin and at Paris would afford the opportunity of achieving this evacuation before it was due.

The pure Alsatians were genuinely inconsolable at being severed from France; but the Swiss and the numerous Germans in the south, who had been attracted to Mulhouse by that town's industrial prosperity, tried to profit by recent events. Not content with having obtained, by a recent ordinance, the freedom of the German market, they dreamed of keeping as long as possible the freedom of the French market as well, which according to the Treaty of Frankfort was to be closed to them in September 1871. If this dream was realized, Alsace, bitterly stricken in its patriotic feelings, would have a kind of recompense in the increase of its wealth, and Prince Bismarck, in order to win over this newly annexed province by a fresh favour, was disposed to obtain for it the longer period asked for by the manufacturers. On our side we did not ask anything better than to make this concession, if in return we were granted an antedated evacuation.

To open negotiations upon this matter, Prince Bismarck sent Count Harry von Arnim to Paris, as a Minister Chargé d'Affaires, the only title under which he could, at the moment, represent his Government in France, since we ourselves had at Berlin only a Chargé d'Affaires, the very distinguished M. de Gabriac. Count von Arnim was not accredited as Ambassador to us until some months later. As negotiator of the Treaty of Frankfort, he was in every way marked out to hold this post; but because of his morose nature it was not a very fortunate selection for Paris, where the victor should have been represented by the sunniest and most affable person they could find.

Immediately on arriving, 24th of August, Count von Arnim opened the negotiations. Our aim was the immediate evacuation of the six departments due on the 1st of May, 1872. We were asking the German Government to accept, in place of the territorial pledge of these departments, the financial guarantees it might think necessary; and to hasten its consent to this substitution of guarantees, we would then show ourselves disposed to continue beyond the 1st of September, 1871, under conditions to be agreed upon, the favourable treatment granted to Alsatian industries for sending their products into France.

Unfortunately, our manufacturers were unwilling to concede this favourable treatment to the Alsatians unless with reciprocity for French goods to enter Alsace. That was asking for free entrance, or at a reduced tariff, of all French goods into Germany through the open door of Alsace-Lorraine. This condition of absolute general reciprocity, which had been imposed upon the French negotiators by a decision of the Assembly, could not possibly be accepted by Germany, and made an agreement on the question of excise almost impossible.

Great difficulties arose also on the question of the financial guarantees. Of the first two milliards of the whole indemnity we still had to pay, on the 1st of May, 1872, five hundred millions, to which would be added on the 1st of March, 1872, the interest of the three milliards making up our *ransom, a total of six hundred and fifty millions. As guarantee for this sum, the German Government demanded the signature of France, backed by the first banking houses of Germany, France, and England. It insisted, moreover, that these bills should be negotiable at the will of the German Treasury.

The French bankers and the French Government, however secure was their solvency, rightly refused to accept this condition, which exposed them to the possibility of seeing their signatures cast into circulation unexpectedly, before they could have made any preparations to meet such tremendous engagements.

Faced with these difficulties, I determined to send M. Pouyer-Quertier to Berlin, to make every effort to solve them by addressing himself to the Chancellor direct. M. Pouyer-Quertier had relations with Germany that might be useful, and when he had gone there to negotiate the final treaty of peace, he had been well received by Prince Bismarck. He had even been *persona grata* with the latter. He went to Berlin in the early part of October, and Count von Arnim was not long in following.

On the question of the guarantees, Count Bismarck began by insisting anew that the bills backed by the bankers should be negotiable when and as he pleased. I telegraphed a formal refusal to accept this condition, which from the financial and political point of view alike exposed us to serious difficulties. The Chancellor then offered to bind himself not to negotiate the bills except in case of a change of Government, which was to say, in case of my retirement.

However flattering this mark of confidence in me, I refused this solution, which would have imposed me upon the National Assembly by the threat of dangerous financial pressure, if they had wished to get rid of me.

M. Pouyer-Quertier, seeing these awkward points, went more to the heart of the matter. Our solvency, as we were every day proving, was as sure as our goodwill to pay. Henceforward there was nothing to be gained by taking precautions against us, precautions which besides the difficulties they raised had the inconvenient result of costing us millions that must go not into the Prussian Treasury, but simply into the bankers' coffers. Would it not be better to display confidence in us by being satisfied to accept month by month up to the following spring the fourth half milliard in successive payments, which we were offering because we were in a condition to make them?

Prince Bismarck readily understood that a prudent policy counselled that instead of taking precautions suggested by mistrust, he ought on the contrary to give us a mark of confidence, which would be a great help to the French Government in carrying out its obligations. He went one morning, therefore, to M. Pouyer-Quertier, without previous warning, and found him at table with his Berlin friends.

He took him apart, announced that he was giving up bankers and their demands, that there would be no more question of bills negotiable or not negotiable, and that they would be satisfied with my signature for the fourth half milliard, which would be paid by fixed instalments fortnightly, beginning from the 15th of January up to the 1st of May, 1872. The one condition attached to this concession was, that until the full payment was made the evacuated departments would only receive the number of French troops necessary for the preservation of order. A very considerable advantage was coupled with this restriction: the army of occupation would be reduced to fifty thousand men.

M. Pouyer-Quertier hastened to inform me of these important stipulations in a series of dispatches, the last of which, dated the 11th of October, 1871, is couched in the following terms:

" . . . At noon I went to see the Emperor; he received me most kindly and told me that the German Government had every reason to congratulate themselves upon the punctuality with which France was carrying out her engagements; that it was on account of this punctuality that his Government was waiving the financial guarantees that had originally been asked for.

"He was happy to order an immediate evacuation of the stipulated territories, in return for a simple promise to pay the fourth half milliard in eight instalments from January to the 1st of May.

"He expressed all his admiration for the results obtained by M. Thiers' Government, the only one rational and possible in the present condition of affairs in France.

"He found the task enormous, yet not beyond the energy and patriotism of the President.

"He eagerly desires the complete evacuation of France by his troops, and also desires that we may be able to find financial combinations to hasten it as much as possible. Germany will gladly do all she can to help.

"The question of the customs did not seem to me to preoccupy him to any extent.

"I have asked for an amnesty for the prisoners who remain in Germany, and who have been sentenced for other than misdemeanours of war.

"With the exception of professional thieves and murderers (not a very numerous class) he has allowed me to hope that all the others will speedily be released.

"POUYER-QUERTIER."

I replied by a full consent to the proposed conditions and profound thanks to the Emperor and the Chancellor.

With the financial question M. Pouyer-Quertier had settled the question of the customs of the annexed provinces. In accordance with the decision of the Assembly the French Government proposed to allow manufactured goods to enter free from Alsace-Lorraine from the 1st of September to the 31st of December, 1871, to impose one-fourth rate from the 1st of January to the 1st of July, 1872, a half from the 1st of July, 1872, to the 1st of July, 1873, on condition of reciprocity for French goods going into Alsace-Lorraine.

The German Government, which, I repeat, refused absolutely to accept this condition of general reciprocity for French products, only consented to a reciprocity limited to products employed by local industries in Alsace-Lorraine.

After lengthy discussions, M. Pouyer-Quertier was obliged to waive the clause anent general reciprocity, and Prince Bismarck on his side, in return for this concession, consented to reduce by a period of six months the favour accorded for Alsace-Lorraine, by limiting its duration to the 1st of January instead of the 1st of July, 1873.

The two conventions, relating one to the financial guarantees, the other to the system of customs for the annexed provinces, were signed at Berlin on the 12th of October, 1871; and the evacuation, with a view to which they had been concluded, began immediately after in the six departments which were to be freed the first.

The Assembly was not sitting, but the country signified to me in the most marked manner its joy and gratitude on this occasion. I did not wish to claim all the merit of this success for myself, and I proposed to the Council, which approved, to raise M. Pouyer-Quertier to the rank of Grand Officier in the Légion d'Honneur, at one stroke passing over all the inferior grades to this high distinction.

Good M. Pouyer-Quertier was moved even to tears by this honour. He might well be proud of it, having thoroughly deserved it by the skill and vigour with which he had conducted and brought this difficult negotiation at Berlin to a successful conclusion.

Count von Arnim came back shortly after M. Pouyer-Quertier, and I thought it right to give him the best possible welcome. He had served us well during this negotiation. I received him therefore with the greatest distinction, and had the salons in which we had influence thrown open to him.

I was thus putting in practice the instructions previously given to the functionaries of the departments under German occupation, among whom many, seeking vulgar popularity, had been rude to the Prussian officers. I had directed the prefects of these departments to accept and return any polite attentions that might be shown them by the heads of the army of occupation, and particularly General Manteuffel's dinner invitations; I had repeated to all of them that the slightest offence to the pride of the heads of this army would expose the people to the harshest treatment.

Before long I had reason to congratulate myself upon these provident instructions. The Prussian generals, very susceptible gentlemen, living in the midst of an enemy populace, were on the other hand very sensitive to the least friendliness, to which they responded with good treatment for the inhabitants; but they became intolerable if we were not as polite to them as they were to us. General Baron von Manteuffel, a cousin of the former Prime Minister of the same name, was at their head—one of the most distinguished minds of all his nation and one of the best men I have ever known. Commander-in-Chief of the army of occupation, he ended by winning the affection of the whole population of Nancy, where his headquarters were.

When he had come to Versailles, he had accepted the hospitality I offered him at the Présidence. All who had occasion to converse with him were touched by his ideas, as lofty as they were generous, and charmed by his fine, brilliant, cultivated mind. After the peace was signed, I had given orders to show every attention to his nephew, the son of the former Minister, who had fallen ill at Clermont (Oise). Appreciating this kindness on my part, he showed his gratitude in a thousand friendly acts for the French prisoners.

We very soon became fast friends, and directly there was any serious collision between German soldiers and the inhabitants, he interposed and ended by amicable arrangements conflicts that might easily have resulted in sentences of imprisonment or penal servitude, or even in heavy exactions upon our villages.

I had chosen as Commissioner Extraordinary at the headquarters of the army of occupation Count Saint-Vallier, a young diplomatist of the greatest distinction, intelligent, not very robust, impressionable to the highest degree, working himself to death almost in devotion to his task, and also a friend of General Manteuffel. I could never tell what great services this friendship rendered us.

The question of lodging the troops in occupation was the one that most frequently gave rise to difficulties. To spare the inhabitants the presence of foreign soldiers in their families, we had decided to put the German soldiers into barracks at the State's expense, especially in the six departments that were to be the last occupied.

The departments next to these, impatient to see the departure of the foreigners installed among them, hardly left us time to finish the barracks as soon as the day fixed for the evacuation had come. On their side the German officers constantly complained of the unhealthiness of these newly built barracks; one day they even abandoned them, to billet themselves on the inhabitants by military authority. These were so many opportunities for violence and brawls.

I spent many hours writing, and issuing orders to put an end to these troublesome incidents, and I always found Count Saint-Vallier and General Manteuffel before me with the same intention. It can, then, be understood how much I valued the friendship of General Manteuffel, a friendship I shall continue to cultivate as long as I live.

One of the visits he paid me at Versailles gave rise to two disagreeable incidents. I had asked him to come to see me. He arrived twenty-four hours earlier than I expected him, and precisely on the day I was to have a great dinner-party of deputies and generals. Certainly General Manteuffel was in no way out of place in this assembly; everybody had the good taste to give him a suitable welcome, and M. de Mérode, who was placed beside him, was delighted with his conversation. General Ducrot alone, before we sat down, expressed to me his regret at having to dine at the same table as a Prussian general. I was not responsible for the meeting, since I myself had been taken by surprise by General Manteuffel's arrival.

"It is for the greatest interests of the State," I said to General Ducrot, "that we should behave with propriety towards a personage who has a right to our regard as much on account of his official position as for his own worth. However, if you cannot endure to meet him, I shall leave you at liberty to withdraw."

And the General took advantage of my permission to leave the Présidence.

Marshal MacMahon, too, who no more than General Ducrot could ever forgive the Prussians their victories, could not control his feelings, and refused his hand to General Manteuffel, who before leaving Versailles had come to pay him a visit.

General Manteuffel went at once to the Minister for War to give him to understand, with all propriety, that such an occurrence could not be passed over without explanation. The Marshal had the good sense to make amends; for in him the tried soldier could afford to stoop a little without loss of countenance; he only pressed that the affair should be kept from me, and General de Cissey, very tactfully, mentioned it to me only when the impression made by this scene was almost wholly forgotten.

The close of this year, 1871, was marked by the beginnings of a monetary crisis which gave me a very anxious moment. To prevent this crisis I had recommended the diminishing of purchases of bills on Germany. But M. Pouyer-Quertier had not watched these purchases with sufficient attention, and M. Dutilleul, the directeur du mouvement général des fonds, whose chief care was to contrive means of paying Germany while displacing specie as little as possible, had continued to accept all the exchange bills offered to him. He had received from the Bank of Paris, in particular, two hundred millions' worth. The exchange on London, which regulates all the rest, consequently went up considerably, which entailed a rush of precious metal to that city. From one single port, in one single day, some eighty millions in gold left France for England. And so the dearth of gold and silver money soon began to hamper the daily transactions in the markets and the retail houses.

For the first time since the re-establishment of peace, the payment of our ransom became a source of embarrassment to the public at large. As soon as I was informed I renewed the order to suspend the purchase of bills, in order to bring down the exchange and stop the export of specie.

This first remedy, good for the future, was not enough for the present. We had recourse then to a measure at an ordinary time questionable, but at the present moment legitimate, which was to create temporarily, and under the guarantee of certain houses of great credit, a kind of emergency paper money, confined to local use. We were in this merely imitating the action of certain managers of great works. These, in short, lacking actual cash, pay their men vouchers of twenty, ten, five, two francs, and even one franc, after arranging with the tradesmen, bakers, butchers, wine sellers, etc., to pay off these vouchers in amounts of a hundred, five hundred, or a thousand francs.

This method having succeeded, it became the type of a more general measure which was immediately effective. We authorized certain great banking houses, such as the Comptoir d'Escompte and the Société

Générale, to issue each a certain quantity of these small notes, provided they deposited with establishments of high credit, placed under State control, recognized securities to an equivalent amount as a guarantee.

The refusal to buy bills brought down the rate of exchange, at the same time as the premium on gold; the thousand franc note, which had lost no less than thirty francs of its face value, began to recover; and the small notes, widely put into circulation, ended the complaints of the public. In this way terminated the monetary crisis, which might easily have grown serious.

What disturbed me more than this monetary crisis was the sudden persistent drop in the price of the loan. Issued at eighty-two and a half, at first it had moved steadily upward and had reached ninety-six in November: one moment it had been thought likely to go to par.

This undue rise, due to the small investors represented by the Bank of Paris, had been opposed by a syndicate of bankers who in turn had forced the price down. If this downward movement had been carried too far, and especially if it had gone below the issue price, it would have involved a real disaster for the great mass of small investors, the consequence of which would have been to compromise the success of the next loan.

I was greatly absorbed in this matter of the price of our public funds, when I learned that the Bank of France, by selling its stocks on the Bourse, was one of the chief causes of this fall.

At once I summoned the Board of the Bank of France, or rather a committee of the most influential members of the Board, among whom were MM. Mallet and Davilliers, men of conspicuous honesty and excellent common sense.

They explained that the Bank was selling off its stocks to get back its notes, which offered it a double advantage: first in raising the value of the note by making it less common in the currency, and secondly by putting these notes at the disposal of the Bank, which, having reached the legal limit of its issue, would soon be forced to draw upon its gold reserves in order to meet the exchange.

I answered that the value of the note was already rising in consequence of the drop in the exchange, and that this rise would become more apparent every day as gold became more plentiful, that besides, if they wanted to raise the value of their notes appreciably by withdrawing them from circulation, they would have to withdraw a capital of at least a hundred millions, which would necessitate the sale of five or six millions of stock. So considerable an operation could not fail to bring about an immense drop in the price of the loan, perhaps below the issue price, which would be a real catastrophe.

These arguments being unanswerable, the Board recognized that they could not persist in selling stock.

We next proceeded to examine what would have to be done to cope with the difficulty arising from the scarcity of notes. Under the Empire, the Bank of France had authority to issue fifteen millions in notes. After the declaration of war, this authority was raised to two milliards four hundred millions, an increase of nine hundred millions, to-day almost exhausted, representing the specie taken from circulation to pay the instalments of the indemnity. We might calculate at four hundred millions the specie that would still be exported from France to complete our foreign payments. It would therefore be necessary to raise the note issue of the Bank of France to two milliards eight hundred millions.

It was consequently agreed that the Bank would cease to sell its stocks, and that the Government, as soon as the Assembly should meet, would bring forward a measure to raise the note issue to two milliards eight hundred millions. If before this became law the Bank should reach the present limit of two milliards four hundred millions, it would meet the needs of the exchange with its gold reserve.

In this way both the monetary crisis and that which would have followed on a drop in the price of the loan below issue price were averted.

During the last three months of this year, 1871, we had been occupied with difficulties arising from affairs. They were soon to be complicated by those for which individuals were responsible.

The important session of 1871-2 was about to open, and the deputies were beginning to arrive. They say that during vacation-time deputies steep themselves again in the feeling of the country, and that they return to their labours inspired by the same dispositions as their electors. That was not the case when the Assembly came back to Versailles.

It is certain that no Government ever had the approval of the country to the same extent as we had. The great majority of the middle class, the commercial classes, the country people, without declaring themselves for a Republic in so many words, said " *We are for the Government of M. Thiers.*" This saying came to us from all quarters.

But in the Assembly, among the Monarchists, only the Moderates were disposed to uphold the Government, because they had been impressed by its popularity, and furthermore because they perceived the impossibility of restoring the monarchy, at any rate for the present.

One section of the Assembly, then, arrived much less influenced by the general satisfaction of the electors than might have been imagined, and a very disturbed existence was in prospect for us for the year 1872, on which we were about to enter.

The session was opened on the 4th of December, 1871, and I read my presidential message in the sitting of the 7th, after the preliminary labours of the Assembly, which had re-elected M. Grévy as its President and M. Martel as its chief Vice-President.

In this message I gave a full account of the position of affairs. To begin with, I recalled the fortunate results of our policy, which after assuring the financial present and prepared the financial future of France, had reduced the number of departments under foreign occupation from forty to six. I then entered upon the most difficult part of the message: the outline of the Government views upon the reorganization of our military forces.

There reigned at this time in France one of those ideas that sometimes take hold of men's imaginations and dominate them irresistibly. It was believed that our reverses were due to the fact that our army was not organized in the same way as the Prussian. Universal compulsory service, sending the whole nation into war, was the only thing, they said, to bring back to France the power she had lost. Such was the opinion of the Left as well as the Right—in a word, the opinion of everybody, except some very few men of unusual good sense.

The inevitable consequence of calling to the colours all the men liable to be chosen by lot is the reduction of the period of service to two years or three: for the more men called up, the less time can they be retained, if the finances of the country are not to be ruined. Convinced that real soldiers cannot be turned out either in two or in three years, I declared my opinion on this subject in set terms. And so the message, religiously heard so long as I said nothing about military reorganization, evoked some murmurs when I touched on this question. At the same time it was approved, as much for what it contained as for its evident sincerity.

Before discussing plans dealing with recruiting the army, the Assembly had to consider the not less pressing matter of the new taxes. Already it had voted three hundred and sixty-six millions by surcharging nearly all the old taxes to the utmost point; it remained still to find, at the least, two hundred and fifty millions in new taxes in order to meet the six hundred and fifty millions which, according to the last reckoning of the war expenditure, must still be added to the normal expenditure expected by the budgets before 1870.

The Commission charged with the examination of the law revising the budget for the financial year 1871 had proposed, through M. Casimir Perier, who presented its report, to obtain these two hundred and fifty millions by a tax, not on income, but on incomes—that is to say, upon four particular kinds of income, viz. (1) income from various French and foreign shares, except the Rentes and other French public funds; (2) pensions, official emoluments, public or private salaries; (3) interest upon credits of every possible kind; (4) the net profits of banks, of industry, of commerce, law officials, etc.

Already this report had been given to the Assembly on the 31st of August, 1871, and the discussion, then postponed until after the vacations, opened on the 22nd of December. M. Pouyer-Quertier, in the name of the Government, rejected all these taxes except that on shares, which he had himself introduced in his budget bill for 1872, presented to the Assembly on the 9th of December, 1871.

Following M. Pouyer-Quertier, M. Germain in his turn attacked the tax on these returns, for which he proposed to substitute an income-tax in the full sense of the word. M. Teisserenc de Bort, a modest and well-informed person, replied with an excellent speech.

M. Wolowski, with his usual fluency, let himself go to prove that an income-tax was the most natural of taxes in a moment of distress, and, to support his contention, quoted the example of England, where this tax, he claimed, was finally and firmly established, without any element of arbitrariness. His ardour and exaggeration proved only one thing: that the spirit of a system, in its mistakes, is nearly as violent as the party spirit.

After him I addressed the House (at the sitting of the 26th of December, 1871), and was heard with profound attention. The Assembly waited with a favourable mind for the blow I was about to strike at revolutionary finance.

My task then was easier than it was to be some days later, when I had to support the tax on raw materials. At first I applied myself to showing clearly the fundamental difference between the financial system of France, a continental country, and that of England, an island country, where a great proportion of all goods of general consumption, arriving by sea, pass through the customs, and where all spirits, being made in immense establishments, offer great facilities for the collection of duties.

Under such conditions, I said, nearly all the revenues of the Treasury are indirect revenues that do not burden landed property. In France, on the contrary, almost all objects of general consumption are produced by the soil, and in consequence taxation is of another kind. Objects of consumption not passing through the customs are here much less frequently taxed than the land which produces them.

I proved this very carefully, insisting on the strict justice which since 1789 had presided over the distribution of taxation in France. I proved that among us the propertied and leisured classes bore at least two-thirds of the public burdens, and the populace less than a third. In England, before the income-tax, it was in a contrary proportion. It was natural, then, that in times of difficulty acquired wealth should have been called upon to come to the help of the British Treasury.

This demonstration produced a real sense of relief in the Assembly. It had been said for so long that the proletariat paid nearly everything and the rich almost nothing. Loud signs of approbation came from three-fourths of the Assembly, which felt, at this moment, that I was a true Conservative.

I went on to explain why the income-tax in England was less arbitrary than it would of necessity be in France. To establish it in England, land, rents, and professional profits had been adopted as the basis, because since none of these sources of income were taxed, they could bear fairly high levies. But in France, if we turned to the land, it could show that already it pays its heavy share through the land-tax and the extra hundredths; in the same way rents and professional profits carry the property-tax and the tax for licences. There would remain, then, for an income-tax in France only one basis, wealth presumed and valued by political rancours and passions.

Lastly, to prove the dangers of arbitrariness in the incidence of income-tax, I went back to olden times, and with Vauban's *Dime Royale* in my hand, I showed that the *tailles* had been simply an income-tax arbitrarily struck; I cited the passages of this famous book where Vauban, with the eloquence of the most straightforward of men, inveighed against the iniquity of this tax, and I asked what it would become in our days of trouble and faction, since already under the peaceful royal days of Louis XIV it had provoked so just a wrath.

The effect of my speech was decisive. There was still a little skirmishing. My friend M. Rouveyre, and M. Wolowski, also my friend (for all called themselves my friends), again began some unfortunate attempts, which were not well received, and in the end the Assembly, wearied and convinced, irrevocably condemned by a great majority the principle of an income-tax.

After this vote the Commission, foreseeing that the same fate would befall the various taxes which together made up what they called a tax upon returns, withdrew their scheme.

Three days later, on the 29th of December, I had again to address the Assembly in the discussion of the Government measure presented on the 9th of December, 1871, to authorize the Bank of France to increase its issue of notes by four hundred millions.

I have already said that the limit of the issue of these notes, raised on the declaration of war to two milliards four hundred millions, was almost reached by the end of 1871, and that it was most urgent that it should be extended up to two milliards eight hundred millions; if not, the Bank would soon find itself reduced to one of two things: either to refuse discounting business, or to fall back upon its metallic capital, which is, and should remain, in its vaults as the guarantee of its notes, and the foundation of the confidence reposed in it throughout the world.

There was, then, no time to be lost, and the introduction, on the 9th of December, of the measure authorizing the Bank of France to raise its issue immediately to two milliards eight hundred millions would have to be followed, without any delay, by the report of the Committee, the public discussion, and finally the taking of the vote upon it. But by a singular inconsistency the Assembly, which was not ill-disposed to the scheme, had appointed to the Committee members of the contrary opinion to examine it. Among these hostile members, in particular, was M. Bocher, a friend and adviser of the Orléans princes, and M. Buffet, since called upon to play a conspicuous part.

M. Bocher, a former prefect, subtle, an agreeable person, clever in affairs, a clear and sometimes a brilliant speaker, originally very modest in his pretensions, had, little by little, grown more ambitious. M. Buffet, a man of dry intellect, reducing everything to formulas of political economy, didactic in speech, but industrious, serious, exact, had all the external qualities that captivate Assemblies. Both displayed themselves, in this discussion, as little gifted with understanding in finance as evilly intentioned towards the Government.

According to them, to extend the note issue of the Bank of France to two milliards eight hundred millions was to create paper money, to engrave the die for assignats. As soon as it was ready to hand, we would flood the country with milliards in paper. The one proper way of dealing with the difficulty, they said, would be to raise a loan of fifteen hundred millions, with the help of which the State would pay its debt to the Bank of France, which would then be in a position to resume its payments in specie.

Several times I visited the Committee to oppose this scheme of a loan, the danger and even the impossibility of which I showed them. On each occasion I reduced my opponents to silence; but barely had I left them than they took up their thesis about assignats and a loan, and time was passing without arriving at any conclusion.

The obvious aim of the Committee was to drag matters on and on so as not to make the report we needed before the Assembly. We had now reached the 27th of December, and at any moment the Bank, which was upon the very edge of the two milliards four hundred millions, was exposed to the danger of no longer being able to undertake the discounting of bills, which was always very heavy at the end of the month, and especially in the closing days of December.

Urged by the necessity, I begged the Assembly to compel the Committee to make its report. The Committee asked for more time, alleging that the subject was too serious, too difficult to be dealt with so hastily. So much ill-will made me indignant.

Addressing the House with the utmost heat, I said that such a report could be written in a few hours, that it would be sufficient even to make it orally, and that in a sitting of two hours I could undertake to exhaust the subject and reduce the whole question to the utmost degree of clearness.

The Chamber, comprehending the urgency of the matter, the frivolity of the Committee's objections, and its malice as well, insisted on the immediate presenting of the report. This was at last done, on the 29th of December.

Before the Assembly, M. Germain and myself annihilated the Committee's arguments. I said that I had no need to be taught the dangers of paper money, I who had passed judgment so severely upon all who in other days had had recourse to this expedient in order to ward off the financial troubles of the State; that to compare the present difficulty to those that it had previously been attempted to solve by an issue of assignats was to misrepresent the truth.

When the State, I said, creates paper money for its needs, it enters inevitably on the path to ruin; but to-day the State has no need. All its services are secured by its actual receipts. The present embarrassment weighs only upon commerce, and arises from the fact that the exceptional movements in specie, occasioned by our foreign payments, have impoverished our monetary circulation. The notes for whose issue we ask authority are called on to supplement the insufficiency of the circulation. Lastly, they are not, as were the assignats, exposed to depreciation, since they will have their equivalent in metal in the vaults of the Bank of France.

I then showed the absurdity, the incomparable madness of the proposal to repay what the State owed to the Bank of France by means of a loan of fifteen hundred millions, interest on which must be paid at the rate of 6 per cent., while the Bank was satisfied with 1 per cent. Furthermore, this loan would make utterly impossible that which we should have to issue the following year, in order to complete the payment of the war indemnity, and to achieve the freedom of our territory.

M. Germain had most brilliantly opened this discussion which my speech brought to an end. Our opponents, constrained to realize the impossibility of doing anything but what the Government proposed, endeavoured to mask their defeat by reducing the four hundred millions we had asked for by one hundred; but the Assembly gave them to us by a very large majority, and at the same time authorized the Bank of France to issue small notes of ten and five francs, which would serve the needs of petty transactions, and would allow the withdrawal from circulation of the notes for one and two francs issued by other houses. Facts before long proved that the Government was in the right.

Barely had the law been passed on the night of the 29th of December, when the very next day demands for discount facilities came in a rush. Without this law, the Bank would have been reduced either to violate the legal limit of its issues, or to surrender a part of its precious metal reserve. Furthermore, the value of the bank-note rose and all monetary embarrassments disappeared.

The Assembly, having taken a few days' vacation, from the 30th of December, 1871, to the 6th of January,

1872, met again to deliberate upon the budget of 1872, presented the previous month.

In this budget the Government had proposed to impose a tax on personal property which would yield about thirty-seven millions. The discussion of this tax, opened on the 6th, was still proceeding on the 8th of January. I then interposed in the debate, and at my request the Assembly decided first to examine all the proposed taxes, and not put them to the vote until after this scrutiny of comparison.

Following this procedure, we came to the discussion of the tax on raw materials, as it had been presented to the Government on the 11th of the preceding June, in the bill to amend the budget for 1871.

The discussion of this tax brought to the tribune the manufacturers, who were interested in preventing its acceptance. Most of them spoke of what they knew, and spoke well; but they reasoned badly under the influence of their frightened interests. They were nevertheless heard with, in a way, a favouring ear, because it was difficult to disentangle the truth from the error in their speeches. The Lyons people went beyond all the others in their forebodings of ruin, although they represented the wealthiest of our industries, and the one least touched by our plans.

It was time for the Government to intervene; and on the 13th of January I made a speech, to the satisfaction of the Assembly, which was beginning to grow uneasy under all these threats of universal ruin.

At the outset I gave a rapid sketch of our financial position, reminding them that after surcharging our existing taxes with all they could bear, asking from personal property a round thirty millions, we still had to find one hundred and ninety millions of new resources to balance our budget. The idea of an income-tax having been cast aside by the Assembly, the only thing possible was to re-establish the tax on raw materials, which had been done away with by the Empire.

From past experience, we knew for certain the yield we could look for from this tax. Its collection would involve no new expense; the customs, which already collected three or four hundred millions, would undertake to recover another hundred or two hundred, practically without increased cost to the Treasury. To unprejudiced minds these two considerations would have been enough to justify the Government proposal.

It remained to estimate the weight of the tax, the dangers it might entail for industry. Now, the proposed tax had this great advantage: that it was split up among manufactured objects, so much so that it would be hard to discern who might have paid it, the producer or the consumer; and to support this contention I gave incontestable and convincing figures. I said again that when the demand for an article is thoroughly established, the increase in cost of its raw material cannot injure its sale, if this increase is not excessive; and to prove this assertion I cited three recent experiments which were fresh in every one's memory.

Transitory causes, among others the American Civil War and silkworm disease, had sent up the prices of cotton, of wool, and of raw silk; yet the consumption of the manufactured article had shown no diminution. Much less, then, could the few centimes we proposed to add to the prices of raw materials injure the prosperity of the industries that used these materials.

When I left the tribune, the members pressed round me, and I was assured that I had carried the day.

Unfortunately, M. Grévy did not put the question to the vote as soon as the discussion was ended. Satisfied with our victory, which doubtless he did not imagine would be compromised by his postponing its proclamation, he put off the voting to the next sitting—that is to say, from Saturday the 13th to Monday the 15th of January.

In this interval, the vanquished rallied and tried a new line of opposition. They pretended that we could only impose a tax on raw materials if, by way of compensation to our manufacturers, we taxed at the same time foreign goods made with these materials; but as these taxes were forbidden by commercial treaties, the Powers to whom we were bound by these treaties would certainly not authorize us to establish them. Therefore, according to our opponents, the tax we proposed was impossible. Never had any one behaved with such blatant anti-patriotism!

All our commercial treaties contained a clause of incontestable clearness, and until this day uncontested, which provided for the case of our needing to impose a tax on raw materials. In these various treaties it was laid down, in language that differed from one to another but in each case corroborating and explaining one another, that if France came to tax certain raw materials, foreign goods made of these materials would, on entering France, pay a compensating duty.

The meaning, then, was obvious. If, for example, the French weaver of a cotton fabric was obliged by a tax on cotton to pay twenty centimes a pound more for his material, to re-establish an equality in the conditions of foreign competition it was quite equitable to lay a compensating duty of twenty centimes on competing goods.

The common sense and force of this stipulation which appeared in all the treaties had never been in doubt, and England had recently interpreted it in the same way as ourselves. The date when our treaty of 1860 with England would expire was approaching, and we had had to confer with that Power as to our commercial policy. We had shown the most conciliating disposition, the least reactionary from a commercial point of view. We had consented not to touch the treaty of 1860, except for a slight increase of from 3 to 5 per cent. on linen, woollen, and cotton threads and fabrics. With this condition, the duties on iron, coal, chemicals, earthenware, glass, and a great many other articles were to continue as they were.

Entering at the same time upon the question of raw materials, we had said that, applying the clauses of the treaty, we should lay upon these materials a tax which would lead to the establishing of compensating duties remaining to be fixed.

The reply had been, and with no objection raised, that when these compensating duties had been fixed, they would be added to the increases we had already asked for, and that a decision would be made upon the total, not upon the compensating duty solely, the legitimateness of which no one denied, but on the increases asked for in the case of linen, woollen, and cotton thread and fabrics. Lord Lyons, the English Ambassador at Paris, always sensible and straightforward, had even said to me in one of our earliest conversations on this subject: "The treaty is so clear as to the compensating duty itself, that you need only enact it and we could have nothing to say."

Not one of us (by that I mean the Ministers of Finance and of Commerce, the Director-General of

Customs, and lastly myself)—not one of us, I say, had any doubt as to France's right to tax, not manufactured articles, but raw materials. And I said as much from the tribune, expressing my astonishment that the rights of France should have been called in question by Frenchmen in their own country, when they were not contested abroad. "But, perhaps," I added, "they will be contested to-night or to-morrow, as soon as what has been said from this tribune is known."

And in fact the very same evening M. Kern, the Swiss Minister in Paris, a most scrupulous defender of the interests of his own people, went to the Minister for Foreign Affairs to lay before him objections which he had never before raised on a subject which had nevertheless been under discussion for a considerable time.

This obstinate debate went on for several days, with great violence on the part of the regular partisans of the income-tax, in coalition with the manufacturing aristocracy. Even good M. Feray was brought upon the scene, one of our political friends, but who had been excited to such a point that he was barely recognizable.

M. Pouyer-Quertier spoke in his turn; by his enthusiasm, his warmth, his lively gestures, and a well-chosen theme he produced a very great effect, and we could think our cause won afresh; but the Lyons folk were moving heaven and earth. They sent to the tribune M. Lucien Brun, a talented lawyer, an ardent Legitimist, who at this juncture acted more through electoral than from party interest. It had been said, and not without reason, that only the big manufacturing class shrank from taking up its share of the sacrifices imposed on the country. M. Lucien Brun protested against this accusation. He was empowered, he said, to bring a declaration from a hundred and sixty-five big manufacturers of Lyons who, with other French manufacturers, undertook to find a sum of one to two hundred millions, by taxing themselves in proportion to the volume of their business. This declaration, made at the last moment, read and commented on with heat, was certain to have its effect upon certain Legitimists who, as great landowners, were on our side.

It was a decisive moment. I mounted the tribune once more, and directly challenging M. Lucien Brun, I asked him who were the signatories of this declaration of his, and what sort of undertaking did they offer? Would they pay a hundred or two hundred millions into the Treasury every year? If they undertook to do this, what guarantees did they propose, and of what financial or commercial value? Would their signature be good, as good as what the State must expect from its receipts? Obviously their private fortunes were not enough to guarantee the annual payment of such a sum; they must, then, inform us from what spring of riches they proposed to draw in order to honour their word. And as this spring did not exist (for it would have been discovered before), their offer was worthless and unworthy of such a serious object.

This was an embarrassing attack, but like a lawyer accustomed to opposition, M. Lucien Brun mounted the tribune again to affirm both the high repute and the solvency of the signatories to the declaration.

I replied that affairs of state were not dealt with in this way, and that the Bank of France, for example, would not on allegations of this kind advance millions if we asked for them.

This effrontery on the part of the coalition of interests angered a considerable number of deputies; everybody was weary, and the ballot was asked for.

Two questions were put to the House. The first, moved by M. Marcel Barthe, proposed to accept in principle the tax on raw materials *as an addition intended to establish the equilibrium of the budget:* a committee would then be appointed to determine the tariff of the tax. According to the second, moved by M. Feray, the principle, instead of being admitted, would merely be held in *reserve,* and a committee on tariffs would be instructed only to have recourse to taxing raw materials if it was absolutely impossible to discover other sources of revenue.

I mounted the tribune to declare that I would never accept any other wording than that of M. Marcel Barthe; that in the present condition of the country it needed to be ruled by a strong will; that if I gave way to a shameless coalition of selfish interests, I should be unworthy of the weight of responsibility laid upon me; and finally I asked that the principle of the tax should be adopted in the words of the question as put by M. Marcel Barthe.

The Assembly understood the gravity of the situation. The Left, which in the hope of making an income-tax inevitable had pronounced against the tax on raw materials, began to regret their attitude. The Right, notwithstanding its sympathy for M. Lucien Brun, feared lest the check on the taxation of raw materials might make an income-tax inevitable, a tax which it looked on as purely revolutionary; but the manufacturers of every shade of party, the Orléanists delighted to have the chance of giving the Government a shake, many of the Centre, inspired by electoral interests—all these were against us. We took the vote, and, contrary to expectation, a majority—a weak majority it is true—rejected M. Marcel Barthe's motion and adopted that of M. Feray.

The Assembly rose, surprised and uneasy. A great number of those who had just set their electoral interests above the public interest pressed about me to tell me that I must not be offended by this vote, that it was without political significance, and that after all if it did not terminate in the adoption of the tax on raw materials, neither did it reject this tax. What did a simple verbal distinction matter?

I gave a fairly rude reception to these people of no pride who, when their own interests were safe, had no thought for the dignity of those whom they advised, and I went back to the Présidence, disgusted to see that mercantile calculations, party passions, the spirit of system, had caused the true interest of the country to be ignored in such a way, especially in the difficult circumstances in which we were placed. I was also deeply wounded that the Assembly, as a body, should so little appreciate the devotion I gave to the service of France.

I had held power for a year, and I had a right to feel proud when I compared the state in which I had received France with that in which I was about to leave her. My colleagues had met; while realizing the great difficulties my retirement might cause, they did not venture to ask me to sacrifice myself and remain in power. M. Dufaure, however, emphasized the importance of the work of freeing our territory, which I had begun and would leave unfinished. I replied that I had done half of it, and that from most unworthy motives I had just been deprived of the means of finishing it.

Next day, the 20th of January, 1872, I sent my resignation to the President of the National Assembly. Although the Assembly expected it, after what I had said the previous day, it was profoundly moved on hearing this communication.

In the ranks of the Left, those who had voted against M. Marcel Barthe's motion blamed themselves for following an impulse whose consequences they now felt acutely. The members of the Right and the Right Centre, having as yet found no one to take the place of power in case it was left vacant, broke out into reproaches against those among them who had just prematurely provoked a crisis in the Government.

Those alone who were so short-sighted as to set the interests of their party above those of France felt a real joy, which they did not seek to hide. When they were asked by whom they proposed to replace me, they dared not yet pronounce the name of the Duc d'Aumale, and timidly put forward that of Marshal de MacMahon. But they could not, as yet, say anything that would allow them to hope that he would accept. For if the Marshal had about him ambitious persons devoid of prudence, he had also a friend full of discretion, M. de Melun, deputy of the North, a stranger to ambition of any kind, who advised him, as I was told, to keep the high position to which M. Thiers had raised him.

After a vain attempt on the part of the Left Centre, which begged me most urgently to withdraw my resignation, after an evening spent in comings and goings of the Left, both Centres, and the Moderate

Right, they resolved to make the Assembly vote on a motion whose mere wording would morally oblige me to retract my decision. This motion, which was carried almost unanimously, was couched in the following terms:

"Considering that the Assembly, in its resolution of yesterday's date, confined itself to holding a question of economics in reserve, that its vote can in no way be regarded as an expression of lack of confidence and hostility, and would not imply a refusal of the support it has always given to the Government,

"The Assembly hereby makes a fresh appeal to the patriotism of the President of the Republic and refuses to accept his resignation."

The Committee of the Assembly was directed to convey this resolution to me. The words "the Assembly makes a fresh appeal to the patriotism of the President of the Republic" made a refusal on my part, if not impossible, at least extremely difficult.

I was perplexed for a moment, for I was already taking some pleasure in my own mind in the idea of devoting myself, in my leisure, to a book that I should have liked to finish before my death, and which now perhaps I shall never be able to finish. The fear that the country's interests might be compromised by the prolonging of this crisis which I had not provoked, but which it depended on me to bring to an end, was the one thing that decided me to waive my determination.

I therefore gave the Committee of the Assembly an amicable reception, and declared that in spite of the difficulties of my task, I resumed it since they made it my duty.

"In face of this fresh appeal to my patriotism,"

said I to the President of the Assembly, "I cannot return a refusal. You may thank the Assembly on my behalf for this mark of confidence, and tell it that I shall vow myself afresh without reserve to my country's service."

We took leave of each other—they satisfied, I regretting my vanished leisure, which I had caught a glimpse of for a moment, though I was consoled by the thought of continuing the work of freeing our territory.

In France, as outside France, there was great satisfaction, not unmixed with apprehensions in the minds of people of discernment, who saw an evil presage in this first rupture.

The keen agitations of these last days were followed by a lull, during which no one would have cared to attack the Government, which the friends of the Orléans princes themselves despaired of overturning. Only the Bonapartists continued to keep up the struggle. One of them had resigned his seat in the Assembly in order to have elected in his stead M. Rouher, whose friends announced his coming appearance in the tribune as a great event and the opening of a new era. As for M. Rouher, he let every one say what they pleased, showed himself little, and spoke little; barely did he address a few words to the fifteen or twenty deputies who still avowed themselves partisans of the Empire.

We were now in the month of February. The Assembly was waiting until the committee instructed to find some tax to substitute for that on raw material should have succeeded in its task. But this search must needs be in vain, for the budget committee had exhausted all its skill in the same search, and the new committee could not succeed where the former one had failed. It had only to confess its powerlessness, after which, for want of anything better, the tax on raw materials, mutilated, less simple, and especially less fruitful, would be voted as necessary.

While the committee on taxation was exhausting itself in barren efforts, I was carrying on negotiations in London to bring England to conclude an arrangement with regard to the commercial treaties, which had become difficult to obtain for several reasons. To begin with, England, having found an unexpected support in the Assembly, was in no hurry to listen to our proposals, hoping that her cause would carry the day in Paris without her having to take any steps in the matter; furthermore, we were feebly supported in London by the Duc de Broglie, our Ambassador.

To help him in his task, I had sent him M. Ozenne, the General Secretary to the Ministry of Commerce, a gentleman well versed in all questions of commercial treaties and tariffs. But M. Ozenne had speedily come to Versailles to tell me that instead of seconding him, of putting him in touch with the right people, our Ambassador had left him to go alone, saying that commercial treaties were outside his sphere, and thus countenancing the idea that it was all a matter of opinions peculiar to M. Thiers, and that he had no share either in the latter's enthusiasm or his responsibility.

And so in London as in Paris, the questions of tariffs and taxes, upon which depended the financial equilibrium of our credit, and by consequence our freedom, moved with the utmost difficulty.

But these were not the only difficulties to occupy us at this moment (February and March 1872). Public opinion, excited against Marshal Bazaine, was accusing him of treason.

The Marshal had, it is true, committed the gravest of strategic blunders. After winning a battle which allowed him to disengage his army, he should have evacuated Metz without losing a moment, and by some marches to the rear escaped the danger of being surrounded, while through fear that he would be blamed for abandoning Metz, he shut himself up in the fortress, allowing a wall of iron to be thrown around him that it had later been impossible for him to break through. That is what was then known with any certainty of his conduct. That is why I had resolutely replied to those who demanded that I should give him up to the rage of the crowd:

"No, I will not fling the country into a disturbance like that aroused in 1815 by a trial of bitter memory, and I shall only submit the Marshal to the judgment of his peers if he demands it himself."

The Marshal consulted the Minister for War and myself as to what he should do; but when he had learned that the Government would not take any responsibility in answering this request, in the end he yielded to the outcries of public opinion, and, in a letter which I made public, demanded a trial.

Then, and not till then, did the Government make a decision in pursuance of which it sent the Marshal before a Council of War, a decision couched in the following terms:

"Marshal Bazaine having demanded a trial," etc.

I gave orders that a convenient abode, near

Versailles, should serve him as a prison. He is still there now as I write.

At the same time General Trochu desired to institute proceedings against a journalist who had violently attacked him. I knew the General's qualities and his defects; I knew that at Châlons he had promised too much to the Emperor Napoleon III, and that on the Fourth of September he had too little held to his promises; that during the siege of Paris he had not understood how to use the resistance of that stronghold for the safety of France, and had directed that resistance badly. I knew all this, but I also knew that everybody had made mistakes in that cruel year, that none the less the General remained a gallant soldier, a noble heart, a brilliant mind, a lofty and very engaging character.

I regarded as profoundly to be regretted recriminations which after our misfortunes could only discredit us in the eyes of Europe, and I disapproved of all the prosecutions set on foot by these retrospective animosities. This one of the General's against the Press immediately roused the whole of the Imperial faction, to which the former Governor of Paris was an object of hatred. I had not to meddle with the affair, and I did not meddle with it; but it was my duty to observe the movements of a society I sought to pacify. I tried sometimes, when the occasion offered, to set an example of the forbearance that so many Frenchmen owed to each other at that time.

So it was that, talking with Marshal de MacMahon of the judgment that had just been delivered in the affair of General Trochu, I expressed the regret that the sentence on the journalist had been so light, that it seemed a reprimand to the General. Marshal MacMahon, laying aside his customary reserve, rejoined :

"Believe me, President, this judgment is a good thing for the army, it is a lesson for it. It must understand that a man ought not to be the Emperor's General in the morning and a General of the Republic at night on the same day."

And the following day, talking over this conversation with General de Cissey, he added to what he had said to me the previous day these words, which the General reported to me verbatim :

"As for me, having received the command from M. Thiers, I will not go to take M. Thiers' place as President. Say so to him in order that he may not believe the absurd sayings that are being put about."

Another and not the least serious cause of trouble at this moment was the affair of the contracts. On the 3rd of March, 1871, the Government had asked and obtained from the Assembly the appointment of a committee to investigate all the purchases sanctioned by the different official departments since the 18th of July, 1870, to meet the needs occasioned by the war. The Assembly then ordered an inquiry into the acts of the Government of National Defence and into the causes leading to the insurrection of the 18th of March. These two latter inquiries, the one presided over by M Saint-Marc Girardin, the other by Count Daru, were directed towards a purely political end : the opening up of grievances against those members of the Assembly who had taken part in the revolution of the Fourth of September, and against those who were held to have been more or less avowedly among the promoters of the Commune. On the contrary, in calling for an investigation of contracts the Government had been influenced by no political prejudice. It had merely wished, in the interest of our finances, to examine the conditions and the fulfilment of the contracts that were sanctioned by the administration under exceptional circumstances. The committee nominated for this purpose was presided over by the Duc d'Audiffret-Pasquier.

M. d'Audiffret-Pasquier has imagination, felicity of language, a real though uneven talent as a speaker, and an excessively versatile mind. The affair of these contracts was an opportunity for him to show his qualities and his defects. An irreconcilable enemy of the Empire, which he had always opposed, no less hostile to the men of the Fourth of September, especially to M. Gambetta, he directed the labours of the committee in accordance with his own passions. Carried away with his accustomed fervour, he often undiscerningly fell upon the innocent as well as the guilty. He came in this way to accuse General Susane, the Director of War Stores, one of the most upright men in the whole administration, a man of frank and blunt character, a very distinguished officer, and highly esteemed by everybody.

The General, in face of this attack on his honour, answered M. d'Audiffret-Pasquier by an abusive letter, and an impudent one, since it was addressed to the president of a committee appointed by the Assembly, which took up the cause of its representative, and I was forced to interfere in order to keep the affair from becoming more serious. I was asked to dismiss the General. On no account would I have been willing to sacrifice this honest man and excellent servant to the State; but I got him to resign his post as Director of War Stores, in which, working hard and loyally, he had had nothing but trouble; I put him back on the Artillery Board, of which he had previously been a member, and where he would find *otium cum dignitate*. By means of this satisfaction to the Assembly's claim, without injury to General Susane, everything was smoothed over.

M. d'Audiffret, continuing his campaign against the Imperial administration, made his first appearance in the tribune with a speech on the contracts, which proclaimed an orator. His success was very marked, even among the Radicals, who rejoiced to see the blows they thought themselves exposed to diverted to fall upon the Empire.

The attack that fell upon the fallen régime was a rude one, but easy to repulse, so shaky was the logic of its assailant. M. Rouher, whose friends every day promised and bragged of his coming debut, could not let slip this opportunity for speaking, and the day for the reply to the Duc d'Audiffret-Pasquier being fixed, curiosity ran high among the benches to which all the Bonapartist public had thronged.

Speaking before the Versailles Assembly for the first time, M. Rouher, once a Minister in power, had become a Minister impeached, bearing the weight of all the mistakes of a régime of which he was the most deeply compromised representative. It was a dangerous position for him, and he presented himself like one conscious of the danger. A vigorous and sensible reasoner, when he showed up all the shortcomings of the committee, he had the advantage of it, yet without obtaining the applause of the Assembly. But very soon, by a premature resumption of assurance, by a few tactless justifications, he raised one of the most violent storms in the Assembly that I have ever witnessed. Assailed with invectives, even insults, for half an hour he presented, in the tribune, the spectacle of a terrible punishment, well deserved but cruel. For my own part, though assuredly I could not congratulate myself on his behaviour to myself, I was seized with pity. I demanded, though it is true vainly, that the agony should be brought to an end. Dominated by the fury of these attacks, M. Rouher was forced to endure them to the very end, and thenceforward we never saw him recover from this defeat.

At this time, too, was raised the question of the representative body of the nation making its abode in Paris. Since order had been re-established, this question had frequently come up in our minds, and every time it was touched upon, directly or indirectly, in conversation or from the tribune, it had been the theme of hot discussion. At Versailles, the Assembly believed itself safer than in Paris against popular violence, and freer to give itself up to its monarchist tendencies. And so all attempts to bring it to the capital had only resulted in irritating without convincing or moving it. It was then highly impolitic to renew the attempt, which did not prevent young Count Duchâtel, the distinguished and very liberal son of the former Minister, from making the formal proposal that the seat of the Assembly should be transferred to Paris. As it was not an urgent proposition, and as it required only to be sent before a committee, we might have expected that this would be ordered. M. Casimir Perier was of his opinion, and had pledged himself strongly in the matter. For my part, not being convinced like him of the certainty of success, I communicated my doubts to him, very circumspectly; but he did not share them, putting too much trust in friends who urged him forward without having determined to support him.

The event very soon justified my fears. M. Duchâtel's motion for the transfer of the Assembly from Versailles to Paris having reached the agenda, M. Casimir Perier supported it in the tribune with great skill, in a simple, short, and forcible speech. But the Centres and the Right, encouraged in their opposition by a member of the Left, M. Cézanne, refused even to accept the Duchâtel motion for consideration. If M. Casimir Perier had not obtained what he asked, he had certainly won a personal triumph by his speech.

I drove him away from the sitting in my carriage to talk with him alone, and first of all, about this awkward contretemps, and I parted from him in hopes that I had decided him against giving his resignation. Unfortunately, I had not convinced him. Irritated against his friends who had deserted him in spite of their solemn promises, he came to announce to me his irrevocable determination to leave the Ministry. It was not an easy matter to replace one so considerable and so highly esteemed as M. Casimir Perier. The Ministry for the Interior could only be held by a man who, while a Republican, would reassure the Conservatives. I chose M. Victor Lefranc, a witty, ingenious individual, who had on occasion managed to please the Centres by his engaging personality and his easy talent, without becoming an object of suspicion to the Republicans in whose ranks he had been born and had never ceased to live. With the goodwill of his colleagues he passed from the Ministry of Commerce to that of the Interior, and the Chamber was not displeased at this change.

His successor in the Ministry of Commerce was M. de Goulard, who had already represented the Government in the negotiations of Brussels and of Frankfort, in which he had displayed tact and *savoir-faire*.

Easter was approaching, and the Assembly, which had been sitting from December to the end of March, wished to have a vacation in order to attend the General Councils, as a new law had instituted two sessions for these Councils, one in April, the other in August. The vacation was settled to last from the 30th of March to the 22nd of April.

Paris had just had a set-back in the resolution of the Assembly refusing to transfer itself to the city. I wished to give it a kind of compensation by spending my days at the Elysée, for I went back to Versailles every night, as the Permanent Committee, an offshoot of the Assembly and sharing its prejudices, pretended that I had no right to leave Versailles, its legal domicile. Though this exaction had no serious foundation, I resigned myself to it.

I took advantage of these appearances in Paris to invite to dinner at the Elysée, followed by a reception, first the Diplomatic Corps, which was very assiduous in its visits to the Présidence; then in succession, the municipal authorities, the representatives of the great and the middle commercial classes, the magistrature, the most distinguished men in letters, science, and art. These receptions had an excellent effect, and I may say that if sometimes I had unpleasantness where the Assembly was concerned, from the country in general, and from Paris in particular, I had only testimonies of sympathy.

At the end of April I resumed, at Versailles, in the

midst of party agitations, the most difficult tasks, and especially that of effecting the final evacuation of our territory. Although accepted in theory by the Prussians, I could only ensure its execution, as will presently be seen, by a most laborious negotiation. And at the same time, in the Assembly itself, we were about to have to take up the reorganization of the army.

The reorganization of our military forces was at the moment occupying the whole country, eager to resume its rank in the world. Europe also was paying close attention to what was about to be done in France on this question.

Among the foreign Powers, several were ready to applaud our military resurrection, as they had applauded our financial resurrection. The Berlin Cabinet, on the contrary, was beginning to take alarm, and observed us with unconcealed preoccupation. They said that the adoption by France of compulsory service would be the signal for a new war, and the Emperor shared this fear, which Count von Arnim, his Ambassador in Paris, did all in his power to instil into the mind of his Government and fellow-countrymen. The army, then, was a French and European question at the same time.

I have already said how many false notions upon the causes of our misfortunes had been the offspring of those misfortunes. The great majority of the French, among Republicans as much as among Monarchists, was persuaded that the Prussians had conquered us because their military organization was founded upon universal and compulsory service. I was far from sharing this opinion. We had been conquered because:

1. The war had not been prepared for. Never, in any time, in any country, had a war been undertaken with less means to make war. We had not two hundred and fifty thousand men to put in our fighting line; our artillery in quantity and in quality was deplorably inferior to that of the Prussians; our magazines were empty; the stronghold of Metz, which was to be the pivot of our operations, was not even armed; and finally, we had no settled alliances.

2. To our insufficient means were joined incompetence in handling troops. Fifteen days had been spent on a line fifty leagues long, without making a single movement; the army had been split up into five corps that could not help one another, and the right wing, posted without support on the other side of the Vosges, could not fail to be swept away, however heroic its resistance. Only by going strongly forward with a mass of two hundred and twenty thousand men, and on condition that they left thirty thousand on the crest of the Vosges to guard its right, could our army have discomfited the Prussians, cut their lines and flung their troops into an irretrievable disorder.

3. Even with all these mistakes, all would not have been lost if, after the disaster of Reichshoffen, we had adopted the course, a grievous one no doubt, of abandoning Metz, and making two or three marches in retreat to escape the danger of being surrounded, instead of remaining where we were and giving the Germans time to envelop us with five hundred thousand men, and every facility for taking all our *cadres* at one single stroke, and with them all means of remaking an army. After this disaster the height of

stupidity had been reached in marching on Sedan instead of falling back on Paris.

Such were the real causes of our misfortunes and not a pretended superiority of organization in the Prussian army resulting from universal and compulsory service. On the contrary, this system of filling up the ranks by sacrificing the quality of the soldiers to their numbers is a source of weakness rather than of strength to an army.

This theory is not mine only, but also that of Marshal Bugeaud, of real soldiers and statesmen, expert in these things, who one and all declare that an army of soldiers who know and love their profession is by far superior to a more numerous army which includes only men insufficiently penetrated with the military spirit.

The first thing we ought to take in hand with a view to the recruiting of the army was, in my opinion, to base this recruiting on certain principles which, while procuring the necessary number of men, would above all assure us of their quality. To ask for an army of fifteen or eighteen hundred thousand men denotes a complete ignorance of these difficult questions in those who speak in this way. Nine hundred thousand men, or a million, are enough for the safety of France, and besides it is all her budget can endure. Now, a million men on a war footing supposes five hundred thousand on a peace footing. To embody them in their units demands not less than one hundred and fifty regiments of infantry, forty of artillery, and seventy-two of cavalry; and these units, if they are to be given a substance that will not leave them in the condition of hollow lifeless skeletons, will entail an expenditure of five hundred millions.

For all these men to become real soldiers, one, two, three years' service is not enough. Not in so short a period can we obtain passive obedience from them, and inspire them with the religion of the flag and the contempt of death—indispensable conditions for victory. Such self-abnegation can only spring up and take impregnable root in men's minds by dint of long association with minds themselves penetrated by it.

In the same way non-commissioned officers are not made in less than three years, and after spending three years in making them, it is not exorbitant to demand two years " to enjoy them," as a certain general, a man of sense and intelligence, once phrased it.

But if the universal compulsory service of Prussia is bad for France, because it would reduce men's stay with the colours to too short a period, their system of regional or provincial armies gives them a real point of superiority over us which I did my utmost to take from them, and which I will have the merit of taking from them if the permanent formations of army corps, which I brought into existence, are retained.

In Prussia soldiers from the same province serve together, commanded by officers from their home country; their material is close beside them, a very great advantage for the change from peace to a war footing. But in this way they have whole army corps made up of Westphalians, of Silesians, of Pomeranians; and if a similar system were practised in France, we should have army corps of Parisians, of Burgundians, of Provençals, etc., which would run the risk of compromising or even destroying our unity, the greatest element in the might of France, and giving civil war opportunities it has not had since 1789.

Without adopting the Prussian system, we might

attain a speed in mobilization not less than hers by means of what I called permanent formations, which consist in the existence before war time, not of regiments, but of complete army corps.

In this way, with nine hundred thousand men on a war footing, serving for five years and *encadrés* as I have just explained, so as to give, on a peace footing, five hundred thousand men divided among army corps organized permanently, I was certain of procuring for France the greatest military power she had ever possessed. But for that we would need a war budget of five hundred millions. This budget, thanks to an increase granted me already by the Assembly, I had nearly obtained, and I hoped with perseverance to bring this annual increase up to a hundred millions.

While preparing this scheme of military reorganization which I wished to submit to the Assembly for sanction, I was busily studying the actual condition of the army. In order to become better acquainted with it than through mere official information I had got into direct correspondence with the colonels of all branches of the service, and demanded frequent reports from them. This plan had very great advantages. It let the colonels know that the higher authorities had their eyes upon them, which obliged them to keep watch over everything in their regiments; and it allowed us to estimate the merit of each officer. I found, besides, in these reports, which I read regularly, though it was a lengthy task, invaluable hints upon the spirit of the army, the progress of its education, the condition of its armament, equipment, etc.

There was one measure especially to which I attached very great importance. In the days before the war we had allowed regiments to be divided up into battalions, half-battalions, sometimes even into companies at the pleasure of the various towns, which all wished to have a garrison large or small so as to help the octroi. The consequence was the impossibility of training the men and the annihilation of all military spirit. Another inconvenience was that certain regiments, sent to do garrison duty a hundred or a hundred and fifty leagues away, were entirely separated from their depots, which made it very difficult for their colonels to keep them under inspection. Lastly, and above all, the artillery being split up into isolated batteries, the regiments of this arm had batteries almost in every corner of France. I wanted to put an end to these dislocations, and already I had obtained some improvements in the matter; however, in May 1873 this work of concentration was far from finished.

I was also engrossed in the question of fortresses, war material, the system of supplies, the permanent formations, and the great experiment in encampment, which had given such remarkable results at Versailles that I had established two new camps, one at Avord, near Bourges, the other at Ruchard, near Tours.

While I was busy over the reorganization of our military forces, the Assembly gave a committee charge to draw up a digest of proposals on the recruiting system of the army. The majority of this committee, composed of forty-five members, generals, economists, financiers, lawyers, at first wanted to adopt the Prussian system in all its details, without omitting anything; then, as I had foreseen, it finished by dividing, and wiser ideas found support in it.

One of its members, M. de Chasseloup-Laubat, who had been chosen to draw up the report of its proceedings, was a suave, experienced man, but perhaps lacking the full courage of his good sense. Two soldiers, also on the committee, Generals Ducrot and Chanzy, after showing themselves strongly opposed to my ideas at the outset, had been brought round to them by the consideration of the period of service. Two years, three years had not seemed enough to them, and they had rallied to the five years' service which I had taken as the foundation of the whole system.

Once this point was reached, the cause of the proper organization of the army was won. As soon as they were willing to keep men with the colours for five years, the whole class could not be called up, and on this point the Prussian system was discarded. And since, besides, there had never seriously been any question of adopting the territorial system of army corps, we were going back to the old French organization except for certain modifications seen to be necessary. But to win the reality of things we had to sacrifice words. M. de Chasseloup-Laubat advised me to this effect, and I did not hesitate to follow his advice. It was agreed, then, that the words "compulsory service" should be set at the head of the law, but that the principle would be applied in the following way:

The annual draft eligible for military service, or not by law exempted, being about one hundred and fifty thousand men, would be obliged to serve, without exception, if the Government should judge it necessary; but the Government would be free to take in only seventy-five thousand men each year. Under these conditions compulsory service presented only advantages, among others that of relieving the Government from the necessity of voting the law of the contingent year by year. There was only one objectionable feature in it: the suppression of military substitution, instead of which volunteer service of a year was introduced, which consisted of authorizing, under certain conditions, volunteers to serve only for one year, provided they paid for their own keep—a bastard institution which none the less might prove very fruitful for the army budget.

Unhappily, the bases of this agreement, arrived at between the committee on the army and the Government, were discussed before the Assembly starting from the month of March on till the month of June, precisely at the moment when we had come to negotiations with Germany for the evacuation of our territory.

Immediately after the convention of the 12th of October, 1871, which had fixed for the 1st of May, 1872, the payment in full of the first two milliards, I had arrived at the certain conviction that even before this we might perhaps occupy ourselves profitably in paying the last three milliards. The reports I received from Nancy and from Berlin, besides, made me hope that the Emperor and the Chancellor would be disposed to listen favourably to proposals from us on this subject.

According to the third article of the Versailles preliminaries, the Emperor, in the matter of the payment of the last three milliards, might substitute for the territorial guarantee, consisting in the occupation of part of French territory, a financial guarantee, if it was offered under conditions recognized as sufficient for German interests.

Before speaking of this substitution, we thought it wise to convince Germany that we had both the will and the means to pay. Our creditors, very eager to have our money, would so much the more easily enter upon the path laid down in the peace preliminaries, and we would have fewer entreaties to make. Accordingly M. de Rémusat and myself, who invariably consulted together, had said to Count von Arnim in January 1872, when he had just been accredited as Ambassador in Paris, that we would consider negotiating this serious business after the payment due on the 1st of May, and at the same time I instructed M. de Gontaut Biron, whom we had just sent to Berlin as Ambassador, to speak to the same effect.

It was for financial as much as diplomatic reasons that we had deferred opening these negotiations until after the payment of the first two milliards, for it was proper to terminate this operation before embarking upon another. But as our abundant resources made it possible for us to pay in March what was due only in May, there was no longer any reason to delay moving in the matter until this date, and we were about to do so when Count von Arnim announced to us on the 27th of February that he was starting for Rome. His absence was to last only for two weeks.

When he took leave of me I told him to hasten back, as we were awaiting his return to speak of the engagements we still had to fulfil, and at the same time I informed M. de Gontaut of my conversation with Count von Arnim, warning him that I was waiting for the latter's return to Paris before opening negotiations.

M. de Gontaut had arrived in Berlin at the moment when General Manteuffel was there also, summoned by the Sovereign to receive the order of the Black Eagle. The General having made use of this occasion to reassure the Emperor and the Chancellor upon the internal condition of France and on the disposition of the Government, M. de Gontaut had been well received at the Court, but coldly enough by Count Bismarck, who put himself about very little for foreign diplomats when they were merely men of the world.

Our first news, then, from our Ambassador was reassuring. But immediately after the coming of Count von Arnim, who had gone to Berlin first, before Rome, their friendly attitude gave way to the most violent feelings of hostility towards France. The war party, with Count Moltke at its head, after having for a moment effaced itself before the peace party, to which the Emperor and the Chancellor were attached, had resumed a strong influence over public opinion.

Our schemes of military reorganization, imprudently discussed in the Assembly, exaggerated and misrepresented by the Press, and also the intention attributed to us of asking for the immediate evacuation of our soil in exchange for payment made before it fell due, had been sufficient to arouse all the susceptibilities and fears of Germany. And this hostility, sad to relate, found a basis in letters sent from Paris to Berlin by Frenchmen, who represented the evacuation as the greatest blunder. It would be, they said, the signal for the immediate dissolution of the existing Assembly, followed by the election of a Radical Assembly—in other words, the general disturbance of Europe.

Carried away by all these exciting causes, the war party demanded that they should hurl themselves at once on France before she should have reorganized her military strength. This opinion was being loudly expressed, especially in the higher ranks in the army, although Count Moltke showed himself reserved upon this point in the presence of our representative.

The Emperor, who was anxious above all things to be paid by France, would very gladly have seen negotiations opened to bring about this result, but not being insensible to the argument that war might recur in no distant future, he feared to dispossess himself of the occupied territory before finishing the fortifications he was constructing in Lorraine, in Alsace, and along the whole of his new frontiers. These were also Count Bismarck's feelings on the subject.

M. de Gontaut kept me informed of this state of ideas. The same intelligence coming from Nancy, from General Manteuffel, always friendly and always well informed as to the Emperor's mind, I understood that the one way to avoid the most serious difficulties was to inform Berlin, without waiting for Count von Arnim to return to Paris, of our intention to open negotiation in the matter at once.

I sent to General Manteuffel, and I directed M. de Gontaut to say in Berlin that our offer to pay in 1872 a debt due only in 1874 proved how little disposed we were to make war. On the eve of war we should not be so mad as to fill their Treasury at the expense of our own.

M. de Gontaut was to seek every opportunity to inform Prince Bismarck, not only that we were eager to free ourselves from our debt, but that we left to him the selection of the financial combination which would be most agreeable to him to guarantee this payment; that we only asked him, in his turn, to explain his views as to the method and the time for the restitution of territory due to us.

Unfortunately, Count von Arnim, now returned from Rome to Berlin, was interested in not allowing us to open a negotiation the discharge of which he wished to reserve for himself on his return from Paris, and he managed to persuade M. de Gontaut not to approach this subject with the Chancellor, who, besides, rudely enough affected to avoid meeting with diplomatists.

It is true that at this time Prince Bismarck was very much occupied with his struggle against the particularism of the Catholics. After having conquered the resistance which the federal party had from all time opposed to the attempts towards the unification of Germany, he thought he perceived this resistance springing up anew in the opposition of the Catholics to a Protestant Empire, an opposition similar to that of the Protestants to the Catholic Empire of Charles V. This last difficulty, and the refusal of the war party to evacuate the French territory, a refusal that made impossible any negotiation for a payment in advance of the three milliards, were perhaps sufficient to explain why Prince Bismarck avoided seeing our Ambassador, and kept Count von Arnim in Berlin.

However that may be, after delays that had taken up the whole month of April, Count von Arnim presented himself at Versailles in the beginning of May.

I received him most cordially, and I noticed that he eyed me very attentively, to assure himself, doubtless, whether all he had been told of my health was true. Count von Arnim was charged by his Government to convey their utmost confidence in me, personally, but to express extreme distrust with regard to the situation, a distrust that extended to all parties alike. In Berlin they were uneasy about my health, and feared the possible consequences of my retirement.

Count von Arnim, then, in a fashion, wished to defend

his Government against the rumours that had filled the English papers, in consequence of which it might have been thought that war was imminent. We should see in these rumours only Stock Exchange manœuvres. This was the only real truth: Prince Bismarck was powerful, but not the master. His influence with the Emperor was great without being always decisive. Now, the Emperor had been inspired with very serious misgivings.

"Were not these misgivings, perhaps," I said to Count von Arnim, "aroused by our armaments? Possibly some one has told you that I am preparing a formidable army?"

"No," he replied; "I am and always have been kept informed by you with complete candour."

"I want to restore to France," I continued, "the rank she ought to hold, and without a real army one has no rank. But I want peace also; I have promised and I will keep my word."

"My Government," repeated Count von Arnim, "trusts to your word; I have orders to tell you so."

He then explained his position with regard to the negotiations that were about to open. According to his instructions he was to omit nothing to bring it to a speedy termination; and he asked us, therefore, not to be too exacting at the outset upon the question of the evacuation of our country. After a first concession from the Emperor another might follow; but if we asked for all we should be granted nothing.

"Make us," he said, "a definite, positive offer; I shall send it to Berlin, and you shall have an answer before long."

I took care not to seem resigned to piecemeal and successive evacuations, and I answered that I would not delay to send him the definite and positive proposal he asked for.

On the 5th of May, as I had promised, I dispatched to the German Embassy a note relating to the payment of our debt and the evacuation of our territory. In this note we made the following declarations:

1. That we were disposed to pay the three milliards still owing by means of a loan of this sum raised at one operation, and whose total would be paid direct to the Prussians, at intervals as short as the payment of the subscribers' instalments and the state of the money market would allow. If any other scheme would suit Prussia better we were ready to entertain it, provided it was practicable.

2. That, our obligations once fulfilled, we asked how Germany would fulfil hers—that is to say, the restoration of the territory occupied by her. We pointed out, besides, that we were two years in advance of the date on which we had engaged to pay, without ever suggesting that in our opinion this sacrifice should entail, on Germany's part, a corresponding anticipation of the time of evacuation of our territory.

This document, dispatched to Count von Arnim by the intermediary of the Ministry for Foreign Affairs, remained unanswered for two or three days.

Count von Arnim had without doubt consulted Berlin by telegraph. When these few days had elapsed, he sent us a memorandum, not harsh, but cold and intricate, replying, in answer to our note, that the forestalling of our payments was merely apparent, for in order to pay the enormous sum of three milliards by 1874, we should have begun our instalments long before the present moment. This meant that they did not consider themselves as obliged, by our pretended anticipation, to anticipate the time of evacuation.

While I was having an answer to this tardy objection prepared by the Minister for Foreign Affairs, I received from Count von Arnim a note couched in curious terms, which mysteriously requested me to give him an appointment to see me. This was the 15th of May. I replied immediately accepting the rendezvous, and Count von Arnim kept it most punctually.

He began, with genuine embarrassment, by asking me to preserve absolute secrecy.

"Our negotiation is not progressing," he said, "and I have come to propose a way of advancing it more rapidly. With your loan scheme you need too much time for payment. Here is the plan that would be proper to adopt:

"1. A milliard, in a loan by lottery that would immediately be placed in Germany, perhaps in a month.

"2. A milliard in foreign values, to be collected by bankers and deposited in the hands of Prussia immediately, which would answer to the famous financial guarantees.

"3. A loan of a milliard in 5 per cent. stock, equally deposited direct in the Prussian Treasury."

Count von Arnim did not say, but left it to be understood that, in consideration of these operations, Prussia would consider herself as sufficiently secured to take part in a speedy and satisfactory negotiation, without saying in what particular it would be satisfactory for us. At the same time he begged me not to let it be known that this plan came from him, and finally spoke to me of the financier Henckel, asking me to help him in society in Paris by preventing the recurrence of certain disagreeable manifestations of which he had been the object.

I gave a sufficiently obliging answer to these requests, but I made inquiries regarding Henckel. I soon discovered that he was a friend of Count von Arnim's, and the rival in finance of Bleischröder, who was said to be in Bismarck's confidence.

Seeing at once that the rivalries of business magnates might complicate the negotiation, I was on my guard.

The day after Count von Arnim's visit I received a visit from Herr Henckel, who had let me know by one of his friends that he desired an opportunity for a conversation with me.

He painted the situation in very dark colours; spoke of Berlin's misgivings as most grave, most disquieting, assuring me, however, that they were not directed towards me, and announced himself as the friend of Prince Bismarck, whom he was shortly to see and of whom he would presently give me news.

From his way of talking I perceived that he was the author of Count von Arnim's scheme.

I saw the latter gentleman again. I declared to him that every plan was the same to me so long as it was possible, that I was ready to add to my previous proposal the one he had suggested, leaving his Government free to choose between them; and on May 17th I sent him a second proposal entirely in accordance with his views.

We remained for several days with no answer, trying to divine the reason for this inexplicable silence on the part of the Prussian Government, and the reserve in which Count von Arnim and Henckel secluded themselves, when the rumour of what was passing in Berlin fell upon our ears.

Herr Henckel, returning from Silesia, had told an intermediary whom he employed with me, that things were going badly; that Count Bismarck had fallen into a violent rage on receiving the dispatch in which the French Government gave him to understand that it proposed to begin paying the three milliards only from the month of March in 1874; that according to him this was contrary to the text and to the spirit of the treaties; gave grounds for assuming an intention not to adhere to the treaties, and that there was nothing left for him but to mobilize the Prussian army.

I suppose that Herr Henckel had exaggerated the gravity of the situation, but I did not doubt that there was some truth in what he had said of Prince Bismarck's ill-humour at the thought of a delay in paying the indemnity, as well as the hostile dispositions manifested by the military faction as soon as they had a complete and immediate evacuation mooted. This would explain the temper of the one and the threats of the other at receiving our first overtures. I was confirmed in this idea by an interview I granted Herr Henckel on the 24th of May. After recalling the very hostile disposition of the Prussian Government, he said that all this storm came solely from our not having been explicit.

"What?" said I. "I wrote twice: the first time I offered three milliards at 5 per cent. payable in thirty months; the second time, to fall in with German wishes (I did not say it was at Count von Arnim's suggestion), I proposed three milliards as follows: one milliard in a lottery loan, a milliard in

5 per cent. stock, and a milliard in foreign values, adding at the same time that if these proposals were not suitable, I would accept others, so long as they were practicable. I made, then, two successive proposals; I have had no reply, and yet you say I am not explicit enough! I cannot understand; I can see nothing through these clouds! Can you have something behind all this? Can you be thinking of making war upon us? Do you wish another negotiator than myself?"

"No," exclaimed Herr Henckel, " there is no question of such a thing. The whole difficulty comes from your not mentioning the evacuation in your proposals."

"But it is not our part to speak on this subject. France is pledged to pay; she offers the payment. Germany is obliged to evacuate; it is, then, for her to say when and in what way she means to fulfil her obligation."

"So," replied Herr Henckel, "but I know the lie of the land, and I assure you that you must open the question of the evacuation, and that you will then be listened to."

He then took from his pocket a paper, which he read to me. It was somewhat confused and unfinished, and I could discern in it that they reserved to themselves the right of evacuating the fortresses, and especially Belfort, only at the latest possible moment. He added that he would finish it next day, and would send it to me that I might judge it better as a whole. I agreed.

I then asked him if Count von Arnim was apprised of our interviews. He replied that he knew of them, and as I desired to see Count von Arnim to bring him to be more explicit, he undertook to let him know that I would expect him next day, the 25th of May, at the Elysée.

Next day, before leaving Versailles, I received Herr Henckel's note. It contained a scheme of piecemeal and successive evacuations, corresponding to payments successive in the same way, and reserving the evacuation of the fortresses until the very last. Thus was confirmed the apprehension that M. de Rémusat and I had always had, that we should not be able to obtain complete evacuation before the end of our payments.

Count von Arnim was waiting for me at the Elysée at the hour appointed. I told him I knew from the document Henckel had just sent me, the bases on which negotiation would be possible. I would resign myself to an evacuation by successive instalments, but I did not wish on any consideration that there should be any question of confining the territorial guarantee exclusively to any particular places, while taking good care not to name any, in order to avoid any discussion on the subject of Belfort.

Count von Arnim, this time eager to act, offered himself to transmit my proposals to his Government, and promised to have a speedy answer. Fearing the obscurity native to German versions, I invited him to come next day to the Présidence to luncheon, to communicate his dispatch to me before sending it, and he accepted.

Next day he came to read it to me. It was far from clear, as I expected, and he consented to join it to a note which I sent him, after having a copy made. In this note I reproduced the financial scheme extolled by Henckel and Count von Arnim, and I accepted the principle of successive evacuations. I wrote at once to the same effect to M. de Gontaut.

Believing that I had thus brought the negotiation on to solid ground, where it would be easy to make it go forward, I awaited with some confidence a favourable answer from Berlin, when, on the contrary, once more one piece of the worst possible news followed another.

That which General Manteuffel sent me from Nancy on the 27th of May was disturbing to this extent, that he did not look on a resumption of the war as impossible. A letter from our Ambassador in Saint Petersburg also gave a picture of the state of Germany that was most alarming for France.

These manifestations of hostility on the part of the German nation, were they not stirred up in order to frighten us, to make us more plastic in the negotiations we were pursuing? I could not believe that the Emperor or anybody else wished to reply by a war to the offer to pay in 1872 what was not legally due till 1874. The whole of Europe would protest against such an infamy.

But a word uttered in Berlin and re-echoed throughout the whole of Germany, filled me with fear—*Belfort*. In Bavaria, in Würtemberg, in Baden, men never spoke of Belfort without blaming Prince Bismarck because he had given it up to us, and said quite openly that they would never give it back. This saying, repeated even as far away as Rome, had found echoes in France. A more disturbing matter was that an important member of the Federal Council had said to M. de Gontaut:

"The military party is beaten; we will treat with you about the evacuation; but as for Belfort, we will give it back at the latest possible moment, and in the last extremity."

This language meant clearly that in order to get our money they would begin to give back our territory piece by piece, but that at the last moment Belfort would be the difficulty.

I talked of my anxiety to M. de Rémusat, who shared it.

"A formidable question may arise in a year or two," said I. "Will an infamy like the refusal of England to restore Malta to us perhaps be attempted on the subject of Belfort? I do not think they will dare it, in the face of all Europe. Nevertheless, we must foresee everything, and I could not for my part accept this treason, if our conquerors wished to impose it on us."

"Nor would I accept it either," answered M. de Rémusat.

"France alone," I continued, "will have the right to decide the question. What we must do is from henceforth to put her in a position to find another reply to it than mere resignation."

I informed the Minister for War of what was on our minds, and of my design, and in the utmost secrecy we took in concert the steps the situation demanded. Not long after, we were assured that from 1873 France would be able to enforce respect for her treaties if any one wished to violate them.

In the midst of these preoccupations, the discussion of the military law was dragging on in circumstances little calculated to calm the fevered spirits on the other side of the Rhine.

The Bishop of Orléans, addressing the House in the interest of the religious schools, had found an opportunity in this discussion to make a violent outburst against Prussia. After the Bishop of Orléans, it was General Trochu's turn, who obstinately supported the three years' service, contrary to the opinions he had previously expressed in his book on the French army. He spoke with talent, even brilliantly, and greatly stirred the passions of the Left.

On the 8th of June, 1872, I addressed the Assembly. In a ripely studied speech, I defended the principle of compulsory service as the committee had accepted it, that is to say, modified by the power left in the hands of the Government to take only the half of any class. I showed the Assembly that since this power allowed us to make the period of military service sufficiently long, our army would soon be numerous enough and strong enough to master every violence from within as well as from without, and to give France back her position in the world.

With regard to our recent misfortunes I spoke of the Emperor of Germany, and said that by seconding instead of being jealous of the men of high talent in his entourage, he had in a way made one man of them all, and so given another Frederick the Great to Prussia.

If such a eulogy of our conquerors had not been skilfully introduced and interwoven into the texture of the speech, it would never have been tolerated; but the passage was listened to in profound silence, and with no signs of disapprobation. The Assembly understood my aim, and was satisfied that the disagreeable effect of the preceding speeches should be effaced, without itself being compromised.

The five years' period of service was adopted, and this vote brought the whole discussion to an end, to the great advantage of the country.

Furthermore, affairs in Berlin were tending to

become calm. Bleischröder, Prince Bismarck's banker, had said that the Chancellor rejected the lottery loan—the deposit of securities—and cared only for a loan of the same kind as had succeeded for the two milliards.

We had replied that we, too, preferred the simple means that had already been employed successfully; and Bismarck, thus informed of our intentions, put the matter clearly.

According to him, our payments were to be accepted in the manner previously adopted. In return we were to be granted a gradual evacuation, or immediate if we could pay the three milliards in one instalment. By candid behaviour towards us the hate that divided our two countries would not be embittered. Then, to escape the opposition he met with at Court, both on the subject of the negotiations he advised them to open with France and on the religious question, Prince Bismarck had retired to Varzin, where he was resting, while at the same time threatening the opponents that were hampering his plans.

At Berlin there were various conferences between the Emperor and his principal Ministers, especially his Finance Minister, Count Camphausen, and his Minister for War, Count Roon, and the Prussian proposals, freed from all that had appeared unacceptable, and simplified from a financial point of view, were dispatched to Count von Arnim at Paris. Von Thile, who took the place of the absent Bismarck as Minister for Foreign Affairs, informed M. de Gontaut and said :

"You may be easy in your mind. His Majesty the Emperor desires peace, and means to second your Government in its labours. He has just sent Count von Arnim instructions which will assuredly hasten the termination of this important business."

The war party was obviously vanquished, and we now had only to await the notifications whose coming had been announced.

At last, on the 14th of June, 1872, Count von Arnim sent me a summary of the conditions in accordance with which the Cabinet at Berlin was willing to negotiate. I proposed that he should come next afternoon to the Elysée Palace. He arrived punctually, and under the beautiful trees in the garden we went to confer with each other upon the German scheme.

"Well," said he, "we are practically agreed. You wish to pay, we to evacuate your country; so that little or nothing can stand between us. As for war, you may be fully convinced that it is not desired. The Emperor, Prince Bismarck, and the politicians are in the ascendant, they desire peace and will prevail. This is the moment to put the seal upon it by an agreement which will establish the parallel progress of the evacuation and the successive payments of the indemnity."

I replied that I, too, wished for peace, that everybody in France wished it also, but that it depended on the conditions that were to be laid down to make it possible and lasting. I then expressed once more the desire that Berlin would accept my proposals of the 24th of the preceding May, aiming at obtaining in 1872 the evacuation of two departments against the payment of a half milliard, and in 1873 the evacuation of the other four departments immediately upon our handing over to the German Treasury fifteen hundred millions in specie and the same amount in financial guarantees.

Count von Arnim stopped me here:

"I must let you know the truth without evasion. I can be easy with regard to the first part of the evacuation; I have sufficient powers for that, and I will immediately give over to you Marne and Haute-Marne for a half milliard paid presently; then two other departments after the payment of fifteen hundred millions, or possibly only a milliard; but to evacuate all on the conditions you offer is impossible; for the Emperor's mind is irrevocably fixed on this point. He does not wish to make war on you, but he wishes to keep territorial guarantees in case you might happen to leave power. However, when two milliards have been paid, I believe you will get him to give up the two last departments in consideration of bankers' guarantees."

These determinations, which I already knew, being thus confirmed, I no longer hesitated to reckon upon them, while doing my utmost to take out of Germany's hands, after a short delay, the greatest possible part of our territory. I asked, then, that the departments of the Marne and Haute-Marne should be evacuated immediately in consideration of five hundred millions down (we had them in securities secretly purchased in the German markets, and in offers of cash from the Bank of France); I asked for the subsequent restoration of the Vosges and the Ardennes after the payment of a milliard or fifteen hundred millions in the spring or during the year 1873; and finally, in 1873 or 1874 we would give solid financial guarantees for the third and last milliard, and would receive in return the remaining departments, and with them Belfort.

In all this Count von Arnim showed himself easy. We agreed that I should put a draft convention in writing and send it to him next day at Versailles.

Returning to the Présidence, I wrote out, without mentioning the lottery loan, which I knew had been rejected by Prince Bismarck, a scheme exactly in accordance with what had been agreed at the Elysée Palace. It was approved by the Council, and finally sent by M. de Rémusat to Count von Arnim.

The latter, after reading it, made a few objections, without pressing them.

At the same moment, Henckel, Count von Arnim's confidant, sent me a memorandum, saying if I was willing to adopt its essential clauses, I would forestall difficulties on the part of Berlin.

Finally, on Tuesday the 18th of June, Count von Arnim brought M. de Rémusat a new draft, and confessed with some embarrassment that on some points it differed from our conversation at the Elysée Palace. To begin with, after having agreed that the second phase of the evacuation, that which was to free the Ardennes and the Vosges, should take place after the payment, of a milliard and half, he now spoke of two milliards. He had, besides, suppressed the first article of our scheme in which there was clearly expressed the reciprocity of obligations of Prussia and of France. As to reducing the numbers of the troops in occupation, and the consequent reduction in the expense of maintaining these troops, he held out in a way that was remarkable, but no longer surprising to us, since the Germans had displayed the utmost obstinacy several times already in the discussion of their smallest pecuniary interests.

I went into this new scheme with M. de Rémusat, and we adopted a new version which contained a preamble reproducing the gist of our first article that had been suppressed, without mentioning direct payment by the subscribers to the loan into the Berlin Treasury, because this payment could not be carried out; once again we asked that the evacuation of the Ardennes and the Vosges should follow on payment of fifteen hundred millions; the date of 1875, taken as the time of final payment, was only indicated as the latest permitted, and we reserved the right to anticipate this period if our resources allowed; finally, we submitted the reduction of the army of occupation and the cost of its maintenance to the Emperor's pleasure.

To sum up, this draft of agreement presented the advantage of allowing us either to delay the full payment of our debt until the 1st of March, 1875, if our financial system obliged us, or to obtain the total evacuation of our territory in 1873, in case we might have at this date the means of paying in cash or in financial guarantees accepted by the Prussian Government. Some subordinate clauses were joined to the preceding, among others that which forbade the two contracting parties to execute any works of fortification in the occupied departments. This clause was aimed at Belfort, where the Prussians were constructing works, in spite of their declaration to the contrary. Finally, speaking of the two departments to be evacuated last of all, Meurthe and Meurthe-et-Moselle, I had expressly mentioned the Belfort district.

This fresh defining of our right made it almost impossible to put any disloyal intention into action. Doubtless there was no such intention, but the great majority of the French people believed in its existence.

This new scheme, after having been submitted to and approved by the Council, was sent to Count von Arnim on the 18th of June, 1872.

On the 19th M. de Rémusat received a letter from the Ambassador of Germany desiring certain explanations.

I sent M. de Rémusat to give them by word of mouth. He did not find him, and asked him to come to see me next day.

Count von Arnim wished to know why, in our draft, there was no longer any mention of direct payment by the subscribers to the agents of the Prussian Government.

I replied that, as the loan was to be raised by public subscription and not through a syndicate of bankers, direct payment into German hands by subscribers scattered over all quarters of the globe was impracticable; and that, besides, each section of territory was only evacuated after payment had taken effect; Prussia therefore had no interest in the retention of this clause.

Count von Arnim comprehended this; he only expressed one regret, that he would be obliged to give Berlin explanations as to this change.

On the question of the evacuation of the Ardennes and the Vosges after the payment of fifteen hundred millions only, he said he would plead our cause, but feared he would not be successful. As for the article relating to the reduction of the army of occupation and the cost of its upkeep, he accepted this hypothetical wording:

"In case the army of occupation should be reduced, there would also be a reduction in the cost of its maintenance."

He added that he thought it certain that fifty thousand men would not be left in two departments, and that the expenditure would therefore necessarily be reduced.

Finally, on the question of reoccupation in case we failed to carry out our engagements, he asked for what reasons we wished to apply this clause only to a failing in our *financial* engagements.

By this wording we had desired to circumscribe and define the right of reoccupation by the Germans, in the fear of giving them an opportunity to meddle in our affairs, and especially to refrain from evacuating Belfort, on the pretext that we had not kept such or such an engagement. I did not say so to Count von Arnim, so as not to inspire him with an idea he had never had, and I extricated myself from an awkward moment by agreeing to substitute for the words *financial engagements* the words *engagements undertaken in this present agreement*, the latter phrase having the same meaning as the former, though in different terms.

M. de Rémusat introduced the changes agreed upon into the last French version, which, immediately sent to Count von Arnim, was dispatched to Berlin.

On the 27th of June, the German Ambassador received from Berlin and addressed to the Minister for Foreign Affairs the final draft of the agreement, entirely conforming to that which we had proposed, except as regards the evacuation of the Ardennes and the Vosges, which the Germans still placed as conditional on the payment of two milliards, and not of fifteen hundred millions as Count von Arnim had allowed us to hope.

This agreement was signed on the 29th of June, 1872, by Count von Arnim and by M. de Rémusat, for whom I had wished to reserve the pleasure of sealing with his signature this considerable step taken along the path of freedom for our territory. Next day I presented the agreement to the Assembly, to which I explained that the periods 1873, 1874, 1875 fixed for the payments were optional for us, and guaranteed us against exactions that might forestall our means of paying, without limiting our right to pay and secure the evacuation before these periods matured, and that our liberation depended only on our credit, which was now greater than ever.

The Assembly, which ought to have been grateful to the Government for these successes, persisted, on the contrary, in its hostility towards it, and in order to display this took for a pretext the fact that the departments of the Nord, the Somme, and Côte d'Or had just elected three very pronounced Republicans: M. Derégnaucourt, a wealthy manufacturer, and MM. Barni and Paul Bert, distinguished professors.

Though this choice could not be looked on as a menace to public order or to society, the Monarchist section of the Assembly was none the less disturbed by these three elections, in which they pretended to discern the complicity of the authorities with the revolutionaries. They wanted without fail and at once to call upon the Government to explain itself as to which side it meant to take.

The Moderates, however, and particularly the Right Centre, showed themselves more reserved. These elections, said they, were of no more significance than those of the previous year which had sent a hundred Republicans to the Assembly. No doubt it was very glaring, but the Government was far from having favoured them, and it was difficult to point out ways of resisting so as to conquer so general a trend of opinion; the wisest added that moderation was perhaps a more effective means than violence.

These arguments, not being to the taste of those to whom they were addressed, were regarded by them as confessions of weakness. Accordingly, they wished to make their protests heard. To avoid challenging the Government from the tribune, which on their part would have meant calling for the system of official candidates for which they had so bitterly blamed the Empire, they decided upon an application which some among them were to make to me.

I might have refused to receive them, but this would have been insulting, and I preferred to hear what they had to say. The selection of my visitors indicated the spirit of the application. They were the Duc d'Audiffret-Pasquier, General Changarnier, MM. Saint-Marc-Girardin, Batbie, Depeyre, de Cumont, de Kerdrel, the Duc de la Rochefoucauld-Bisaccia, and the Duc de Broglie, who had in the previous April resigned his post as Ambassador at London.

On the morning of the day on which they presented themselves at the Présidence M. Vitet was breakfasting with me, and I invited him to be present at the interview. He accepted, and his presence was welcomed by my visitors. I gave them the most courteous possible reception, and invited General Changarnier, who had seemed to me to make himself sponsor for the rest, to begin.

The General at once explained the motive for their visit. It was inspired, he said, by the desire to direct my attention to the last elections, to have an explanation with me in the matter, and to inquire as to the course the Government intended to adopt in order to save the country from the perils that threatened.

After the General, whose tone in any case was affectedly mild, other members of this deputation that had no mandate but its own, spoke to the same effect, to justify their uneasiness.

Having heard them attentively, I replied that two out of these three elections had taken place in departments administered by prefects, MM. Séguier and de Guerle, who were not suspected of any love for the Republican party; and that for the third the defeat of a moderate Republican by an advanced Republican was due to the Conservative party, which had split the vote.

These facts were so indisputable that there was nothing so say by way of answer. The Duc de Broglie, in measured but somewhat acrid tones, said that it was not the behaviour of the prefects they found fault with, but that perhaps the general attitude of the authorities was not wholly innocent of the recent electoral results; that I had a great and legitimate influence on the country, and that the electors, wishing to please me, thought, no doubt wrongly, that they were succeeding by choosing such candidates.

I replied clearly that having accepted the charge of the Republic, and meaning to keep it faithfully, I had no right to oppose the election of Republicans; that to ask any other behaviour of me was to wish to have me depart from my avowed and constant rôle; that I had, besides, no way of estimating the degree of republicanism in various candidates, nor of controlling the vagaries of universal suffrage. I had merely the conviction that the impartial policy pursued by the Government was more apt to inspire electors to choose properly than the opposite policy.

My reply, precise, clear, and firm without sharpness, shut the Duc de Broglie's mouth, and he assumed thenceforward an attitude of affected coldness.

Others of my visitors having manifested their anxieties for the future with greater cordiality than my first interlocutors, I told them that, in my opinion, to escape from our serious if not alarming situation the organization of a Conservative Republic was a safer means than the re-establishment of Monarchy, which was made impracticable by the rival claims of three dynasties.

"By a few wise laws," I said, "let us entrust the legislative power to two Chambers; let us give the Upper Chamber and the Executive together the right to dissolve the Chamber of Deputies; let us then make an electoral law guaranteeing universal suffrage, as far as possible, from its own impetuousness, and in these conditions I am persuaded that the Government will be sufficiently armed against the worst enterprises of demagogy."

I was not the only one to speak during this interview; but if my interlocutors did not accept the efficacy of the means I thought proper for safeguarding the future, they proposed no others. And yet they were every one, in fidelity to their memories of the past, partisans of a restoration of Monarchy.

Leaving me, they went back to the Assembly, where members awaited the result of their action with curiosity. They had to agree that they brought nothing very new, for what I had said to them was precisely what the Moderates were saying every day. The Extreme Right, irritated by the failure of its action, declared that since anything was to be expected from a blind and powerless Government, nothing was left but to break away from it; and the same evening M. Saint-Marc-Girardin, in order to provoke this rupture, inspired an article in the *Journal des Débats* which reproduced our interview with very inaccurate details.

Next day, in the Assembly, I addressed myself to

M. Saint-Marc-Girardin, and before M. Vitet, who was as much offended as myself, I accused him for the untruth of the article in question. He excused himself, laying the blame on a correspondent whom he had not had time to inform more accurately.

The desired effect was obtained, and the Right, taking a step farther on the path of hostilities, without carrying the Right Centre with it for the present, pretended that M. de Larcy, its representative on the Ministerial Council, could no longer remain there. M. de Larcy resisted, but was beaten and came in real distress to tell me.

I endeavoured to keep him, showing him the blunder his political friends were making in gratuitously depriving themselves of a representative in the Cabinet. He agreed, but persisted in his determination through fear of being excommunicated by his party.

I regretted his loss as a man and as a minister, and as I did not care to put any one in his place, I amalgamated the Ministry of Public Works and the Ministry of Commerce, which was held by M. Teisserenc de Bort, whose energy and capacity would be enough to deal with this increased work. In this way the gap was promptly filled.

These difficulties, little or great, fortunately did not succeed in disturbing the country; the time had therefore arrived to begin the vast financial operation of the loan of three milliards to pay off the war indemnity. As the month of August was approaching, and the Assembly was disposed to take its summer vacation in order to attend the second session of the General Councils, I did not wish it to break up before passing the taxes which, by establishing the equilibrium of the budget, would strengthen our credit; I had consequently had the vital question of raw materials brought up again. The discussion had once more taken the same line as in the month of January. The whole survey of possible taxes was repeated, including the income-tax, which once more I managed to have rejected, to admit merely a tax of some thirty millions upon personal property and a new surcharge on licences.

These poor resources being far from sufficing for our needs, the committee which the Assembly had, on the 19th of the previous January, directed to propose new tariffs for the tax on raw materials, was obliged to comply. After sufficient trouble I obtained its report, which I supported from the tribune, and which was adopted by a very large majority at the sitting of the 26th of July.

But this tax, which might have yielded one hundred and eighty millions, had been reduced to ninety-three millions. The balance of the budget was thus obtained with great difficulty.

The tax on raw materials, as far as its collection went, was subject to the success of our negotiations with the various Powers to whom we were bound by commercial treaties, which postponed this collection until 1873. The budget for the current year, 1872, could do without it, as the expenses of the new loan were only to fall upon the next year. We had even contrived a surplus, in 1872, to meet the delays that would occur in the yield of the now taxes through the difficulties of their first establishment. No service was in difficulties, the advanced evacuation was certain, and the task of calming agitated passions was making visible progress.

It was in these encouraging circumstances that, on the 15th of July, 1872, the Assembly passed the law which gave the Government authority to borrow by means of a public subscription in 5 per cent. stocks the sum of three milliards five hundred millions, three milliards of which represented the debt to Germany, and five hundred millions were to be set aside for the costs of the loan. These costs, which included, with the expenses for purchasing exchange bills and for transferring the money to Germany, the interest on the capital up to the payment in full of the debt, would not absorb the whole of the amount provided for, and there would be a surplus left, perhaps five millions, which I intended to place to the sinking fund.

It was permissible to ask ourselves if we should find still three milliards available among the body of capital, especially so soon after our loan of two milliards.

I did not doubt the confidence that would be inspired by an investment at 6 per cent. on the security of the ledger of France, and this confidence was not long in showing itself by the overwhelming demand for the loan. Many foreign bankers had come to Paris to ask for the greatest possible share, not merely in the subscription, but also in the subsidiary profits of which the subscription might be the opportunity. Before this eagerness on the part of the capitalists it was unnecessary to have the loan guaranteed, as we had done for the first two milliards. But there was another precaution to take in order to facilitate our payments in Germany: this was to secure bills drawn on that country.

M. de Goulard, who had taken M. Pouyer-Quertier's place at the Ministry of Finance, gave M. Dutilleul directions to arrange for this operation with the banks. They engaged, in return for a fixed premium of twenty-five millions, to procure us seven hundred millions in bills on Germany.

On our side we had secretly brought up about four hundred and fifteen millions in such bills; and finally we reckoned on receiving about three hundred and fifty millions more, representing the subscriptions to the loan that would be made on foreign stock exchanges. We were therefore assured of fifteen hundred millions in foreign bills, or half the whole of the amount to be paid out of France.

Besides, as the banks, through their treaty with us, were interested in seeing that the exchange rate was not raised against us, we had less reason to fear a scarcity in specie such as had followed the payment of the first two milliards.

Furthermore, precautions were taken against the risks of a financial crisis. For example, the law authorizing the loan had also raised from two milliards eight hundred millions to three milliards two hundred millions the limit of the issue of notes by the Bank of France. We had, besides, handed over to the Bank to be coined some thirty millions of bar silver we had procured from the Hamburg Bank in exchange for its paper known as *bancos de Hambourg*, of which we held a great quantity among our bills on Germany.

If these measures were not enough to prevent a financial crisis, at least we could say, with Bossuet, that we had taken out of Fortune's power all that could be taken from her by dint of counsel. But they were enough, and the success of our financial operations was complete.

The eagerness displayed in France and abroad to subscribe to the loan allowed me to raise the issue price of the stock above the ninety-two and a half which had been fixed for the earlier loan. By a decree of the 20th of July I made it ninety-four and a half, with a first payment fourteen and a half francs more than had been demanded in 1871. The complete payment for the stock was to be made in twenty monthly instalments, beginning with the 1st of September. These conditions were unanimously approved, and every one agreed that no one could display more resolution in defence of the interests of the State.

By the evening of Sunday, the 28th of July, the day fixed upon for opening the subscription lists, already we knew that the most sanguine hopes were surpassed, and the next day, when all telegraphic communications had been compiled, we learned that the financial world had offered us forty-four milliards, or nearly thirteen times the amount asked by France!

The great number of subscriptions from foreign countries gave us the three hundred and odd millions of bills on which I had counted to complete our means of paying our debt abroad.

By the first guarantee payment, and the anticipatory payments of subscribers, we could realize a sum of eleven hundred millions, which, with the resources already in the Treasury, allowed us to pay the first half milliard at once, and to secure the evacuation of the departments of Marne and Haute-Marne. From that moment I saw with delight the possibility of obtaining the liberation of our territory for 1873.

The Assembly prorogued itself from the 4th of August to the 11th of November. On the 5th of August, by physician's orders, I left Paris to go to Trouville, where I had chosen a house looking over the whole gulf of the Seine, from le Havre to the cliffs of Calvados.

I was followed by the Minister for War, his executive staff, the principal members of the Artillery Board and the Commissariat, with whom I meant to occupy myself directly and with my own eyes with the question of war munitions and stores, and many other matters from which I had been heretofore kept by the presence of the Assembly. The guns with which we were to carry out artillery experiments had been transported to Trouville, and with them the officers and men capable of serving them.

Before describing in detail these experiments and their consequences in the remaking of our war material, I wish to recall or to indicate briefly the chief results already attained in our task of reorganizing the military power of France.

Shortly after the defeat of the Commune, I had instituted a Superior Council of War, presided over by the Minister for War and composed of twenty-four members, among whom were the two Marshals, de MacMahon and Canrobert, Generals de Ladmirault, du Barail, Forgeot, de Berckheim, Deligny, several Commissary-generals, a member of the Cour des Comptes, and an Inspector of Finance.

This Council, made up of experts, had, after very serious discussion, approved of the principal provisions of the recruiting law, later sanctioned by the vote of the Assembly. It had subsequently adopted my scheme for *permanent formations*, which consisted in creating and maintaining in time of peace as in time of war twelve army corps of three divisions, with their complement of officers, magazines, and stores under their hand, having only peace effectives in the ranks, but in a position to rise to war strength in a few days.

Together we had appointed the following stations for these corps: four would be at Paris and Versailles; two in the East, with Châlon for their centre; one at Lille; two on the Loire at Bourges and at Tours; one at Lyons; one between Toulouse and Bordeaux; and one at Marseilles, where the African troops would be mustered. This distribution was aimed at facilitating a rapid concentration of our forces towards the East.

But there was one question of immense importance, that of works of fortification, which according to the law could only be decided by a special commission whose views would, so to speak, be final.

This Commission included ten or twelve members, among them Marshal de MacMahon, Generals Frossard, de Rivières, de Courville, Forgeot, de Berckheim, Ducrot, and Chanzy.

I put before them the following proposals:

To construct certain new works on the East, to strengthen Besançon and Langres;

To raise a huge network of defence works at Belfort, allowing us to make an entrenched camp of this stronghold;

To perfect the fortifications of Verdun and the fortresses of the Meuse and the Ardennes;

And above all to create a powerful military centre at Châlons.

I said that by creating there, between Paris and Bordeaux, a *Paris without population*, which could contain immense quantities of provisions and stores, and two or three hundred thousand men, resting on almost impregnable works, a march upon the capital would be almost impossible, for any invading army that should neglect this obstacle would have on its flank or in its rear the two or three hundred thousand men entrenched in this outwork of Paris. I looked on the creation of this place as likely to be the safeguard of Paris in the future.

I wished to have another work at Rouen to protect Paris, in case of an invasion of Flanders and Picardy, and to secure its provisioning if a siege was expected. But I was most of all eager for the carrying out of my project for Châlons, and the Commission adopted it unanimously. That for Rouen, not so obviously useful, was also adopted in spite of some opposition.

For Paris, General de Rivières, of the Engineers, had devised a scheme of works that would have cost more than a hundred millions, and which was unnecessary since Paris, even as it was, had held the Prussians for four months. It would have sufficed to add to the existing defences four or five forts, at Saint-Denis, at the confluence of the Seine and the Marne, at Hautes-Bruyères, at Châtillon, at Montretout. Paris would thus have become impregnable, and these works would have cost thirty millions.

But General de Rivières held to his plan, which received the approval of the Marshal, though General Frossard and General de Berckheim had shown its uselessness. I joined myself to the latter two, and the majority of opinions was on our side. Nevertheless, the matter was not yet settled when I left the Présidence.

Thus, at the time of my coming to Trouville several of the essential matters with regard to the re-establishing of our military forces had been considered and most of them settled. I had reserved the question of our war material, to make it the principal object of my studies while I was at Trouville.

First of all our attention was fastened upon possible improvements in the rifle and in the gun. As for the rifle, I left it to General Douay, the creator of the school for marksmen at Vincennes, to see about correcting its shortcomings.

As for the artillery, which the recent war had equally shown to be inadequate, the difficulties we had to overcome were infinitely greater. The substitution of the percussion fuse for the time fuse was an important improvement and easy to carry out, but the inferiority of our fire in comparison with that of the Prussians came also from the shape of our pieces, their way of loading, and chiefly from the metal of which they were made.

On the unanimous advice of the generals and officers of land artillery and naval artillery, one of the most distinguished among whom was General Frébault, the system of loading by the breech was adopted. This system, it is true, was only possible with steel guns, and ours were all made of bronze. Happily we had at the head of our armament works at Tarbes an officer of exceptional merit, Colonel de Reffye, who had found a way to fit movable steel breeches to bronze guns. I summoned him to Trouville, where he brought several of his converted pieces. The trials we made of them proved their excellence both for range and accuracy. It was consequently decided that our artillery should be transformed in accordance with this system, which would place at our disposal from fifteen hundred to eighteen hundred pieces of 7 for 1872, and two thousand four hundred pieces of 4 for

1873. Without any doubt it would suffice to restore our divisional artillery and our reserve artillery. Colonel de Reffye, having been decorated Commander of the Légion d'honneur on the very ground where the trials were made, was sent back to Tarbes to begin his manufacturing without delay.

The employment of bronze, which we had in abundance, meant a saving in money for us, and especially a still more precious saving in time; but the qualities of steel had not escaped me. Accordingly, it was settled that by way of experiment some guns should be forged of the latter metal at Creusot, where, as our officers averred, they had succeeded in producing a steel superior to Herr Krupp's in the Rhine provinces and Mr. Firth's in England.

In any case, if we did not succeed in forging an infallible metal, it appeared certain that we could do away with the danger of bursting by binding the inner tube of the gun with forged iron.

These matters pertaining to war material being settled, I directed my attention to the administration and maintenance of the troops, including the soldier's rations, which I improved. In particular we discussed the advantages and disadvantages of the service corps. The advantages seemed considerable, from the point of view of the convenience of having men always at hand, and the excellent quality of the supplies they provide for the corps; but they deprive the fighting strength of at least twelve thousand men, and their work costs more than the general stores.

On this point I gave a long hearing to a very well-known manufacturer, M. Godillot. He would undertake, he said, to keep the stores of twelve army corps always full, so that in case of a sudden campaign we could from one day to the next clothe and equip eight hundred thousand men! That would be an immense help in accelerating mobilization. I was shaken by this consideration, and resolved to submit the question to the Superior Council of War.

The time of my vacation was not therefore lost as far as affairs went.

I received numerous visits at Trouville. First one from M. de Vogüé; he was coming back from Constantinople, and told me he had had no little trouble to save the Sultan from the lightnings of the Court of Rome over the Armenian business. M. de Gontaut came after him. Everything, he said, was placid in Germany, and the final evacuation of the territory now depended solely on the rapidity of our payments.

My friend Prince Orloff was also among my visitors. No one could be more amiable, or simpler, or more sensible with less pedantry than Prince Orloff. I had a very lively affection for him, equal to his for me. He was at Berlin at the moment of the meeting between the three Emperors of Austria, Russia, and Germany, a meeting that stimulated the curiosity and the imagination of politicians to the highest degree.

As far as France was concerned I heard most accurately, from M. de Gontaut and from Prince Orloff, of the intentions of the Emperors of Russia and Austria. Scarcely had he arrived in Berlin when the Emperor Alexander had sent for our Ambassador to tell him that if there had been any plot whatever to be hatched in Berlin against France, he would not have come, and Prince Orloff was charged to confirm this speech to me.

The Emperor François-Joseph had given the same assurance to our Ambassador, which did not prevent the Legitimist and Bonapartist newspapers from pretending that the main object of the Berlin meeting was to sanction, by the signature of the Emperor Alexander, the treaty that had torn Alsace and Lorraine from us.

In reality, the three Emperors were not sorry to show their unity, both to England, which had not been invited to this meeting, and to the trouble-mongers of every country—Germans, Austrians, Spaniards, Russians, or others. The German Emperor had also arranged the meeting of the sovereigns of Russia and of Austria with intent to make them forget their mutual resentments, and to bring about a reconciliation from which he would have nothing to fear, since it was his own achievement.

To this information sent by M. de Gontaut, Prince Orloff added more interesting details, which only he had been able to discover, thanks to his intimacy with all the important personages of Saint Petersburg—details that proved the sympathy of the Russian nation for us, and its desire to see our power completely re-established. The Khiva Expedition was starting just at this moment. It had been preceded by an explanation between Russia and England. The latter, regretting the part she had played at the denunciation of the Treaty of Paris, had shown herself extremely distrustful and very exacting towards Russia in the matter of guarantees, to such a degree that the Emperor Alexander, usually so pacific, had uttered threats which, indeed, had not moved England. Prince Orloff went so far as to say to me:

"We shall fight, if we must, with or without allies."

I took particular care to throw no fuel on this fire. While expressing every interest for the greatness of

Russia, I said to Prince Orloff that the moment did not seem to me opportune for settling by war the great Asiatic conflict that is always threatening to break out between Russia and England. To-day everybody wished for peace, and France in particular, doomed as she was to bend all her resources to the payment of her debt to Germany, could only think of freeing her territory from foreign occupation.

The Prince asked nothing, but he was too intelligent not to understand and not to profit by what I said. Count Schouwalow, sent to London on this occasion, passed through Paris, where I spoke with him to the same effect as to Prince Orloff; and he went on to end, by a betrothal between a daughter of the Emperor and an English prince, a conflict which at the outset had looked very serious.

It was also during my stay at Trouville that I had some anxiety over my three milliard loan. It would be a mistake to fancy that an operation of this nature is terminated when the subscription lists are closed. One must still follow it with keen attention for months, and be ready to stand by it in case of need.

The payment of the subscriptions was made with uncommon alacrity. We had received twelve hundred millions and a half, and deducted from this sum five hundred millions paid direct to the Germans, which with the two milliards already written off represented the half of our debt.

But the September instalment, the first since the floating of the loan, was about to fall due, and the approach of this settlement, extraordinary for the immense size of the sums involved, preoccupied the market in public funds to such an extent that people were asking whether speculators would be able to borrow the necessary amounts to carry over to the following month; if not, they would be driven to sell at any price, and the stock would fall to an alarming figure.

I have never had anything to do with what is called the world of business, but I have always observed it attentively, because it is a considerable section of the public, and when one is governing one must take it into account. In the present case I did not hesitate to take into consideration the very deep anxiety that ruled on the Stock Exchange.

At all periods we were careful not to leave public funds to themselves, even when the loans were placed in the hands of great companies of finance, interested in handling them to the best advantage. With much more reason, when we proceeded by means of a public subscription and no one was responsible for the loan, the Government would have been much to blame if it had not sought means of averting an imminent financial crisis, the consequences of which might go so far as to jeopardize the liberation of our territory.

And what, indeed, was the amount of the help the market needed in order to prevent this crisis? An advance of fifty millions was sufficient, the figure indicated by the Stockbrokers' Union; and the Treasury had about seven hundred millions at its disposal out of the first instalment of the loan!

Accordingly I wrote to M. Teisserenc de Bort, the temporary Minister of Finance, and I summoned him afterwards to Trouville to talk over this matter; for I could not address myself to a wiser, more enlightened, or more upright counsellor. Like myself, he was of opinion that under these exceptional circumstances we ought to keep up the price of the funds, and do it obviously, openly, so as to avoid all suspicion of any clandestine operation. The Treasury would advance to the Company of Stockbrokers, who would be responsible for repayment, the sum of fifty millions to be lent for carrying over. This operation would be advantageous both for the State credit and the Treasury. Our intervention was only to take effect, however, at the last possible moment, and only if the price of carrying over went beyond fourteen centimes, which would answer to 8·85 per cent. interest.

The stockbrokers, according to our instructions, having made no mystery of the help eventually promised by the Government, people were reassured, and when the critical day arrived the carry-over prices fell almost at once. The rate of fourteen centimes was not even reached, and the Treasury had no need to intervene. The mere announcement of the Government's intention had been enough to bring Stock Exchange transactions back to normal conditions.

I had spent the month of August and a great part of September at Trouville, surrounded by signs of sympathy from the people of all the neighbouring districts. The principal towns had invited me to pay them a visit: Cherbourg, Caen, Lisieux, Honfleur, le Havre, etc. The last-named town was sufficiently near Trouville to enable me to accept its invitation.

The eve of the day on which I was expected there, we saw several cruisers flying the British ensign arrive in the roadstead. The English Government had sent them, by way of courtesy, to escort me to Cherbourg, where they thought I was going. Before entering the harbour of le Havre we passed in front of these vessels to return their salute, and again in the evening when we left on our way back to Trouville.

The next day, the 19th of September, I returned to Paris. I took up my abode at the Elysée, where I received, as I had done before, all the persons who deserved to be distinguished among the various sections of the population of Paris.

During this short absence some troubles had been stirred up against me, as much by the Legitimists as by the Radicals and the Bonapartists. The Legitimists in La Vendée had organized pilgrimages, which they advertised in their papers. These unusual movements of crowds preceded by banners, marching in procession and singing canticles, provoked counter-demonstrations. At Nantes, for example, in spite of all the precautions taken by the prefect, M. Doniol, a gentleman of wisdom and prudence, the pilgrims were greeted, on their return, with hisses and hostile cries.

This was a most regrettable attack on the liberty of conscience, but by what means could it have been prevented? None the less the Royalist papers made it a pretext for attacking the Government with the utmost violence, as though the Government on its side would not itself have had a right to complain that, by political as much as religious demonstrations, the pacification it had with so much trouble brought to men's minds had been compromised.

On their side the Radicals were agitating. I had stopped their campaign to demand in addresses the dissolution of the Assembly; they had submitted without too much complaint; but to console themselves for this constraint they wished to hold certain banquets, and M. Gambetta, not wishing, he said, to make any difficulty for the Government, approached M. Victor

Lefranc to know whether this would be allowed or forbidden. The Minister replied that he would not tolerate any public banquet, adding that while he could not legally oppose private banquets, he nevertheless disapproved of them as against the interests of the Republic. M. Gambetta then assured him that his language would be irreproachable.

At Chambéry there was a first attempt to hold a banquet, which was prevented by the police, because it presented the features of a public meeting; but at Grenoble M. Gambetta, amid the enthusiastic plaudits of his friends, made his famous speech upon the *new social strata*, which produced so bad an effect and stirred the wrath of the Conservative party.

Thus on the one hand the hooting of the pilgrims at Nantes, on the other the virulence of the Grenoble speech became grievances against the Government, which the Royalists accused of being the accomplice of the democratic party in all its violence and the Permanent Committee announced that it would make this matter the subject of questions in the Assembly. I went on the 10th of October, 1872, to the sitting of the Committee, over which M. Grévy presided. My presence controlled the most agitated, who spoke of nothing less than the immediate summoning of the Assembly. M. de Bisaccia demanded explanations on the important matters that were exciting the anger of his friends. I addressed them at once, and gave them the clearest possible explanations on every point.

The campaign that had been announced against the Assembly, to obtain its dissolution, had been stopped, I said, at its very beginning, by means that went to the very limit of the law, if they did not go beyond it. At Nantes, as elsewhere, proper steps had been taken to safeguard the freedom of the pilgrimages; the bishop himself admitted it; but no precaution could prevent whistling and hooting.

Upon this point the Committee did not insist further. M. de Broglie himself, whom I had welcomed at Trouville, where he had come to see me with the prefect of his department on matters relating to his election, M. de Broglie recognized that we had scrupulously observed all our engagements and that there was no reproach that could be addressed to us. This testimonial was not without its effect, and the Committee's ardour began to slacken.

There remained the affair of M. Gambetta's speech at Grenoble. I expressed the greatest disapproval of the tendencies shown in this speech, particularly the doctrine of social strata, so contrary to the essential principle of the French Revolution, which allows of no distinction between citizens except the degrees of their merit, and I had no trouble in proving how baseless in my case was the reproach of being M. Gambetta's accomplice.

M. Grévy, with a few contemptuous words on the subject of these childish accusations, gave the Committee to understand that it was taking too much on itself by adopting towards the Government an attitude that could only belong by right to the Assembly.

After Legitimists and Radicals came the turn of the Bonapartists in the person of Prince Jérôme Napoléon. Since his excursion to Corsica he had not been heard of, till on the 11th of October I learned that he had just arrived with Princess Clotilde and their children, in Melun, and from there had gone to Millemont to M. Maurice Richard, the former Minister of the Emperor.

I summoned the Council and put the affair before them. Evidently the Prince, after recognizing the previous year the Government's right to object to his presence in France, was to-day repudiating this right and wanted to put our force to the proof. Our right, however, was founded on the law of forfeiture, twice passed by the Assembly; if we allowed this law to fall into abeyance with regard to Prince Napoleon, we could not invoke it against Napoleon III, who was being urged to land in France.

These arguments were not contradicted, and the sentence of expulsion, having been agreed upon, was communicated to the Prince, who at first displayed an intention of resisting; then perceiving that his resistance was useless, he returned to the Swiss frontier in a special train placed at his disposal. Princess Clotilde, whom I had informed that there was no objection to her remaining in France, did not wish to be separated from her husband, and went with him.

After these affairs, which caused a certain amount of anxiety to the Government without disturbing the peace of the nation at large, we still had to occupy ourselves with the loan for the October settlement on the Bourse—less troublesome, however, than in September.

The carrying over was still *hung up* (an expression of a language that is foreign to me, but which I use to be understood), and it was necessary to put into the market capital which would naturally reach the point where it would be most serviceable; for it is with capital as with water, you have only to increase the mass to have it rise to the soil you wish to fertilize.

To furnish the money market with the resources it lacked, I had the idea of discounting the seven hundred millions of bills which the banks were to hand over to us for the discharge of our debt to Germany.

Wise and clever M. Dutilleul, whose opinion in these affairs had the most weight with me, because I was sure that he would not advise anything irregular, M. Dutilleul approved of my plan; for it was but fair to return to circulation, where it was needed, a part of the capital that we were locking up in consequence of the payment of the loan instalments.

We therefore informed the banks which were obtaining bills for us that we had at their disposal the money they might need, and there was not one, even among the most powerful, that did not eagerly take advantage of our offer. About a hundred millions were thus, by drawing on the Treasury, restored to the market, and during the few days that preceded and followed the October settlement money was plentiful. Yet in spite of this help, carrying over took place at a fairly high rate, which proved how necessary was the step we had taken.

While we were thus without a crisis passing through the two critical moments of our financial operations, subscribers to the loan were making haste to pay us, and by the help of our bills we were acquitting ourselves of our debt to Germany without any pinch to ourselves.

To these fortunate results were added rich harvests of every kind, especially in wheat and fodder, and as the rest of Europe had not been equally favoured, our commodities went to England to pay for the bills we had received from the banks. Lastly, thanks to the small notes of the Bank of France which had been put in circulation, there was not even the appearance of the money embarrassment that had disquieted us the previous year.

Unhappily, this co-operation of circumstances favourable to the accomplishing of our patriotic task was neutralized by the agitations of the political parties.

Some months before the session that was about to open, the Advanced Left had pretended that the only mandate given by the electors to the deputies was to make peace, and that peace being made, the Assembly ought to dissolve. The majority had properly replied to this species of summons that, besides the mandate to make peace, the Assembly had also been charged with the task of giving France a Constitution, and that, furthermore, even if peace was signed, it would only be completed after the carrying out of the conditions upon which it was concluded—after the payment of the indemnity and the evacuation of the territory. As our punctuality of payment made this evacuation certain for 1873, it was concluded from this that the Assembly would first have to come to definite resolutions in the matter of the Constitution.

The system under which we were living, created by what was called the Pact of Bordeaux, consisted of one sovereign Assembly, with an executive derived from and responsible to that Assembly. Such a system could only be temporary; its continuance was only desired by the extreme parties; the Extreme Left, because one sovereign chamber was in accordance with its revolutionary principles; the Extreme Right, because it hoped to find, in the weakness of a temporary system, facilities for restoring Monarchy. Such was, besides, the conduct recommended by the Count de Chambord to the Legitimists who had visited him at Lucerne.

On the contrary, the Left Centre and the Left wanted definitely to organize a Conservative Republic, entrusting me with the Presidency for a period of more or less duration. The Right Centre itself, hoping that I would give myself up to it, consented to this organization, and wished to offer me the Presidency for life.

Whatever were the intentions of the various parties, my duty was to point out to the Assembly the danger to which it would expose the country by leaving behind it public powers insufficiently organized, and to propose the means of averting this danger.

Personally I did not wish for too long a period as President, still less a term for life. It did not suit me to give myself over indefinitely to politics, as I desired to spend my last years in a repose that only the interests of the State had brought me to abandon; and it did not suit me either to play the part of a little bourgeois usurper taking advantage of the unhappy times to impose himself upon France. I was at the head of the Government through my patriotic devotion, with a sense of the honour involved, which I freely avowed; but I was not an official tenacious of his place, and I had no mind to hand myself over to any one in return for a few years of power.

My ruling principle was the most conservative in the world. I had no fear of future elections; but since the unforeseen always finds a place in political affairs, I desired that during this session, which would probably be its last, the Assembly should pass conservative measures that we should perhaps not obtain from its successor.

Such were the views of the Government. I outlined them in a message which the Council unanimously approved, and which I took to the Assembly on the 13th of November, 1872. I meant to read it myself, to invest it with more formality and weight.

I began by depicting the prosperity of the country, proving by official figures the activity of its trade, which for this year had surpassed the most prosperous year of the Empire by seven hundred and eighty-seven millions. The Bank of France had seen its reserve mount from six hundred to nine hundred and fifty millions; we were on the point of reaching an equilibrium in our budget, and our payments to Germany were taking place punctually and without any financial crisis.

Apart from the material side of things, I said that a great quiet was falling upon the passions roused by our military disasters and our internal troubles, and that Europe saw with a sympathetic eye the reconstruction of our forces. All this part of the message was heard with the utmost attention and obvious satisfaction in the Centres.

At length I came to the political part, and attention redoubled. Addressing myself to the Left, I said that the stability of a Government could only be assured by maintaining public order; and my severe language, which should have been applauded especially by the Right, was only applauded by the Left, eager to prove that it did not take my words as conveying blame to itself. These words: "*The Republic will be Conservative or it will not exist,*" were drowned in plaudits from the Left Centre and the Left, and the Right Centre, embarrassed, not venturing to join the Left, which it appeared unhappy to see animated by such proper sentiments, was silent, and preserved an attitude which it should have left to the Extreme Right.

I quote this part of the message taken from the *Officiel*, so that all may judge whether it would be possible to use more conservative language.

"We have just informed you accurately, gentlemen, of the actual situation of the country, and we have laid especial stress upon its financial and commercial position, because that is what has most importance with regard to our credit, and because our credit, along with our army, which is being reorganized with remarkable rapidity, constitute the two elements of our power. Thus, after a most unhappy war, after the most terrible of civil conflicts, after the crumbling of a throne that had been believed solid as a rock, France has seen all nations eager to offer her their capital, her credit better established than ever, eight milliards paid off in two years, the greatest part of these sums transferred to foreign countries without disturbing our circulation, the bank-note accepted everywhere as cash, the taxes, though increased by a third, paid without crushing the taxpayer, financial equilibrium re-established, or about to be, two hundred millions set aside for the sinking fund, and industry and commerce increasing by more than seven hundred millions in one single year! These results, which we would not venture to submit to you if they were not a striking proof of the vitality of the country—to what, gentlemen, do we owe them? We owe them to one cause, and one only, the energetic maintenance of order! (Hearty assent from a great number of benches.) Yes, it is order that has brought it about that on the morrow of a foreign war, on the morrow of a civil war, with foreign troops occupying our soil, with the ruins of our towns still smoking, it is, I repeat, order, strongly maintained, that has permitted France to produce as much and to command as much credit as in the most prosperous moments of her existence. (Applause from the same benches.)

"I do not fear to repeat it, gentlemen: if you had not enjoyed absolute order, this war, unexampled in reverses, this cruel dismembering of our territory, these tremendous burdens that seemed beyond our power to bear, this throne fallen beneath the weight of its mistakes, this ancient monarchy under which we were wont to live suddenly vanished, this new frame of a Republic, which in the ordinary course agitates men's minds—all this, coming suddenly upon us, all this pouring at once upon our surprised and ravaged country, all this might have become irretrievable disaster! With the preservation of order, on the contrary, our workshops were reopened, men's hands resumed their busy activity, foreign capital, far from avoiding us, sought us out again, calm has come back with work; and already France raises her head again, endures her unconsolable griefs without forgetting them, and, still more astounding! a form of government which, as a rule, disturbs her profoundly begins little by little to enter into her habitual life . . ." (Acclamations of assent from the Left and the Left Centre.)

A voice on the right: "No! no!"

The President.—" . . . does not prevent her from returning to life, to hope, to confidence, confidence she inspires in others as she feels it in herself. (Renewed and hearty assent on the Left.)

"And since I am coming now inevitably to burning questions of the moment, I will say to those who have long given their faith to the Republic, as the ideal of government most in harmony with the thought and the most appropriate to the progress of modern societies, I will say to them, 'It is you who should most passionately pray for order . . . ' ("Hear! hear!" "Excellent!" from the Left. Exclamations and ironical laughter on the right.) 'For if the Republic, already twice essayed without success, can succeed this time, it is to the preservation of order you will owe it.' ("Very true!" "Well said!" from the Centre and the Left.)

"Let this then be your task, your daily care! If the exercise of certain rights that belong to free peoples may disturb the country, learn to renounce them voluntarily, and make in favour of the public safety a sacrifice that will above all benefit the Republic. If it could possibly be said that order is not equally in the interest of everybody, I would venture to assert that it is your essential interest, and that when we work to maintain it, we are working for you, almost more than for ourselves." (Movement of approbation among the Left Centre.)

M. de Belcastel.—" It is France we must work for."

The President.—" Gentlemen, events have given us the Republic, and to go back to its causes in order to discuss and judge them would to-day be an undertaking as dangerous as useless. The Republic exists . . . "

A voice on the right: "No! no!"

Baron Chaurand.—" We said the opposite at Bordeaux!"

The President.—" Gentlemen, have the goodness not to interrupt! You have no right to make personal replies to a message to the National Assembly." ("True!" "Well said!")

The President.—" I ask members of all views to wait and not to be in a hurry to blame or to approve.

"I resume.

"The Republic exists; it is the legal Government of the country; to desire otherwise would be a new revolution and the most to be feared of all. Let us not waste our time in denouncing it; but let us employ our time in imprinting upon it the characteristics that are desirable and necessary. A Committee appointed by you, some months ago, gave it the title of Conservative Republic. Let us adopt this title, and try above all to see that it is deserved. (" Hear! hear!")

"Every Government must be conservative, and no society could live under a Government that was not. (General assent.) The Republic will be conservative, or it will not exist." (Sensation.)

A voice from the Left Centre: "Hear! hear! We accept!"

The President.—"France has no mind to live in continual alarms; she desires to be able to live in peace, so that she may work to maintain herself, and to meet her enormous burdens; and if she is not given the calm which she absolutely needs, whatever be the Government that may refuse her this calm, she will not endure it long! ("Hear! hear! Well said!" from a great number of benches on the Left and the Left Centre.) Let no one delude himself! It may be imagined that, thanks to universal suffrage, and so backed by the power of the mass, a Republic could be established that would be the creature of a single party! That would be a work to endure only for a day.

"But the mass itself needs repose, security, work. ("Hear! hear!") It may live for a few days on agitations, but not long. (Renewed and numerous signs of assent.) After inspiring fear in others, it takes fright at itself, it flings itself into the arms of an adventurer, and pays with twenty years of slavery for a few days of a disastrous licence. ("Hear! hear!" Prolonged applause from a great many benches.)

"This it has often done, as you know; and do not imagine that it is not capable of doing so once again. A hundred times it will re-embark upon this sad and humiliating voyage from anarchy to despotism, from despotism to anarchy, filled with shame and calamity, in which France has met with the loss of two provinces, a tripled public debt, the burning of her capital, the ruin of her greatest monuments, and that massacre of hostages which one would have deemed impossible! (Deep emotion.)

"I conjure you, gentlemen, not to forget these conditions, so terribly bound together: first a Republic in agitation; then a return to a power that is called strong because it is uncontrolled, and with the absence of control, ruin certain and irreparable. (General and hearty assent.)

"Yes, let us break the fatal chain that binds these disastrous conditions to each other, and let us calm instead of stirring up; let us make the necessary sacrifices to the security of all, let us even make sacrifices that seem excessive, and above everything let us not turn our eyes towards the reign of a party . . . ("Hear! hear!"); for the Republic is a misnomer, if instead of being the Government of all it is the Government of a party, whatever may be that party. (Bravos and applause from a great many benches.) If, for example, you mean to represent it as the triumph of one class over another, at once you estrange from it a part of the country, first one part, and then the whole. ("Yes! yes!" "Hear! hear!")

"The Revolution of 1789 was made to abolish classes, that there should be in the nation only the nation itself, the nation united, living all together under one and the same law, carrying the same burdens, enjoying the same advantages, in which, in a word, every man should be rewarded or punished according to his works. ("Hear! hear!" and applause from the Left.)

"Acting in this way, the Republic of 1789 established the existence of all upon the basis of true social justice; and its principles swept over the whole world, because they were nothing else than this social justice proclaimed and applied . . . (Renewed applause from the Left) for the first time in the world's history. And it is because it had this signification that it was possible to boast of the tricoloured flag that it would go the whole world round. Long, in the wake of a conqueror, it moved in victory among the nations of Europe; but its material works have perished, while its spiritual achievements remain and are the most solid glory of France, far more than victories that by the chance of mere force pass from one flag to another. (Movement on the benches.) As for myself, I do not understand, I do not accept the Republic save as it should be, the Government of the nation, which having long and faithfully left to an hereditary power the direction of its destinies, but not having found success, through mistakes that are impossible to judge to-day, at length resolves to rule herself, alone, through her own representatives freely chosen, wisely selected, without question of party, or classes, or birth, seeking them neither above nor below, neither on the right nor the left, but by that light of public esteem in which characters, qualities, defects portray themselves in lines impossible to misread, and choosing them with that freedom that is only enjoyed in the bosom of order, calm, and security! (Bravos and loud applause from the Left.)

"Two years passed under your eyes, under your influence, under your control, in almost unbroken calm, may give us hopes for founding this Conservative Republic, but only hopes; and—let no one forget this—the smallest mistake would suffice to make this hope vanish before an afflicting reality. (Movement and murmurs on the Right.)

"Permit me to add a last reflection. It is not France alone that the Republic needs to inspire with confidence, it is the world. Vanquished though she is, France has not ceased to attract, to fix upon herself the eyes of the nations, which take alarm or are reassured according to what passes within her borders; and this uneasy attention is but a homage paid to her influence on the peoples of the world. Sometimes we hear it said, 'France is isolated.' And most frequently it is with those who say so merely an illusion of their pride. Foreign Governments have in other days had a weakness for interfering in the internal affairs of their neighbours; cruel experience taught them their lesson, and now they no longer think of doing so. But they are masters of their own good opinion, and no one can do without the good opinion of others. Man needs the esteem of his fellows, and nations have need of the esteem of other nations. ("Hear! hear!") A day comes, too, when one needs support, moral support at the least, and one only finds it if one has deserved it. (Assent.)

"Foreign Governments are to-day sufficiently enlightened to see only France herself in France. If she is orderly, it is to the advantage of all; if she is not merely orderly, but strong, it is to the advantage of those who desire a true balance among the Powers of the universe. Now I dare to affirm that the efforts France has put forth, for now nearly two years past, have won her an esteem many tokens of which she has already received. And it is not to this party or that party, to this man or that man, that these tokens have been addressed, but to France, to France alone, and the conduct she is displaying to repair mistakes she did not make, but which she is expiating because she allowed them to be made. (Loud and widespread applause.)

"Well, then, I declare it, because my duty is to keep my eyes fixed on Europe, France is not isolated, and on the contrary it only depends upon herself to be surrounded by trusty and useful friends. Let her be peaceful under the Republic, and she will estrange no one. Let her be agitated under a tottering monarchy, and she will see chaos opening around her under one form of government as well as under another. (Loud approval on the Left. Prolonged interruption.)

"Gentlemen, we are coming to a decisive moment. The form of this Republic has only been a provisional form dictated by the course of events, resting upon your good sense and on your unity with the power you have temporarily selected; but all minds look to you, all ask themselves what day . . . (murmurs on the Right), what form you will choose to give to the Republic that conservative strength it cannot do without."

M. de la Rochefoucauld, Duc de Bisaccia.—"But we do not want it!"

M. le Vicomte de Lorgeril.—"And the Pact of Bordeaux?"

The President.—"It is for you to choose both. The

country, in giving you its powers, gave you the clear mission to save it, by procuring for it peace first of all, after peace, order, and with order the re-establishment of its powers, and finally a regular form of government. You announced it thus, and now it is for you to fix the order and the time of these various sections of the work of salvation entrusted to you. ("Hear! hear!" "Quite so!" from the Right.) Heaven forfend that we should put ourselves in your place! But on the date you have fixed, when you have chosen some from among you to meditate upon this great work, if you desire our advice we shall give it to you loyally and boldly. (Exclamations and murmurings on the Right.) Until then count upon our profound attachment to the country, to you, to this thing so beautiful and so dear to our hearts that was before us, that will be after us—France, which alone merits all our efforts and all our sacrifices. (Loud and widespread applause.)

"A great and momentous session is opening before you; it will be neither deference, nor co-operation, nor devotion, nor determination, on our part that will be lacking in the success of your work, which may God bless and make complete, and above all, lasting, which has not yet been granted to us since the beginning of the world!" (Long acclamations and repeated applause on the Left Centre and the Left.)

Although this language was as moderate and as conservative as possible, the Extreme Right contained themselves with much difficulty.

As soon as I had finished reading, M. de Kerdrel claimed to speak, and was greeted with much whispering from all sides of the Assembly, uneasy as to what he was about to say. The Right seemed decided to show no further consideration, and the Right Centre itself, Monarchist in the depths of its heart, was ready to allow itself to be carried away, though it perceived how dangerous a conflict with the Executive might be. M. de Kerdrel, in a tone full of consideration for me, said that the message inviting the Assembly to enter upon the path of constitutional development deserved on this account to be most carefully examined. He therefore asked that a committee should be appointed to present to the Assembly a draft answer to the Message.

Not fearing the investigation of the Government's views, I hastened to declare that so far from fearing the light we sought it, and that the Cabinet associated itself with M. de Kerdrel's proposal. After my declaration no hesitation was possible; it was decided that a committee should be appointed to draw up a report on this proposal.

Such was the first act of a policy, the aim of which was to delay as much as possible the moment when France would be sheltered from the rivalry of parties by the stability of the institutions I proposed to give her.

In considering the motives which had inspired this Message, it will readily be understood how much the reception given to it shocked me. I gave counsels of political prudence, I asked for measures of social preservation, and I was accused of not being conservative enough! If I had not had before me the unfinished work of the liberation of the territory, I would have resigned the power to this Assembly which was sacrificing the present and certain interest of the country to chimerical hopes.

Incidents could not fail of being plentiful along this path into which the majority had thrown itself, and on the 18th of November, General Changarnier—always in a hurry to provoke crises from which he always emerged disillusioned, his friends never taking any account of his pretended services—General Changarnier mounted the tribune to develop an attack seemingly directed against M. Gambetta, but in reality against the Government, on his notorious Grenoble speech. He was sufficiently rude to M. Gambetta, and accused the Government of weakness and lack of decision.

M. de Broglie then summoned me, not very politely, to repeat before the Chamber the words I had spoken before the Permanent Committee with regard to the Grenoble speech. He would be glad, he said, to hear me once more, with the same fervour, the same accent, combat the socialist doctrines of that speech.

Members were generally disgusted with this impertinence of a novice in parliamentary life, who was putting questions upon his conservative principles to one who, for forty years, had been the constant opponent of anti-social doctrines.

I went to the tribune, and after criticizing the rudeness of M. de Broglie's summons, which I peremptorily refused to answer, I said that in this quarrel picked with the Government there was only one serious question, that of confidence, and I demanded that it should be settled that very moment. This challenge troubled our opponents, who would not have liked so decisive a step. But they had provoked it, I insisted, and we turned at once to the often lengthy agenda before the Assembly.

It being impossible to go on with the business

without further notice, I supported the following motion proposed by M. Mettetal:

"The Assembly, confident in the energy of the Government, and reprobating the doctrines put forward in the Grenoble speech, passes to the business of the day."

Of six hundred members present, there were only three hundred and seventy-nine votes cast, two hundred and sixty-three for and one hundred and sixteen against. It was clear that the Assembly was allowing itself to be carried away by the coalition of Monarchist parties. We were thus entering upon a period of conflicts no longer possible to avert, and which the Kerdrel Committee, with a majority hostile to the Government, was to continue.

While waiting until this committee should be prepared to hear me, I had to occupy myself with a sufficiently serious consequence of our loan. England was threatened with a money crisis as the result of her share in our financial operations. She had sold us a great number of her bills on Germany, and as the inevitable consequence of these sales, the rate of exchange went up in Berlin, in Frankfort, in Hamburg, precious metals were being sent out from London to these places. Our neighbours then found themselves exactly in the position in which we had been after our first loan.

To put an end to this movement, the Bank of England had put up its discount rate from 4 to 7 per cent., and would not have failed to carry this progression to the point where balance would have been established between the discount and the exchange rates. It was the beginning of a financial crisis which, extending to all the money markets of

Europe, would have become a serious danger, especially for ourselves, whom it surprised in the midst of settling our loan and our payments. Our interest was to do away with this danger as soon as possible.

To this end the Bank of France, which at the same moment had eight hundred millions in specie at its disposal, was prepared to advance one hundred or two hundred millions to the Bank of England, and would have authorized it with a justifiable feeling of national pride. I even disclosed our willingness to Lord Lyons; but the Bank of England did not wish to ask us for this service. All the same we came to its aid indirectly.

We had set up a financial office in London, under M. de Maintenant, a very clever and honest inspector of finance. This office was to receive the payments of the very numerous English subscribers to our loan, and in return to deliver the scrip and pay the coupons to the foreign creditors of France. The funds thus centralized came to about two hundred millions, deposited in the Bank of England, whence we were to draw them in order to pay Germany; we preferred to delay this operation, so as not to increase the embarrassment of the Bank of England by depriving it of these two hundred millions; and shortly after, thanks to this considerate behaviour on our part, and to the arrival of gold from Australia and from America, the discount rate fell in London, and the danger of a European financial crisis was averted.

On the 22nd of November, 1872, I went with M. Dufaure before the Kerdrel Committee. The points on which its president, M. d'Audiffret-Pasquier, asked us for an explanation were as follows:

1. The committee thought that, on the 18th of November, by speaking from the tribune of the Grenoble speech as a mere incident, I had not blamed it with sufficient severity.

2. The committee wished to know how the new institutions could be reconciled with the Pact of Bordeaux.

3. Finally, what, according to our idea, were these new institutions that were to be given to France?

To these three questions, put in the most courteous terms, I answered clearly and firmly.

I said, first of all, that the reproach that I showed too much indulgence for the doctrines of the Grenoble speech needed no reply. Everybody knew what I thought of the Radical doctrines, and how I had fought the formidable insurrection they had provoked. The true ground of debate lay elsewhere. It was in the spirit of the Message, which part of the Assembly found too republican.

What, then, I asked, were my motives for speaking as I did? Everybody immediately before the Message blamed the temporary principle, even those who to-day refuse to give it up. If I had associated myself with this feeling, nearly universal in France, it was because it responded to the need of taking precautions against the possible advent of a Radical Chamber, and with it Socialism. Against this danger I saw only one means of resistance; to create an Upper, that is to say a Conservative, Chamber, and a solidly established Executive, sharing with the Upper Chamber the right to dissolve the Chamber of Deputies. This organization would have to be completed by a wise electoral law. With these conditions I judged that there was nothing to fear from the future national representation. I had already the previous year told the members of the Assembly who had come to discuss their forebodings as to our political future, and I took nothing back to-day.

They asked me again how these proposals could be reconciled with the Pact of Bordeaux.

In the simplest and most straightforward manner I told them. At Bordeaux I had promised to keep the Republic faithfully; to-day it was just as I had taken it into my charge on the first day, without any alteration. And yet there was a difference: on the day when it was entrusted to me, the country was disorganized, while to-day it was completely reorganized in its finance, its army, its administration. Did the Pact of Bordeaux mean that we were never to get away from temporary and provisional things? Assuredly not, for at Bordeaux I had said, with the approval of the Assembly, that when our noble wounded (that is to say France, then vanquished, beaten down, covered with blood and desolation) was restored to health, it could then decide upon its own destiny. The end of the provisional régime was then foreseen in the very wording of the Pact of Bordeaux. That is why I had proposed to the Assembly to prepare a number of laws proper to assure the future destiny of the country against the dangers that would result from the prolonging of the provisional régime. In what was this foresighted step contradictory to the Pact of Bordeaux? On the contrary, it was its confirmation.

"Those very same people," I added, "who run to Antwerp or to Chislehurst, offering the crown to their selected princes, are also asking to abandon the provisional régime, and if we were to accept the solutions they pursue, they would never accuse us of breaking our word."

Besides, I did not ask that the Republic should be proclaimed as the final system of government. I merely said, in order to respect every one's susceptibilities: " Let us confine ourselves to organizing the Republic now existing in such a way that it will be conservative as long as it is the Government of the country, the Assembly remaining the sovereign judge of the methods I propose to attain this end. A Government that had neither views nor a voice on so serious a subject would be the most culpable and the most pusillanimous of governments."

Such were my answers, to which no rejoinder was offered. The committee, through its president, confined itself merely to thanking us for our explanations, and chose M. Batbie to make its report, which he read to the Assembly on November 26, 1872.

In a style full of bitterness for the Left and of feigned deference for me, he depicted the present condition of France in the darkest colours; he said that, in such a situation, the irresolute policy of the Government should give place to a *fighting policy*, a wretched phrase that was to have a long re-echoing, and ended by requesting that a committee of fifteen members, nominated by the official departments, should be enjoined to lay before the Assembly a bill upon the responsibility of Ministers.

The Keeper of the Seals was the first to reply. His clear, decided, vigorous speech brought the debate back to the question. Looking to the public interest, the Government, he said, had proposed to the Assembly to take certain constitutional measures proper to assure the immediate future of the country. In reply to this proposal the committee demanded a fresh settlement of the question of the responsibility of Ministers. Although this settlement might bring about a decrease of the influence of the Head of the State in Parliament, the Government did not oppose its submission to the Assembly, on condition that the constitutional measures asked for in the Message should also be submitted. And therefore M. Dufaure moved a counter resolution in the following terms:

"A committee of thirty shall be nominated in the official departments, in order to present to the National Assembly a bill to regulate the assignment of the public powers and the conditions of the responsibility of Ministers."

The Reporter then demanded that this counter resolution should immediately be put before the committee, which was allowed, and the Keeper of the Seals and myself went to uphold it before them. But the Legitimists wanted an immediate and complete rupture. They prevailed in this, and at seven in the evening the Reporter went to the tribune to announce that, the committee and the Government persisting in their respective resolutions, the question could only be decided by the Assembly.

A night sitting was demanded. I declared that I wished to speak, and that I would only speak the next day, which I did immediately the sitting of the 29th of November was opened.

M. Batbie had described at great length what he called the army of disorder, accusing the Government of lacking firmness in dealing with it. Then he had been tactless enough to avow that the majority was dissatisfied at hearing the Left applaud the President.

I replied that no doubt there existed an army of

disorder almost everywhere in Europe, but that no one had fought it more strenuously than myself on every occasion when it had threatened society by insurrection, by strikes, by socialist theories. In all these occurrences, particularly in 1848 and in 1871, I had set myself, not without peril, against the assaults directed against social order, and I had averted them by persuasion or repulsed them by force.

It was said again that we left religion unprotected, regardless of the fact that, under the Empire, I had defended the power of the Church of Rome against the insensate policy of nationalities.

It was pretended that the signs of approval to-day lavished upon me by the Left proved that I was no longer opposing the theories and the systems I had formerly reprobated.

Now these signs of approval were to be explained in a very different manner.

At Bordeaux I had solemnly promised to preserve the Republic; upon the insurrection of Paris, in order to prevent the rising of the greatest towns in France, I had pledged myself not to lend a hand to any restoration of Monarchy. I kept my word, fulfilled my pledges. That was why the Left testified its approval.

Then, addressing the Right, I said that if the Monarchy, recognized at Bordeaux as impossible, was now become possible, I might be told that as I alone had given this pledge it was for me to retire and leave the Assembly free to re-establish the Monarchy. In that case I should retire. But if there was no agreement among all the various parties to decree the crown to one of the three claimants, the Republic, recognized as necessary last year at Bordeaux, was so still to-day; and I added that in proposing to make it Conservative by means of laws which I would submit to discussion in the Assembly, I merely obeyed the dictates of loyalty, the force of circumstances, and the most vital interests of public peace.

Coming finally to the theme of Parliamentary Government which the committee pretended to strengthen, I asked if anything could be more parliamentary than the régime under which we were living, which obliged the Head of the State to submit all his acts to the approval of the Assembly. Certainly it would have been much more easy for me never to oppose myself to its will; but I would thus have failed in my essential duty; for the Assembly being sovereign and uncontrolled, its power would have been of all the most to be dreaded.

When I had returned to the Government bench, many deputies came to congratulate me, and my colleagues told me that they were delighted with the situation I had just created for the whole Cabinet.

After a sufficiently lengthy interruption, the discussion was taken up by M. Ernoul. It was not, he said, a matter of the Republic or of the Monarchy, but of the freedom of Parliament, compromised by the greatness of my position, which meant that when I was present the Assembly was no longer free. He averred that, far from wishing to attack my power, it was sought to make it independent of crises in the Ministry, and he finished by recalling the concluding lines of my *History of the Empire*, in which I had pointed out the danger of giving up the country to one man, whoever it might be.

I asked M. Ernoul at once if in good seriousness he was applying to me phrases that were applied to Napoleon, the absolute master of France and of nearly all Europe. Was it not perceived how misplaced was this pretended comparison between the unlimited power of the great despot and my authority, precarious, limited, and contested day by day?

Finally, to end this long debate, only the essential points of which I have indicated, I declared that behind all the theoretical questions that had just been debated there was a question of confidence in the Government, a question which I begged the Assembly to answer.

It answered by adopting the counter resolution of the Keeper of the Seals by three hundred and seventy-two votes to three hundred and thirty-five, a majority of thirty-seven.

At any other time such a majority would have seemed in my eyes insufficient; but at the point we had reached we must needs be content with it.

This vote was greeted with satisfaction by public opinion; but the Right Centre, upon which thenceforward depended the Government's majority, proved on November 30th how fragile had been that it had given us the day before. It was on the occasion of the addresses that nearly all the General and Municipal Councils had sent me to approve what was called the policy of the Message. I had, though without much success, done all I could to discourage these manifestations, because they amounted to a censure of the disposition displayed by the Assembly. Nevertheless we were blamed for them, and the Minister for the Interior, M. Victor Lefranc, questioned upon these addresses, was defeated by a hostile order of the day. The same evening he brought me his resignation.

The malcontents of all parties in the Assembly pretended that M. Victor Lefranc was merely the mask of M. Calmon, the Under-Secretary of State for the Interior: a most ill-founded reproach, for M. Victor Lefranc had in his ministry all the authority that was implied in his functions; but it is true that M. Calmon exercised a very vigorous supervision over the holders of prefectures and sub-prefectures, an important part of the Government. The son of the former Director-General of Registration, who had been a very considerable personage, and highly considered under earlier régimes, M. Calmon, a man of clear and decided mind, firm, pre-eminently a man of order, was also an administrator of the greatest merit. Like us he desired the Republic to be conservative, and endeavoured to inculcate the same idea throughout the administration. That sufficed to make him the target for the attacks of the Right in the Assembly.

Faced with these difficulties, I proposed to M. de Rémusat and M. Dufaure a combination consisting of transferring M. de Goulard from the Ministry of Finance, in which he was not specially essential, to the Ministry for the Interior, in which he would have the advantage of pleasing the two centres by his amenability. I would next call the Prefect of the Seine, M. Léon Say, a man of incontestable worth and of sound liberal opinions, to the Ministry of Finance, and M. Calmon would replace him in the Prefecture of the Seine, where he would render immense service. There was still one Ministry to dispose of, the Public Works, which was held provisionally by M. Teisserenc de Bort, the Minister of Commerce. For this post I thought of M. de Fourtou, a young deputy who appeared to have a certain political insight along with the gift of speech.

This combination, adopted and approved of by the Council, was announced in the *Official Gazette* on

December 7, 1872, and was well received by the Assembly and the public. And my complaisance towards the Assembly, manifested by this change in the Ministry, and more particularly by the selection of M. de Goulard for the Ministry of the Interior, had so great a success with the Right that we could believe that we had made peace with it.

A few days later the Right again had reason to feel keen satisfaction, this time over the petitions for the dissolution of the Chamber.

It seemed a favourable opportunity for a great display of Republican and anti-Republican passion. I did not go to the sitting, in order to leave it for M. Dufaure to speak, as he was set on measuring himself with M. Gambetta, whose intervention in the debate was announced.

This encounter took place and was extremely hot. M. Gambetta, very downright and incisive in his manner, having displayed a certain arrogance towards the Chamber, M. Dufaure called him strongly to order and moderation, and roused the greatest enthusiasm in the centres, which were delighted to have this vigorous talent at their service for a moment. A majority of nearly five hundred votes to two hundred (it is true that this was against dissolution) declared itself in a way that made it possible to believe that the majority of earlier days was reconstituted. But at what price could it be held together?

The famous Committee of Thirty, created by the vote of November 29th, had just been elected after lengthy discussions. It was merely a doubling of the Kerdrel Committee, to which had been added fifteen new members, with a hostile majority as usual. M. de Larcy had been nominated president. This choice of a former colleague who had always remained a friend was, they said, a sign of goodwill which the Committee had wished to give me.

On January 1, 1873, the customary receptions were held at Versailles, as in 1872, with a great crowd of deputies of every shade of opinion; for even the Right, which since the last change of Ministry and the speech of M. Dufaure affected to be satisfied, did not fail to come to the Présidence.

The Diplomatic Corps also came to assure me of the friendly sentiments of which the European Cabinets had already given me proof in our negotiations relating to the commercial treaties.

With England the compensating duties, consequent on the imposition of a tax on raw materials, which had been declared impossible of acceptance of our neighbours, had just been agreed to in a new treaty substituted for that of 1860, a treaty which assured the return of a hundred millions indispensable to balance our budget. To attain this result I had been obliged to set the interest of our finances above that of our mercantile marine, by provisionally abandoning the application to England of our new law of super-tax on shipping. I had still another motive for giving way on this point. I reckoned that as soon as England accepted the compensating duties, Belgium and Italy would accept them in their turn, since they could no longer cite the example of England to justify their opposition. And our treaty once signed with that Power, Belgium hastened to sign a similar one, and Holland showed an intention of following suit. As for Italy, she was of no very great importance to us as far as raw materials were concerned, except for raw silk and hardly at all for manufactured silk. We had, therefore, only a very little interest in obtaining compensating duties on this last commodity. Besides, the Cabinet of Sella-Lanza, weakened by the internal difficulties springing from the law relating to the religious houses, was neither disposed nor prepared to enter upon a discussion concerning Italy's commercial system. He asked us to be satisfied for the moment with a convention by which, accepting the principle of compensating duties, he engaged to transform this convention into law during the course of the year.

We owed this pledge to the goodwill of King Victor Emmanuel, who was satisfied with France's policy towards Italy, and therefore disposed to make concessions likely to facilitate relations between his Government and ours. Accordingly, when the Pope complained to us of some difficulty emanating from the Italian Government, I addressed myself to the King through M. Visconti-Venosta, and I obtained all right and possible satisfaction until the famous *modus vivendi* between the Papacy and Royalty had been discovered and had been accepted by the Holy Father.

With Spain our relations were equally good, in spite of some trouble caused by the fall of the Savoy dynasty on the other side of the Pyrenees. King Victor Emmanuel had allowed his son Amadeus to accept the crown of Spain, an error similar to King Leopold's in authorizing his son-in-law Maximilian to accept the throne of Mexico. The young King Amadeus, courageous and intelligent, who, in order to follow in his new country the excellent examples of King Leopold and King Victor Emmanuel, allowed his subjects to govern themselves, had gone too far in this path when he chose Republican Ministers such as M. Zorilla and his friends. And so after King Amadeus, had reigned three years, a Republic came to be proclaimed in Madrid.

I had been loyal towards King Amadeus, opposing the Carlist attempts against his authority as much as I could. I say "as much as I could," because on the Spanish frontiers I was not always obeyed by certain prefects, who had no more republicanism than the mere word. I maintained an equally loyal attitude to the Spanish Republic, and if I was a little tardy in recognizing it, it was merely to wait until the Government *de facto* should have acquired the characteristics of a Government *de jure*. I simply promised my best services to M. Olozaga, the representative of this Government in France, and I kept my word through all the affairs to which the Carlist insurrection gave birth upon our frontier. I pointed out to him, at the same time, the grave difficulties to which the Spanish Government would expose itself if it disturbed Portugal, which at the moment was seriously alarmed. Happily, in eloquent M. Castelar we found a Minister of the greatest ability and wisdom, our relations with whom were excellent, and the Cabinets of Europe were very grateful to us for our behaviour at this juncture.

Abroad, then, our affairs were going as well as possible; but at home I had to seek some way of putting an end to the difference that had arisen between the Government and the Committee of Thirty, a difference that held the attention both of our own and foreign countries; Germany especially, which held to the idea of settling her accounts with us, was uneasy at what might be a cause of trouble in France, and Count von Arnim, as often as I met him, asked me what point the work of this Committee had reached.

And so from the month of January I had several times attended its sittings, in order to spur it on to finish its report.

"The Assembly," I had said to one of the members, "has charged you to present to it a scheme for the organization of the responsibility of Ministers and a scheme of organization for the public powers. In my opinion the responsibility of Ministers is already adequately established by existing laws, and what you are looking for under this name is a means of weakening my influence on the deliberations of the Assembly by forbidding me the tribune. I am nevertheless disposed to show myself as conciliatory as possible on this point, provided that you at the same time occupy yourselves with the second part of your task."

Following my observations, the Committee of Thirty at length decided to divide itself into two sub-committees, which should each examine a part of the resolutions before it.

As I have said, I lent myself to everything desired by the sub-committee that was to concern itself with the responsibility of the Ministers. Its members were, they said, so far from any intention of limiting or cramping my freedom of action that they wished to ask a right of suspensive veto for me, allowing me to resist the headstrong impulses of a single Assembly, and if they aimed at curtailing my right to take part in the debates from the tribune, it was chiefly for the sake of my own dignity, to withdraw me from the violence of those debates. They did not find that I was sufficiently safeguarded from them by the article of the Rivet Constitution, which obliged me, on each occasion when I wished to speak, to inform the

Assembly by a message; and they proposed new formalities to make access to the tribune more difficult for me.

Thus, directly I should announce by message my intention of intervening in any debate, all discussion should cease, and I could only speak in the next sitting. When I had been heard, I should withdraw without discussion, and the sitting would again be suspended. I would be replied to at the next sitting. And as I could not be deprived of the right to reply in turn, I pointed out to them that discussions would in this way be exposed to the risk of becoming everlasting and losing themselves in absurdity, if some day a mischievous President, without fear of hearing Cato's quip on Cicero applied to himself—*habemus consulem facetum*—wanted to go on indefinitely making trips from the Présidence to the Assembly.

When the Committee unfolded all these devices before me, I could not prevent myself from calling them, laughingly, *chinoiseries*, a word that stuck to the work of the Thirty. I accepted them all the same, in a spirit of conciliation. For at the same time as I was taking part in these discussions, I was preparing the basis of a new and last convention with Germany, to ensure the final liberation of our territory.

The fourth milliard was to be paid on the 1st of May following (1873), and the departments of the Ardennes and the Vosges would thereupon be evacuated, that is to say nearly a year before the period fixed by the convention of 29th of June, 1872. There would then remain only the Meuse, Meurthe-et-Moselle, and the territory of Belfort to be liberated, the last pledges for the fifth milliard, payable 1st of March, 1875.

Happily our abundant resources gave me the certainty that we would be able to anticipate this date, and pay the fifth milliard in the year 1873, without having recourse to financial guarantees, and I arranged, in co-operation with M. de Roussy, the Directeur-Général de la Comptabilité publique, and M. Dutilleul, Directeur du Mouvement Général des Fonds, the following scheme :

Immediately after the payment we were about to make, on the 1st of May, of the five hundred millions completing the fourth milliard, we would offer Germany to pay the fifth and last milliard in four equal instalments, on the 1st of June, 1st of July, 1st of August, and 1st of September, 1873.

Unfortunately, the twenty-five thousand men who would withdraw from the Ardennes and the Vosges on the 1st of May, when the fourth milliard would be paid, would go to join the twenty-five thousand that already occupied Meurthe-et-Moselle and the Meuse, and would crush these two departments under the burden of fifty thousand German soldiers until the 1st of September. To prevent this painful necessity, as well as to avoid the expense of providing quarters for the troops, I resolved to propose to Prussia the evacuation of all four departments at once on the 1st of July. The Meuse, Meurthe-et-Moselle, and Belfort would in this way be free two months sooner, but by way of compensation the Ardennes and the Vosges would be two months later than our conventions allowed. This measure seemed an equitable one, and I arranged a meeting with Count von Arnim in Paris on the 4th of February, to propose it to him.

"I have considered our resources," I said to him. "On the 1st of May next, at the latest, you will have received the fourth milliard in full, and from that date you are to restore us two departments. How do you expect to set about this evacuation?"

"The simplest thing," replied Count von Arnim, "would be to send the twenty-five thousand men occupying these departments back to Germany. But our army would be reduced by so much, and our poor General Manteuffel would think himself dishonoured if he no longer had fifty thousand men under his command."

Count von Arnim, who loathed General Manteuffel, never let an opportunity slip for uttering his antipathy in malevolent speeches.

I said then that if the withdrawal of the twenty-five thousand men was not possible, the simplest thing would be to carry out the total evacuation of all four departments at the same time, and I explained the scheme set forth above. He found it acceptable.

"Only," he said, "you are asking credit for five hundred millions, since we should be evacuating all we hold two months before being fully paid, and it will perhaps be insisted that on your part you should leave a pledge in our hands until the full discharge of the debt."

He then expatiated on a theme he had often treated: the difficulty of getting the King to evacuate the territory he held, as he was persuaded that the departure of the Prussians would immediately be followed by a revolution in France.

After this interview, on the 10th of February, I wrote to Nancy so that General Manteuffel should know of our plans and lend us his concurrence.

Our proposals reached Berlin and were satisfactory to Count Bismarck; but it was difficult to make them agreeable in the eyes of the Emperor, who would have liked to make no concession before an agreement had been reached between the Government and the Committee of Thirty.

Fortunately, this agreement was near at hand, thanks to my acceptance of the scheme of the law on the responsibility of Ministers. It remained only to get the Committee to add to this draft the one demanded by the Assembly, upon the organization of public powers, and they determined to charge the Government with presenting this.

From this moment, union between the Government and the majority was regarded as re-established, which facilitated our negotiations with Germany. On March 1st M. de Gontaut announced to me by telegraph that the Emperor would accept our proposals as to the payment of the last milliard, but that he wished to keep Belfort until September as pledge for the final clearance of our debt.

Immediately Count Bismarck informed him of this condition, M. de Gontaut had hastened to declare that the intention to keep Belfort until September was a mark of distrust that would antagonize and alarm public opinion in France, and on March 3rd I received an identical communication from General Manteuffel, by the intermediary of M. de Saint-Vallier, who also had addressed the very same protestations to the General.

Our two representatives to the German Government thus expressed the feelings which they knew animated me. To sever Belfort from the territories to which it was joined by the actual wording of the treaties, and to reserve it as the last pledge for our debt, made the fate of this fortress depend on an accident or some subtle interpretation of texts.

Accordingly, when Count von Arnim came officially on behalf of Count Bismarck to inform me of the conditions imposed upon the evacuation, I declared to the Ambassador of Germany that the clause in which his Government asked to retain the fortress of Belfort until September was unacceptable.

Count von Arnim, who expected my objections, granted that this clause was regrettable, that he would not have himself cared to propose it to me, and he took the greatest pains to persuade me that it concealed no dishonest *arrière-pensée* on the part of either the Emperor or Count Bismarck. Of his own accord he promised to interpret my objections to Berlin. In displaying this good disposition Count von Arnim was perhaps sincere, since he had an interest of pride in signalizing his mission to Paris by the conclusion of a treaty definitely settling all matters between France and Germany.

This conversation allowed me to hope that the Belfort clause was not irrevocable, and, like me, M. de Rémusat was of opinion that by discussion we might perhaps arrive at getting rid of it. But hardly had we come to join forces on the subject, when M. de Saint-Vallier added to his previous communication the summary of a dispatch from Count Bismarck to General Manteuffel, in which the acceptance of this clause was expressly represented as the *sine qua non* of the evacuation of the last four departments in July.

This determination, which Count von Arnim had not indicated as firmly decided upon, obliged us to accept Prussia's conditions, since a refusal on our part would have exposed us to the loss of the benefit of the evacuation of the four departments from July 1st. But we could yet hope that by accompanying our acceptance with certain reserves, the negotiation would be prolonged, and that in this way Count Bismarck, impatient to make an end, would in the long run make us some concessions.

I therefore sent Count von Arnim, on March 8th, a draft agreeing in nearly all particulars with the proposals he had communicated to me.

The same day Count Bismarck, having sent for M. de Gontaut, had intimated his dissatisfaction at our delay in replying to his proposals, which, according to him, were very advantageous to us. He considered it a success to have got the Emperor to sanction them, and could not imagine that we should have any serious objections to make on the score of Belfort. As he had written to Count von Arnim, these conditions were for us *to take or leave*, and if we did not accept them, they would fall back upon the terms of the convention of the 29th of June last. At the end of this interview the Chancellor had allowed him to understand that, possibly before the complete payment of the last milliard, if circumstances permitted, we might obtain some mitigation of these conditions.

On March 9th, a dispatch from M. Gontaut informed me of this conversation. I replied to him the same day, that I had already sent Count von Arnim a draft in which I accepted the Belfort clause, but that I accepted only with regret and on condition that it was drawn up exactly in the terms of which I sent him a copy. Then, by a postscript, and to mark more clearly the value I attached to having Belfort restored to us at the same time as the last four departments, I said that if Count Bismarck would consent to accept only a small part of our debt in notes of the Bank of France, we would be in a position to pay in full on August 1st. In that case the evacuation could be delayed until that date, and agreeably to the treaties the Germans would withdraw simultaneously from the four departments and from Belfort. In this way I avoided opposing an absolute refusal to the Prussian proposals, while at the same time not giving them a definite assent.

The next day I received from M. de Saint-Vallier the official text of the Prussian proposals; it differed, on points, from that which Count von Arnim had communicated to me. M. de Saint-Vallier pointed out to me at the same time several modifications he thought prudent to make in the periods for evacuation laid down in these proposals. I telegraphed immediately to him that I would have accepted the text he sent me if I had known it earlier, but that I had already sent to Count von Arnim and addressed to M. de Gontaut a draft falling in with the proposals of Prussia. I authorized him, however, to request General Manteuffel to communicate to Berlin my preference for the Nancy text, except for the modifications deemed necessary on the subject of the periods of the evacuation.

On March 11th M. de Gontaut brought my answer of the 9th to Count Bismarck, who showed himself still very much displeased with Count von Arnim, having had from him no definite answer on the part of the French Government, and very much annoyed at having to discuss the conditions attached to my acceptance of the Prussian proposals. He again protested that there was absolutely no *arrière-pensée* on the subject of Belfort, and said, with a smile, that if the treaty was not punctiliously observed by the Germans, he engaged to go and deliver himself as a prisoner in Paris. Then he added, abruptly:

"Are you very anxious to recover possession of

Belfort a little earlier? Is it the occupation of this fortress that torments you? Leave us another material pledge until the full payment, Toul or Verdun, for example. We shall then evacuate Belfort at the same time as the four departments."

When I sought by temporizing to overcome Prussia's insistence I never expected to succeed so speedily or so completely, and the offer to substitute Verdun for Belfort was almost unhoped for. Nevertheless, M. de Gontaut almost let it escape him, by answering Count Bismarck that he would have to ask for fresh instructions from his Government to cover this point.

The same evening, in a telegraphic dispatch, he gave me an account of his conversation with Count Bismarck, and informed me of the offer to substitute Toul or Verdun for Belfort as the last pledge for our ransom. This news filled me with joy, for neither Toul nor Verdun could be the object of suspicious coveting on the part of the Germans. M. de Rémusat shared my satisfaction, and we hastened, on the 12th of March, to enjoin upon M. de Gontaut to accept the substitution of Verdun for Belfort.

At the moment when the dispatches relating to this substitution were being exchanged between Paris and Berlin, the Emperor, in the speech from the Crown at the opening of the Reichstag, had spoken of the fortunate re-establishment of everything in France, hinting at a speedy evacuation of French territory in return for the payment of the war indemnity in full. This speech produced a great effect at Berlin and in Paris, both alike interested in a speedy settlement of the difficulties pending between the two States.

By the 14th of March we had come to an agree-

PRESIDENCY OF THE REPUBLIC 317

ment on all the details of the convention. But Count Bismarck, as he confessed afterwards, regretting that a desire to convince us of his straightforwardness had brought him to offer us the substitution of Verdun, sent word to me by M. de Gontaut that if I consented to give up this substitution, the convention could be signed at once; that if not, it would be necessary to increase the Verdun garrison, place at least two stations between that fortress and Metz, and establish a military road—formalities which would delay us considerably.

To this new proposal I replied by telegram at five o'clock in the evening of the 14th.

"I hold absolutely to the substitution of Verdun for Belfort. . . . The difficulty of the stations is no difficulty. I have consented to it. . . ."

Then, fearing lest Count Bismarck might make a last effort to withdraw his concession of Verdun, I telegraphed anew to M. de Gontaut on the 14th, at six o'clock in the evening:

"I hold absolutely to the substitution of Verdun for Belfort. . . . Such a definite engagement cannot be repudiated. As for the two stations, I consent to them. As for the numbers of the garrison I am willing to increase them. . . . Regarding payment, I will lend myself to any demand. But for Verdun I insist, and you will insist upon it. . . . Hold fast, and you will win. . . ."

Count Bismarck, informed of my reply during the evening, put off signing the convention until next day, the 15th of March. What I had foreseen happened.

At two o'clock M. de Gontaut was waiting for Count Bismarck for the signing of the convention. The Chancellor came punctually, not yet to sign, but to make a last attempt to take back the concession he had made, alleging the Emperor's displeasure at having to give way on this point. The perusal of my repeated orders put an end to the Chancellor's insistence. He went back to tell the Emperor of the failure of his attempt, and returned at five o'clock to the French Embassy, where at length he signed the convention.

This day M. de Gontaut was giving a concert at which the Emperor had promised to be present with all the Court. I, too, desired to associate myself from afar with this festivity, recommending the Ambassador to wear the Grand-cordon de la Légion d'honneur, which I had sent him the day before, with the approval of the Council, to mark the share he had taken in this negotiation. The Emperor and the Empress, who, as they had promised, had come to the Embassy, were very eulogistic to France and very cordial to her representative.

Some hours before, M. de Gontaut had announced the signing of the convention to me. In allowing him to append his name to a document of such importance, I had, he wrote, obtained for him an honour that should have gone to M. de Rémusat, and the high distinction the Government had added to that honour seemed to him more than he deserved. However, weighing up his services I had thought it right and proper to accord him this distinction.

This convention of the 15th of March, the crowning of our common labours and the end of my principal task, overwhelmed France with joy, and the Assembly, associating itself with public feeling, declared for the second time, on the 16th of March, that I had deserved well of the country.

The session, beginning on the 11th of the preceding November, had been sufficiently toilsome to make us feel the necessity of bringing it to a close. The Assembly and the Government being at one on this point, it was agreed to break up until the beginning of April; but before that date a very serious trouble was stirred up over the municipality of Lyons.

The situation of this town had become disturbing enough; M. Cantonnet, the Prefect of the Rhône, having been unable to agree with M. Barodet, the Mayor of Lyons, asked that in order to put an end to this conflict the Central Mayoralty should be suppressed. I should have preferred to try, by a system of electoral sections as in Paris, to get a Moderate majority in the Municipal Council. In case of failure, it would always have been possible to propose the suppression of the Central Mayoralty by a general law applicable to all the great towns.

"By taking other measures," said I, "we run the risk of making M. Barodet the great man of Lyons, and through not wanting to have him as Mayor of Lyons, we shall have him its representative in the Chamber."

I did not know how truly I spoke.

The peaceful solution I proposed could not satisfy certain Conservatives in the Assembly. Those in particular who represented departments neighbouring that of the Rhône were in haste to extinguish a fire of agitation that burned too near themselves; and M. de Goulard, wishing to satisfy them, asked the Assembly to suppress the Central Mayoralty of Lyons.

The inhabitants of Lyons defended themselves at the tribune, at great length, but with method and clearness, by the mouth of one of their deputies, M. Ferrouillat.

M. Le Royer, a former magistrate, respectable, but cold and severe, also spoke for them with no little talent. The discussion at one moment became very keen, and M. Le Royer having described the too frequently repeated arguments of the Committee as *lumber*, roused the inflammable temper of the Marquis de Grammont, who called out:

" That is insolent ! "

The word roused both sides of the Assembly. M. Le Royer then stopped, and said with the utmost coolness :

" . . . I am waiting for the word to be withdrawn or rebuked by the President as it deserves."

M. Grévy, who, tired out by the debate, was not following very attentively, was as though waked up suddenly, and seeing that he must take command of the situation if it was not to cause a duel between the two interlocutors, called M. de Grammont to order. The Right protested violently at this. M. de Grévy appeared not to notice this scene; but at the end of the sitting he rose and addressed the House.

"My conduct," said he, " appears not to be approved; it is even strongly blamed by the hostile demonstrations of the Assembly. . . .

"I have neither asked nor sought the duties with which you invested me. I have always fulfilled them to the best of my ability, with all the justice and impartiality of which I am master. Since I do not find in return from you, gentlemen, the justice to which I think I am entitled, I shall know what remains for me to do."

After these words, deliberate or no, the vacancy in the Presidency of the Assembly was to be expected next day. Accordingly, all who sought peace and unity did their utmost to prevent this affair from going further, and told M. Grévy that by resigning he would weaken the Government. That he understood; but he was too deeply engaged by his own words to go back upon his resolve, and the next day he sent his resignation, couched in terms so acid that it was difficult to answer such language by re-election. Nevertheless, he was re-elected by four hundred votes. His friends again wished to persuade him to be satisfied with this majority; but his inflexibility made all their urging in vain.

We chose, therefore, for his successor M. Martel, who had every claim to the sympathy of the Assembly; but M. Buffet, our opponents' candidate, had the majority and took up the function of managing our debates.

Such was the first serious consequence of this Lyons law, without reckoning that the suppression of the Central Mayoralty of that town made, as I had too clearly foreseen, an embarrassing individual of M. Barodet.

Finally, in the closing days of this session we had the affair of Prince Jérôme Napoléon, who appealed against the expulsion to which he had been condemned some months before. The committee charged with investigating this appeal found that it deserved to be taken into consideration, and laid before the Assembly a report in which, without blaming the Government, it raised doubts as to the legality of the expulsion of which Prince Napoléon complained.

I was not present at the sitting in which the discussion on this report opened. It was M. de Goulard who spoke first. He showed himself very firm on this occasion, put the Cabinet question in excellent terms, and got the Assembly to adopt a motion of confidence, but with a majority of only fifty-six! This vote, compared with the crushing majority which had twice pronounced the fall of the Bonapartes, proved that the alliance of the Legitimists with the Imperialists was accomplished.

An incident of this kind foreshadowed others graver still. It showed how fragile was our alliance with the Thirty, since the Duc de Broglie and his friends, after having promised fidelity in return for our complaisance towards their work, had voted against us on this question. The fact of a Duc de Broglie patronizing a Bonaparte, in order to gain the shelter of the Imperialists, showed also to what compromises the party spirit will sometimes carry politicians.

The satisfaction with which the treaty of the 15th of March, 1873 had been received in France, and the declaration of the Assembly that I had deserved well of the State had procured me all these distresses, all these defections of the present moment.

The Assembly broke up on the 8th of April, 1873, and I came to Paris, to spend there in the Elysée Palace the period of this vacation, which was to be about six weeks.

I had first of all to settle our programme of work with the Ministers, who all wished to go far from Paris to take their repose. Their leave having been so distributed that the whole Council should never be absent at the same time, we agreed to meet twenty days before the return of the Assembly, so as to prepare the laws relating to the Constitution. We then fixed for the 27th of April the eight elections that were to be held for the seats that had become vacant. One of these elections, very important already because it concerned Paris, was the most important of all because of the circumstances in the midst of which it was to take place.

The treaty of the 15th of March had produced a great impression, and the public, in its gratitude, very rightly associated M. de Rémusat's name with mine. The mayors of Paris, to satisfy this feeling which they shared, would have liked our Minister for Foreign Affairs to become their representative in the Assembly, and they proposed this on the day on which they came to Versailles to congratulate me on the liberation of the territory.

M. de Rémusat was not a deputy, because he had not wanted to be; but at this moment he was certainly pre-eminently worthy to receive the mandate that was offered to him. We both welcomed the feeling that had inspired this idea, without caring to bind ourselves by a definite acceptance before the apparent goodwill of the public should become certain.

A few days after, the proposal of the mayors seemed to be unanimous, when the Radicals interposed, irritated at not having been consulted about an election in which the city they regarded as their proper electoral domain was interested, and in his newspaper M. Gambetta made no delay in showing himself hostile to the candidature of M. de Rémusat. However, this hostility would have given way before the enthusiasm of the Liberals if the Conservatives, in suppressing the Central Mayoralty of Lyons and its holder, had not allowed the Extreme Left to propose the election of M. Barodet in Paris as a protest against that suppression.

Before this opposition we thought we ought to reserve any decision. But as soon as our hesitation was known, the Conservatives reproached us with abandoning the party of order, who could only accept M. de Rémusat as candidate.

"You will hand Paris over to M. Gambetta," they said. "Support us and we will give you the most active co-operation."

As for the frankly Legitimist sheets, Orléanist and Bonapartist, they went so far as to accuse us of wanting to favour the Radicals by giving them a success that it only depended on ourselves to take from them.

So as not to deserve such a reproach, M. de Rémusat, with my approval and that of the Council, consented to stand, and we prepared to support his candidature with all the influence we could honourably make use of. We saw all the members of the municipal body, and a great number of men of importance in commerce and industry. I found them zealous, even ardent, understanding perfectly that this election in Paris would give us great moral force and prestige.

The Left at this juncture behaved with as much resolution as restraint; but its zeal on behalf of M. de Rémusat chilled that of the Moderate Right, which should, on the contrary, have rejoiced to find allies, through their common interests, without having to sacrifice their own opinions.

Sunday, the 27th of April, was the day fixed for the election; from the morning there was an extraordinary concourse of electors at the booths, and during the whole of the day appearances were in favour of M. de Rémusat. The first figures that we knew made us hope for success; but towards ten o'clock at night the news became less favourable, and at eleven the Prefect of Police announced to us that M. de Rémusat had only polled one hundred and thirty-five thousand votes against one hundred and eighty thousand cast for M. Barodet.

The Monarchists exaggerated the importance of this ballot to give more verisimilitude to their denunciation of the progress of Radicalism, which, according to them, had become irresistible through our fault. The departmental elections, seven in number, in which they had only succeeded in getting two of their candidates elected, furnished them with a fresh pretext for attacking the Government.

We devoted the days that followed, before the resumption of the session, to preparing the law of the Constitution which the Assembly had directed us to present to it, and which, by a wise organization of public powers, was to guarantee France from an excess of democracy.

The discussion of the foundations of our future institutions had been learned and profound, the drafting of M. Dufaure was perfect, and the Council showed itself unanimous upon these grave questions. But this harmony was to be short-lived.

M. Jules Simon, by his astute behaviour, had so far triumphed over all the attacks of his enemies, though in educational matters he had set on foot certain reforms that were open to criticism. In the Administration des Cultes, on the contrary, he had obtained favour at Rome, so much indeed that the Papal Nuncio was his warmest advocate. Nevertheless, those who should have been disarmed by this patronage persisted in seeking to drive him out of the Council, in which they had an ally, M. de Goulard. The latter, at their instigation, very soon adopted an attitude of such pronounced hostility to his colleague, that M. Jules Simon tendered me his resignation.

At first I refused to accept it; however, on the eve of the return of the Assembly, seeing it was impossible to re-establish harmony in the Council without parting with either M. de Goulard or M. Jules Simon, I decided to accept the latter's resignation. I determined, in order to compensate the Left for his going, to replace him by M. Casimir Perier, who was willing to accept the portfolio of the Interior, and I hoped to satisfy the Right by keeping M. de Goulard in the Cabinet, in the Ministry for Education, and transferring M. de Fourtou from the Public Works to the Ministry of Religion.

M. Jules Simon, having approved of this combination, resigned his portfolio with complete disinterestedness, and refused to accept the Italian Embassy, which I offered him.

Although less disposed than M. Jules Simon to make us concessions, M. de Goulard accepted my proposals, and M. Casimir Perier consented to take the portfolio for the Interior. But when I spoke to him of the composition of the Ministry, he refused to be in it with M. de Goulard.

His name, his character, his courage being likely to restore to the Cabinet the strength it was losing through the retirement of M. Jules Simon, I yielded, and informed M. de Goulard of what had taken place. He left me without hiding how deeply he was wounded, and immediately sent me his resignation.

During the day M. Casimir Perier, who had listened to the counsels of his friends, gave up his prejudices and went to M. de Goulard to get him to withdraw his resignation, which I had just received. He found him inflexible, and his disappointment at not succeeding made me afraid for a moment that it might decide him to resign; but he felt that he could not leave us when our enemies were preparing to attack us, and with an outburst that touched me profoundly, M. Casimir Perier declared himself ready to defend the Moderate policy that we had adopted. If all these concessions I was making thus in the interests of this policy could not assure its triumph, we should have at any rate a strong and worthy Ministry to support it.

We agreed, then, with M. Casimir Perier to complete the Cabinet by calling M. Bérenger to the Public Works and M. Waddington to the Ministry of Education. These two deputies had all the necessary aptitudes for directing the ministerial departments entrusted to them.

There was complete harmony among all the members of the Ministry. The constitutional laws were read in the Council to the new Ministers, and the outline of principles drawn up by M. de Rémusat had their entire approbation. They found in it the expression of a frank and reconciliatory policy, which inspired no regret for having associated themselves with it.

On the 18th of May I went to Versailles before the Assembly, which was to meet on the 19th. Taking stock of the gravity of the whole situation, I told myself that my essential task was accomplished, since the liberation of our territory would be complete and final in some months, on the 1st of July, 1873. Without doubt I could be deprived of the joy of presiding over the festival of liberation, but I could not be deprived of the honour of having put an end to the foreign occupation, long before the date arranged by the treaties.

As to the constitutional laws, I certainly was anxious that they should be accepted, since they were calculated to consolidate the work of raising up France again, the work I had nearly finished. But if I was shipwrecked in this last venture, what I had already done was enough to allow me to enter proudly upon a well-merited repose.

As soon as the Monarchists knew of the new rearrangement of Ministers they attacked it violently. The Government, said they, by expelling from the Cabinet men of the Right Centre to replace them by men of the Left Centre, was moving towards the Left itself. They must no longer hesitate, for if they let this occasion pass it would become impossible to retrieve the power from those who were about to make use of it in order to dismiss the Chamber and make or allow detestable elections.

What emboldened them most in this campaign was the hope, if not the certainty, of having found some one to take my place. The announcement, more or less confirmed, of the Marshal's acceptance made a great impression on the dubious. "By the Marshal," they were told, "we shall have the army with us; we shall make ourselves masters of the elections"; "we shall make a Monarchy," said the Legitimists, "with the Comte de Chambord," "a stadtholderate with the Duc d'Aumale," said the Orléanists. As for the Bonapartists, they counted upon a Marshal of the Empire to evict all pretenders in favour of the Prince Imperial.

How much foundation was there in this assertion? I did not know.

The morrow of my return to Versailles, the very day the Assembly was to meet, the Marshal presented himself the first of all at the Présidence, with an air so kind, so friendly, so affectionate, that he seemed to me to wish to protest, by his attitude, against the language of his friends.

To their first approaches the Marshal had answered that he would under no circumstances consent to take the place of one who had shown him the utmost consideration. But they had insisted, representing to him that France was in danger, that it was his duty not to abandon her; and his refusal seeming less determined before these new importunities, they had hastened to repeat everywhere that the Marshal would accept the power.

Finally, in the last days before the return of the Assembly, a friend of the Marshal, from whom I have the tale, having asked him if it was true that he had decided to accept the Presidency, he had replied that he had no ambition for it, but that he would not see France left without a Government if M. Thiers were to retire.

From that time the Right had come to an understanding with M. Rouher, and had obtained from him the promise of twenty or thirty Bonapartist votes if it was decided to bring in the Marshal and not the Duc d'Aumale. This compact concluded, the Duc de Broglie, on the very day of the reopening, the 19th of May, 1873, placed in the hands of the President of the Assembly, in the names of three hundred and twenty members of the Right, a demand for interpellation, couched in the following terms:

"The undersigned, convinced that the gravity of the present situation calls for a Cabinet at the head of affairs whose firmness shall be reassuring to the country, demand permission to question the Ministry upon the last modifications that have taken place in its ranks, and upon the necessity of ensuring that a resolutely Conservative policy shall prevail in the Government."

On the 23rd of May, 1873, the day fixed for discussing this interpellation, M. de Broglie, in the midst of the universal preoccupation, mounted the tribune and reproached us with calling ourselves Conservatives without persuading any one, and with living as protégés of the Radicals.

According to the law of the Thirty, I could not address the House until the following sitting, after asking permission in a message.

M. Dufaure replied that the Government had in no circumstances incurred the reproach brought against it of favouring the Radical party, and that it was, on the contrary, in order to prevent the dangers to which this party would expose France that the Chief of the Executive Power and the Ministry had drafted the bill laid before the Assembly on the very day of its reopening, a bill tending to organize the existing Republican system on Conservative lines.

After this speech my message asking permission to address the House was laid before the Assembly; they decided to give me the next day, the 24th of May, and I began my speech as soon as this day's proceedings opened.

I do not care to give any summary of the speech I made on this occasion; those who are interested in these debates will find it in the Official Report of the sittings of the Assembly. I was not interrupted even one single time, in spite of all that was keen and even rude in my language. They had no wish to compromise anything by imprudent incidents.

Always in conformity with the law of the Thirty, no one replied to my speech, and the President terminated the sitting after deciding that the Assembly should meet again at two o'clock.

At this sitting it was forbidden for me to speak. The orator who addressed the Assembly was M. Casimir Perier, whose speech I sum up as follows.

"M. de Broglie has pretended," he said, "that the last modification in the Ministry, the entrance of MM. Casimir Perier, Waddington, and Bérenger into the Council, is a concession made by the Government to the Radicals. I do not think I need to demonstrate how much my acts, my words, my whole life protest against such an allegation, equally false as regards my colleagues. Not only does the latest modification in the Ministry not announce a step forward for Radicalism, but on the contrary the new Ministers bring to the Cabinet an incontestable force for the defence of Conservative ideas. The interpellation of M. de Broglie is therefore without justification."

This protest remained unanswered: such was the order. The Assembly at once proceeded to vote upon the various proposed orders of the day. That of M. Ernoul, presented in the name of the signatories to the interpellation, was adopted by a majority of sixteen votes, three hundred and sixty to three hundred and forty-four. It ran as follows:

"The National Assembly, considering that the form of Government is not in discussion; that the Assembly is in possession of constitutional laws presented to it by virtue of its decisions, and to be investigated by it; but that from to-day it is of importance to reassure the country by ensuring that a resolutely Conservative policy shall prevail in the Government, regrets that the recent modifications in the Ministry have not given Conservative interests the satisfaction they had a right to expect," etc.

The House rose at once, and was dismissed until

eight o'clock in the evening. I could not accept M. Ernoul's motion, to which I replied by sending my resignation. It was known already that the Marshal would accept the Presidency of the Republic. He was elected by three hundred and ninety-one votes.

Next day I hastened to make preparations for my departure, and to return to Paris after an absence of three years, during which I had governed with moderation and firmness, in the ways of rectitude, sustained by the confidence of France and the esteem of Europe.

APPENDICES

APPENDIX No. 1 (*v. page* 7).

M. Jules Favre to M. Thiers.

MINISTÈRE
DES
AFFAIRES ETRANGÈRES.
Cabinet.

September 11, 1870.

MON CHER ANCIEN COLLÈGUE,

Allow me to thank you from the bottom of my heart, in my own name as much as in the name of the members of the Government of National Defence, for the sacrifice you are so good as to make by accepting the mission I am happy to entrust to you. You have not counted its fatigues or its dangers, you have given ear only to your own patriotism. You will have your reward in the proud consciousness of accomplished action. You will, I am confident, restore peace to the world, and your name, already illustrious, will be immortal as the name of one of the benefactors of humanity. It will be equally dear to the defenders of liberty, it is for the sake of liberty you are devoting yourself. Right is on your side; and the banner you mean to bear to London, Saint Petersburg, and Vienna is that upon whose folds the hand of God has written *In hoc signo vinces.*

For my own part, in the midst of my sorrows I shall keep a lively memory of this day, which can add nothing to my friendship for you, but which increases the burden, which my heart holds lightly, of my deepest gratitude.

Pray accept the assurance of my respectful and sincere affection.

JULES FAVRE.

APPENDIX No. 2 (*v. page 62*).

Monseigneur Dupanloup, Bishop of Orléans, to M. Thiers.

ÉVÊCHÉ D'ORLÉANS.

ORLÉANS, *October* 23, 1870.

MONSIEUR, TRÈS ILLUSTRE ET BIEN EXCELLENT AMI,

I bless God for the knowledge that you are in our vicinity; it is the one ray of light in our melancholy horizon.

I will not speak of our own particular position. It is nothing in the great general posture of affairs.

Although you alone might rescue France from this dreadful invasion and this anarchy that threatens us, it is so difficult that God must indeed be your help.

When you have discovered a ground upon which honest men can find footing and come to an understanding, may they all join with you to choose not merely the *roadstead*, but the *harbour* of which you have so often spoken to me.

M. Cochery will give you news about us. The general, Baron von der Tann, who commands here, has displayed the utmost eagerness and obligingness in giving the necessary safe-conducts, of which M. Cochery is the bearer. He expressed the keenest delight, as well as the generals present at his quarters, on learning that you intended to go to the Headquarters at Versailles, where your coming is very eagerly expected and desired by the King and by Count Bismarck.

He said he had the honour of your acquaintance at Dieppe, when he was there with the late King of Bavaria.

He told me, too, that he had already issued orders so that you would find relays on the whole journey, from here to Versailles; and in these circumstances you will allow me to offer you my carriage, which is really good and comfortable for travelling.

It goes without saying that if you decided to pass through Orléans (which would give me infinite pleasure), my house would be your own, and in it you and the ladies, who will allow me to mention them here, will find a real repose and absolute freedom.

Pray accept the sincere homage of my most cordial and devoted respects.

✠ FELIX,
Évêque d'Orléans.

P.S.—It is absolutely certain and evident that the whole of the Bavarian and Prussian armies here desire peace.

APPENDIX No. 3 (*v. page 62*).

M. Thiers to Monseigneur Dupanloup, Bishop of Orléans.

TOURS, *October* 24, 1870.

MONSEIGNEUR,

I am deeply touched by your unfailing kindness to me, and I thank you with all my heart. I thank also General Baron von der Tann, for his extreme courtesy; but the safe-conducts sent to me are not precisely what I look for and what I need in order to continue my difficult mission. You are doubtless aware, Monseigneur, that Russia, England, Austria, and Italy have put before the belligerents the principle of an armistice that would give France time to convoke a National Assembly. I have accepted this mission, the sequel and continuation of that which I have been engaged upon for the past six weeks, to come to Tours, then to go to Paris to lay the proposal of the neutral Powers before the Government from which I had received my mandate. But this way of proceeding supposes that having come to Tours and received the necessary powers from the delegation sitting there, I shall go to Paris to have those powers confirmed. If I acted otherwise, I should be presenting myself at the Prussian Headquarters without a sufficient mandate, and I could do nothing of any value. There would be a further irregularity in this procedure. His Majesty the Emperor of

Russia was good enough to ask from Saint Petersburg for safe-conducts from His Majesty the King of Prussia to enable me to enter Paris and leave again immediately in order to present myself at the Prussian Headquarters, and there negotiate for the proposed armistice, if I am authorized in Paris to do so.

It is a reply to this request supported by the British Cabinet that I must await, and I should be very happy to receive it through Baron von der Tann, and then to pass through Orléans. If it is understood in this sense, and if I am permitted to enter Paris and to leave it in order to go at once to Versailles, I wish that it may be by way of Orléans, and with the facilities Baron von der Tann is so good as to offer. I should be most grateful to him if he will in this way help me to accomplish a difficult mission, which I am taking up through love of my country and the burning desire for a peace that will bring to an end a cruel and distressing slaughter between two great nations.

I beg you, Monseigneur, to convey my answer to Baron von der Tann, and to accept once more the expression of my unfailing affection and respect.

A. THIERS.

APPENDIX No. 4 (v. page 64).

M. Gambetta to M. Thiers.

RÉPUBLIQUE FRANÇAISE,
LIBERTÉ—ÉGALITÉ—FRATERNITÉ.

GOUVERNEMENT
DE LA
DÉFENSE NATIONALE.

TOURS, October 25, 1870.

MONSIEUR ET ANCIEN COLLÈGUE,

I have the honour, at your request, to forward a copy of various passages from a dispatch I addressed yesterday, October 24th, to my colleagues of the Government of the

APPENDICES

Republic, relating to the proposal for an armistice made simultaneously to Prussia and to France by England and the neutral Powers.

". . . What you are now cognizant of permits me to give a brief summary of the discussions that have taken place in the Council. Three main questions have come up for discussion.

"First: Is M. Thiers to be authorized to return to Paris? On this point the Council was unanimous, with the reservation that M. Thiers should not visit Headquarters on the way.

"Secondly: What view is to be taken of the proposal for an armistice? We were of opinion that M. Thiers should submit it to you with his support, on condition that the armistice should be for at least twenty-five days, with revictualling: our interest in insisting on this is obvious.

"Thirdly: Must we hold an election? You will see by the minutes which M. Thiers will lay before you that my three colleagues were for the affirmative, while I declared myself for the negative.

"The reasons are set forth elsewhere.

*   *   *   *   *

"We must accept no truce proposed to us unless it offers us an advantage from the military point of view."

Such is the opinion I have expressed to my Government. Since you were present at our deliberations, you are in a position to repeat to my colleagues that under the conditions recounted above, I regard the proposed armistice as very advantageous from the military point of view. For this reason I joined my colleagues at Tours in authorizing you to report the proposal and at the same time to recommend it.

Pray accept the expression of my fullest respect and consideration.

LÉON GAMBETTA.

APPENDIX No. 5

M. Gambetta to M. Thiers (*v. page* 64).

RÉPUBLIQUE FRANÇAISE,
LIBERTÉ—ÉGALITÉ—FRATERNITÉ.

GOUVERNEMENT
DE LA
DÉFENSE NATIONALE.

TOURS, *October* 26, 1870.

MONSIEUR ET ANCIEN COLLÈGUE,

I hasten to send you a copy of a dispatch that has reached me during the night, addressed to me by the general commanding the fifteenth military division of Nantes, General Mazure, in whom I have every confidence.

The general writes me as follows:

" Received from absolutely unimpeachable source in which have absolute faith, letter from which extract follows.

"'METZ, *October* 19, 1870.

"'We are not downhearted yet, we eat horsebeef only, we have still a little bread, no sickness; the army in excellent heart. The situation must of necessity resolve itself within a few days *one way or another*. We shall have a hard try at breaking through. Out of my forty-eight guns I can only handle twelve now, the horses belonging to the others have been eaten. These forty-eight guns make up the general reserve for the army, and the divisional artillery is not so much weakened. However that may be, it seems to me to be in the utmost degree urgent to make an attempt to help Bazaine to free himself and prevent a disaster the consequences of which would be incalculable.'

"I have purposely underlined certain words whose effect I do not venture to pronounce upon."

Furthermore I have received from the sub-prefect of Neufchâteau a dispatch that came from Metz at seven o'clock in the evening of Sunday, October 23rd. Unfortunately this dispatch is in a cipher the key to which has been mislaid, and I am waiting for the bearer, whom I have sent for to Tours, in order to have some explanations.

Pray accept the expression of my fullest respect and consideration.

LÉON GAMBETTA.

APPENDIX No. 6 [1] (*v. page 119*).

Comte Beust to Prince Metternich, at Bordeaux.

VIENNA, *March* 3, 1871.

* * * * *

In my dispatch of the 20th of February I had already informed your Highness that we wished to make haste to recognize the new Government, in order to give France a proof of our friendly sympathy.

Subsequent events merely confirm us in this resolve. Accordingly, without awaiting for the arrival in Vienna of an official representative of the French Republic, I send you herewith the letters by which his Imperial and Royal Apostolic Majesty accredits you as his Ambassador Extraordinary to the French Republic.

In presenting these letters to the Chef du Pouvoir Exécutif, your Highness will be good enough to convey to him on our behalf how profoundly the King-Emperor, our august master, and his Government desire to maintain the most cordial relations with France. This sentiment is far from being altered by the present circumstances. We ascribe too great importance to France's holding her accustomed rank among European nations to refrain from expressing to her, in an hour of trial, our signal regard and unchanging friendship.

* * * * *

[1] *Archives Diplomatiques*, 1871-3 (1 and 2), page 43.

M. Thiers, I repeat, can therefore wholly count upon our good dispositions to him personally no less than towards the country he governs. . . .

Be so good as to express yourself in the sense of this dispatch, which your Highness may also read to M. Thiers as well as to M. Jules Favre.

Believe me, etc.,
BEUST.

APPENDIX No. 7 (*v. page 172*).

DRAFT OF A LAW

Presented to the National Assembly, August 12, 1871, by MM. Rivet, Léon de Malleville, Picard, de Tocqueville, de Pressensé, Duvergier de Hauranne, etc.

THE ASSEMBLY.

Considering that it is essential, in accordance with the will of the country and to satisfy the most urgent interests of industry and credit, to give new guarantees of duration and stability to the established Government.

DECREES:

ARTICLE 1.

M. Thiers shall exercise, under the title of President of the Republic, the functions laid upon him by the decree of the 17th of last February.

ARTICLE 2.

His powers are prolonged for three years.

At the same time, if during this period the Assembly should think fit to dissolve, the powers of M. Thiers, bound up in those of the Assembly, should not continue further than the time necessary to constitute a new Assembly, which in turn would be called upon to legislate upon the executive power.

Article 3.

The President of the Republic is charged with the promulgation of the laws.

He oversees and ensures their putting into execution.

He has drafts of laws presented to the Assembly by Ministers.

Envoys and Ambassadors of foreign Powers are accredited to him.

He resides at the place where the National Assembly sits, is lodged at the expense of the Republic, and receives a salary provided for by the budget.

Article 4.

He presides over the Council of Ministers, the members of which he nominates and dismisses.

He appoints a Vice-President in the Council.

In cases where he is absent or prevented from attending, the Vice-President takes his place in presiding over the Council and in the exercise of his other functions.

Article 5.

Diplomatic agents, commanders of land and sea forces, and all magistrates and functionaries of the higher grades are nominated or dismissed in the Ministerial Council.

Article 6.

All acts of the executive power shall be countersigned by a Minister.

Ministers are responsible to the Assembly.

APPENDIX No. 8 (*v. page 240*).

Proposals made to Prussia.

VERSAILLES, *May* 5, 1872.

Count von Arnim has desired to have a summary of the proposals I have made to him in order to establish a definite basis for negotiation, and I hasten to send him this summary.

The two Powers, France and Germany, have two engagements to fulfil: the one, to pay the agreed war indemnity, the other to evacuate that portion of French territory she still occupies. France is ready, on her side, to carry out faithfully and completely the engagements entered into, and even to anticipate them in point of time, since the period fixed by treaty for the payment of the second part of the indemnity is May 1874, and she offers to begin to pay in the course of the present year 1872.

As for the financial means to be adopted, that which seems to her the most natural is that which has already been successful, and which France now offers the Prussian Government, but she would adopt another if this Government preferred, stipulating only that it should be practicable. The French Government, then, would open a loan of three milliards, in which all the bankers of Europe would be allowed to participate, without exclusion or preference, and which would be payable at the smallest possible intervals.

The condition laid upon these bankers would be that they should pay into the Prussian Treasury the sum of three milliards within a time solely determined by the strength of the European market.

The French Government does not think it possible to obtain from this market more than one hundred millions a month, without producing a financial disturbance that it is in the interest of both Powers to avoid.

On this basis the whole of the sum agreed upon could not be realized in less than thirty months; but it would certainly be realized within this time, unless under extraordinary circumstances independent of the wishes of the French Government, and with regard to which the treaty to be drawn up might establish precautions wholly reassuring for the two contracting parties.

This is the offer of the French Government for the discharge of the obligation on its side, it being always fully understood that if another procedure recognized as practicable should be preferred by Prussia, France would offer no objection.

It is now for the German Government to inform France how

it proposes to undertake the evacuation of French territory, the necessary sequel to the payment of the war indemnity.

In the interests of the two contracting parties, for whom it is in the highest degree important to suppress all causes of conflict, and to calm all national passions, it would be desirable that the evacuation should be speedy and as complete as possible. This would respond to the behaviour of France, which offers to discharge her obligations, both in full and as promptly as the difficulties of a colossal financial operation allow.

If the German Government, inspired by a prudence which would seem to us to have scanty foundation, wished to divide the evacuation, the financial operation must then be divided, and we should accomplish in two parts what under every aspect would be better done in one.

Whatever the solution adopted by the two Governments, it is important that a speedy conclusion should be arrived at, for the prospect of a loan inevitable and near at hand weighs upon the credit of Europe as a whole and injures business throughout the world. The French Government, immutably determined in its intentions, not merely for a durable peace, but for a calming of the mind of the nation, promises to bring to these negotiations the most conciliatory dispositions, and furthermore, the sincere desire for arriving at a prompt and satisfactory conclusion.

The President of the French Republic,
A. THIERS.

APPENDIX No. 9 (*v. page 240*).

Reply of Count von Arnim to the proposals made to Prussia.

AMBASSADE
IMPÉRIALE
D'ALLEMAGNE
EN FRANCE.

PARIS, *May* 7, 1872.

The question of the evacuation of the territory is essentially bound up in the declaration formulated in the Versailles preliminaries, announcing that His Majesty the Emperor of

Germany will be disposed to substitute for the territorial guarantee a financial guarantee, if the French Government should offer one that could be considered as safeguarding the interests of the Empire.

It follows therefore that the equivalent of the occupation of French territory should be a financial guarantee offered by France.

The minute of His Excellency the President of the French Republic appears in a certain degree to alter the ground in this question.

He offers to anticipate the payment of the three milliards due on March 3, 1874, by monthly payments of one hundred millions, to begin during the year 1872 and to continue for thirty months.

Even supposing that an agreement could be come to on this basis, it is not misplaced to point out that in all probability the monthly payments could only begin on the 1st of September, 1872, so that the three milliards would not be fully paid up until the 15th of March, 1875, or a full year after they were due.

Now if on the one hand there is an anticipation of part of the debt, on the other there would be a delay of twelve months. In other words, one milliard eight hundred millions would be paid before, one milliard two hundred millions after they were due. It is not easy to see how a modification of the system of territorial guarantee established by the Versailles preliminaries could be compensated for by the method of payment proposed by the French Government.

That is not all.

Germany has only a secondary interest in receiving the three milliards before they are to fall due. Now the Government of the Empire will carefully refrain from burdening France in the sense of anticipatory payments, fearing lest it might by its action embarrass the financial dispositions of France. The French Government therefore, if it desires to hasten on the evacuation of the territory in accordance with the Versailles conditions, ought to declare in precise terms the nature of the guarantee it intends to offer as an equivalent of the territorial guarantee.

The evacuation could not be brought into relation with anticipatory payments, which have no importance save as they will make it easier to find a valid guarantee for the part of the debt whose discharge is deferred until the time it becomes due.

ARNIM.

APPENDIX No. 10 (*v. page 241*).

Count von Arnim to M. Thiers.

PARIS, *May* 15, 1872.

MONSIEUR LE PRÉSIDENT,

I must have a little conspirator's talk with you without the newspapers crying out the details on every roof.

If you can receive me *to-morrow*, about noon, I shall come to Versailles either by rail, or riding.

Pray accept my assurance of the profound respect with which I have the honour to be your most humble and obedient servant.

ARNIM.

P.S.—To give myself an air of mystery, I shall enter by M. de Rémusat's side door.

APPENDIX No. 11 (*v. page 241*).

M. Thiers to Count von Arnim.

VERSAILLES, *May* 15, 1872.

MON CHER COMTE D'ARNIM,

It is very difficult, alas! to escape those evil eyes served by wicked tongues that we call newspapers. Never, indeed, have I known the Press more abject than to-day; and yet our interviews are most legitimate, and I will say, patriotic, since both you and I are serving our countries to the best of our ability. I cannot guarantee that these ill witnesses will not catch you on the way, but you will be received at the hour you mention, and as little as possible will be known of this new interview.

Pray accept the renewed assurance of my feelings of profound consideration and sincere friendship.

A. THIERS.

APPENDIX No. 12 (*v. page 242*).

M. Thiers to Count von Arnim.

VERSAILLES, *May* 17, 1872.

MON CHER COMTE D'ARNIM,

I add to a dispatch from the Cabinet in reply to your first note a confidential letter which will perhaps a little advance our difficult task. I cannot conceal from you that your note, to which the Cabinet has just drawn up the enclosed reply, seemed to me merely an act of obstruction, and I would be glad to arrive at a positive knowledge of your intentions; for if we are not to come to terms this year, the public must know it, so as to put an end to the expectation of a coming loan, which is paralysing our credit and the credit of Europe; and if, on the contrary, we are to treat, we ought to take advantage of the fact that all the capitalists are prepared to employ their capital usefully, and to have our funds resume their upward movement.

This consideration leads me to join to our first proposal another, more definite and, if I am well informed, more in accordance with the wishes of your Government and of the German capitalists.

What is constantly spoken of among you is the *financial guarantees*, which should be *the exact equivalent of the territorial guarantees* that would be relinquished by the evacuation of our territory.

I had originally offered a loan of three milliards, a plain loan at 5 per cent., to be paid within the shortest possible time, that is to say, in thirty months, the amount to be paid direct to the Prussian Government by the European bankers. I have been told that this arrangement was not enough for you, that you would prefer to add to one ordinary loan at 5 per cent. bringing in a milliard within a very short period, another loan of a milliard by a lottery, which, I am assured, would immediately be covered in Germany ; and finally that, having obtained two milliards by this double method, you would wish to receive the third milliard in foreign securities of recognized stability. These three operations, of course, would be in reality one and the same, undertaken by all the European bankers, whose help would be invited, and ought, during the course of the year, to set us free of our engagements to Germany.

It would follow from these arrangements that the discharge of our debt being in full and almost immediate, the evacuation of our territory should be equally complete and carried out as soon as payment is effected.

I have already told you that on our side what would meet the wishes of the German Government would also satisfy us. I repeat the same assurance, with two reservations : the consent of the Chamber of Deputies, and the practicability of realizing the methods proposed.

As for the first loan of a milliard by the means already put to the proof, a loan at 5 per cent., issued on the Paris Exchange, we can see no objection. As for the lottery loan, it had been suggested to us last year, and we had considered it out of keeping with the established ways of high credit. But since we know that it is very much to the mind of German lenders, whose help would be invaluable to us since they would pay actually in Germany, we would not refuse. Finally, as to the deposit of foreign securities for the third milliard, we have always been doubtful whether it would be possible to procure them. But we would agree to this also, if the affair was shown to be practicable by a solid offer on the part of foreign capitalists.

These proposals, though departing from our usual ways, and though in part seeming doubtful of success, would be accepted by us if, I repeat, they were at the same time practicable and sanctioned by the National Assembly, which would probably set up no obstacle.

Here, my dear Count, is what I venture to suggest in order to make you, as you seemed to wish, a proposal more definite and more in accordance with the views of your Government. Look, examine, send to Berlin and persuade them to answer, in order that we may either put off for this year the financial operation that all Europe is expecting, or set them afoot before the summer, when, as a rule, all financial operations are paralysed.

Pray accept once more the assurance of my most affectionate esteem and friendship.

A. THIERS.

APPENDIX No. 13 (*v. page 245*).

Henckel Donnersmack to M. Thiers.

May 24, 1872.

MONSIEUR LE PRÉSIDENT,

I have the honour herewith to address to you my personal ideas, which you have invited me to send to you, upon the subject of an arrangement between France and Germany for the last three milliards.

In case you should consider it important to ask the consent of the German Government for a loan à loterie, I take the liberty of reminding you that the Government would be obliged to submit their authorization to the German Reichstag, which will shortly be prorogued for almost a year.

Pray accept the expression of my most respectful sentiments.

HENCKEL DONNERSMACK.

1. France engages to pay to Germany by the 1st of February, 1873, at the latest, the sum of one milliard of francs. As soon as this sum has been actually received in the Treasury of the German Empire, the evacuation by the German troops of the

departments of Marne and Haute-Marne shall take place within the next fifteen days.

2. France engages to pay to Germany by ... the last two milliards, either in specie and negotiable securities (in accordance with Article 7 of the Treaty of Frankfort of May 10, 1871), or by guaranteeing their payment by the deposit of securities, other than French, that are at the time quoted on all the European exchanges. Germany shall accept these securities at 20 per cent. below the current quotation, reserving the right to reject such securities as may not offer sufficient guarantee.

As soon as these last two milliards are paid or the securities guaranteeing their payment have been deposited, the whole of France shall be evacuated by the German troops, except the fortresses of Belfort, Toul, and Verdun, which shall remain in the hands of the German troops until full actual payment shall have taken the place of the deposited guarantees.

3. Until actual payment has been completely effected, for which Germany consents to an extension of time until May 1, 1875, the departments occupied to-day by Germany shall be declared neutral, except fortified places which may have a garrison of one thousand men in each.

France engages to construct no fortifications in the evacuated departments so long as full payment has not taken the place of the deposited securities and so long as the three milliards have not been received in full by the German Treasury.

4. France shall negotiate a loan in order to carry out her engagements to Germany, and engages to stipulate conditions that shall establish that all moneys paid upon the loan shall be paid direct to the German Treasury.

APPENDIX No. 14 (*v. page 245*).

Minute sent to Count von Arnim by M. Thiers.

May 24, 1872.

A loan of three milliards opened with the assistance of all European bankers, part in a lottery loan, part in 5 per cent.

Government funds, part in foreign securities, accepted by the German Treasury, and guaranteed by France.

In return, after the payment of the first half milliard, the Emperor of Germany would evacuate two of the six French departments he occupies; after the payment of the third half milliard, the Emperor of Germany would evacuate two out of the four departments still occupied; and finally after the payment of the sixth half milliard in foreign securities, accepted by the Emperor of Germany, the last two French departments would be evacuated by the German troops.

It is fully understood that if these arrangements were not recognized by European bankers as practicable, new dispositions would be sought, and in any case, arrangements would be made to begin during the present year the carrying out of this great operation, consisting on the side of France in the speediest possible discharge of her debt, and on the side of Germany in the gradual evacuation of French territory.

If these proposals were not agreeable to the German Government, we would endeavour to modify them so as to come to agreement with that Government.

A. THIERS.

APPENDIX No. 15. (*v. page 246*).

M. le Comte de Saint-Vallier to M. Thiers.

NANCY, *May* 27, 1872.

MONSIEUR LE PRÉSIDENT,

I should have been glad to avoid writing to you at the moment when you have to undergo the burden of the discussion on the question of the army; I should have desired to wait a few days, but circumstances do not permit.

For a week General Manteuffel and von Treskow frequently have repeated to me that their news from Berlin was not good, that misgivings as to France's reservations and secret projects seemed to increase, that letters and newspapers agreed in representing us as burning to begin the war again, that people were readily repeating that our proposals for the payment of the three milliards were not serious and that we were merely seeking to lull Germany's vigilance to sleep, to gain time by making unacceptable offers. The military element was active, and the immediate circle of the Emperor William did not hide that the sovereign was a prey to grave preoccupations.

I answered this uneasiness by the declarations you had authorized me to make; I affirmed with all my power the loyalty and fixity of your resolution for peace; my interlocutors did not contradict, but always returned to the charge soon after with new disquieting information. Unfortunately, for the fortnight since I left Versailles, I have had not a single indication of the progress of the pourparlers begun with Count von Arnim; the preoccupations and fatigues caused by the debates in the Assembly have prevented you and M. de Rémusat from informing me of the position of affairs and what I should say. I left you after having had two conversations with Count von Arnim of which I have not preserved a good impression, and at the moment of my departure, this Ambassador was requesting an audience of you for the next day. Since then I have no information, which prevents me from refuting as decidedly as would be desirable the alarming rumours brought to me by the German generals.

This morning I found General Manteuffel more moved and more troubled than usual: he answered my inquiries by telling me he had received an unpleasant letter from Count Moltke, that this letter was confidential and that he could only impart its tenor to me if I would undertake to keep strictly for you and for myself what he should tell me of it: "Especially," said he, "if you write of it to M. Thiers, take care that Count von Arnim may never suspect that I give you any knowledge of letters so confidential as this; it would be injurious for everybody, and for myself, my position would be compromised." After this preamble to which I replied by promising absolute discretion on your part and on mine, he confided to me that Count Moltke recommended him to take certain military precautions and to be on his guard, as the likelihood of a resumption of hostilities on the part of France seemed to be increasing ; according to Count Moltke we had not made serious proposals for anticipating the payment and the liberating of our territory ; all would be confined to conversations and an exchange of views ; sure information received in Berlin would hardly leave it open to doubt that the appetite for revenge is growing in the French people and even in the heart of the National Assembly ; that universal compulsory military service is on the point of being voted and immediately put into execution ; that the French Government is actively engaged in military preparations ; that the French army is already much finer, stronger, and more formidable than it was before our crushing reverses ; that we are increasing it day by day ; that little by little we are bringing back from Africa our surest and best tried troops, and that even in the last few days two fresh regiments have arrived from Algeria.

After making this communication, General Manteuffel added that personally he was still not without faith ; but that he greatly feared that time was being lost and that on both sides distrust and irritation were being permitted to spring up ; he persists in believing that it is not with Count von Arnim in Paris, but only at Berlin that a speedy result can be attained. He pretends to know that M. de Gontaut has never asked Bismarck *directly and personally* his preference as to the method of negotiation to be adopted, as you had instructed him to do.

I hasten to send you these items of information and these confidences ; I could not, I confess, hear them without replying that these unjust suspicions, this constant and incurable mistrust were calculated to discourage our loyal purpose, and that it seemed as though it was desired to drive us beyond our patience by these continual accusations. You alone, Monsieur le Président, can appreciate the importance of this communication, and judge whether there is any reason to be seriously disturbed by it, or whether it is merely a ruse of Count Bismarck's to screen more effectually real negotiations proceeding between you at the moment. I should be happy, in any case, to know, were it only by a single word, the true posture of affairs; I should make no use of the information beyond what you might think opportune.

Pray accept, Monsieur le Président, the homage of the respect with which I have the honour to be Your Excellency's most obedient and devoted

SAINT-VALLIER.

P.S.—Distrust is so much the order of the day in Berlin, that their preoccupations are concerned with Russia as much as with us; officers of the General Staff are sent to the Russian frontier, the fortresses of Eastern Prussia are put in a state of defence; emissaries are everywhere scattered in Russia as in France before the late war.

APPENDIX No. 16 (*v. page 246*).

General Le Flô to M. de Rémusat.

AMBASSADE DE FRANCE.

SAINT-PÉTERSBOURG, *May* 23, 1872.

CHER MONSIEUR DE RÉMUSAT,

At the moment when the toilsome negotiations are beginning at Paris and at Berlin for speedier financial and territorial liberation of our unhappy and well-beloved country it is especially useful, in my opinion, to keep you well informed on everything that is taking place in Germany, upon the feelings manifested towards us there and upon the state of public opinion. M. de Gontaut leaves you nothing to desire on this head; I think it none the less my duty to convey to you the rumours that are current here. Now *it is certain* that all the reports of the Russian agents in Germany agree in representing that country as animated by the worst possible disposition and given over to an agitation very hostile to us; it is no less certain that people there publicly express a rancorous regret not to have overthrown us sufficiently, sufficiently tormented us, and that the necessity of a new war is there loudly proclaimed. They should, they say, take advantage of France's temporary weakness, the instability of her Government, the ruin of her finances, the insufficiency of her war material, and in short, of the moment when her army is not yet reorganized, to resume a struggle that under such conditions would call for but moderate efforts on the part of Germany and would ensure her fifty years of peace and security. And do not imagine it is the professors, students, bourgeois, and subalterns who use this detestable language ; it is repeated in the highest circles, and even here by Prince William of Baden, with unheard-of brutality. I know this from an exalted member of the Diplomatic Corps to whom the Prince made his confidences, who was indignant at them and came to let me know. I was very much humiliated, for I had been completely duped by this Prince, who had done me the honour to call on me the day after his arrival in Saint Petersburg and at my return visit had showed himself courteous, modest even to a kind of humility, and had left me with an excellent impression of him. They say indeed that he is very stupid ; but no stupidity, however great, could explain such duplicity ; and from the speech of this Duke as of those who come back from every corner of Germany, we cannot but infer that the worst possible feelings continue to be harboured there against us. Are these feelings natural, are they the result of the nightmare of revenge that pursues these people whose astonishing victories have not yet sufficiently reassured them, to whom continually, whatever we do or say, we are a source of fear ; or are they factitious and inspired by a policy that seeks to make out of this odious agitation a fulcrum and an argument for resistance in the negotiations that have just opened ? Both hypotheses may be true. The official world of Saint Petersburg does not believe in Prince Bismarck's good will to treat in all seriousness, and it is thought that he will avail himself specially of these strange rumours about our supposed formidable armaments, which are current throughout the whole of Germany, and which he himself pretends to believe : M. d'Oubril's dispatches prove as much. And as I speak of M. d'Oubril, on the Exchange the day before yesterday a rumour was spread to the effect that he had written that in a conversation with the Chancellor of the German Empire, the latter had said to him that *men's minds in France were in such a state that he would not venture to guarantee peace more than six months' duration.* The authenticity of this was strongly asserted, nevertheless I only take it with a grain of salt. However that may be, it seems to me indisputable that the trend of opinion in Germany is strongly against us, and this makes me regret that the discussion of our military law is down for so early a date ; this discussion might entail some embarrassments. The trial of Marshal Bazaine, too, falls at an awkward moment, from the same point of view. It was written, it seems, in the destiny of this fatal individual that he would spare his country no disaster and no vexations ; but we must now leave it to justice alone to speak.

* * * * *

Adieu, cher Monsieur de Rémusat, etc.

Le Flô.

APPENDIX No. 17 (*v. page 250*).

Count von Arnim to M. Thiers.

Ambassade
Impériale
d'Allemagne
en France.

Paris, *June* 4, 1872.

Monsieur le Président,

I have the honour herewith to hand to you a summary of the conditions upon which they are prepared in Berlin to negotiate upon the payment of the three milliards and the evacuation of the French territory.

While placing myself at your disposal for any further explanation you may wish, I take this opportunity to repeat to you, Monsieur le Président, the expression of the profound consideration with which I have the honour to be Your Excellency's very humble and obedient servant,

Arnim.

I had forgotten to say that the Imperial Government does not think it admissible that a lottery loan should be quoted on the German exchanges.

Pray accept, Monsieur le Président, the renewed assurance of my profoundest consideration.

ARNIM.

SUMMARY OF THE CONDITIONS PROPOSED BY GERMANY.

1. France shall pay to Germany one milliard by February 1, 1873; a second milliard by January 1, 1874; the third milliard by March 2, 1875.

2. Germany shall evacuate the two departments of Haute-Marne and Marne after the payment of the first milliard; the departments of the Ardennes and the Vosges after the payment of the second milliard. The two departments of the Meurthe and the Meuse, as well as Belfort, shall remain under occupation until the payment of the third milliard.

3. France not paying the third milliard until twelve months after it is due, she shall deposit in the German Treasury negotiable securities other than French, declared acceptable and sufficient by the Imperial Government as guarantee for the payment of the third milliard.

4. The territory evacuated under this arrangement shall be declared neutral from a military point of view. France undertakes not to assemble considerable bodies of troops in this territory, and she shall construct neither fortifications nor entrenched camps in it.

It is fully understood that these restrictions cease when the third milliard is paid.

5. The Emperor of Germany reserves to himself the right to reoccupy the evacuated departments, in case of the non-fulfilment of the engagements entered into by France.

6. The interest of 5 per cent. stipulated in the Treaty of Versailles shall be paid at the intervals agreed upon, and on such sums as have not been paid into the German Treasury.

APPENDIX No. 18 (v. page 252).

Draft of a Convention proposed to Germany by the French Government.

June 15, 1872.

BETWEEN THE PARTIES. . . .

It has been agreed as follows:

ARTICLE 1.

The President of the French Republic, undersigned, pledges himself to fulfil to His Majesty the Emperor of Germany as promptly as possible the engagements under Article 7 of the treaty of May 10, 1871, and in return H.M. the Emperor of Germany pledges himself to evacuate French territory as soon as the war indemnity stipulated in the said treaty shall be paid in full.

ARTICLE 2.

The sums still due to the Empire of Germany shall be discharged by means of a loan contracted by France which shall impose upon the contractors of the said loan the obligation to pay direct to the German Treasury the sum of three milliards at intervals as short as can be arranged without going beyond the resources of the money market.

ARTICLE 3.

As soon as the sum of one half milliard is paid, that is to say, in the two months following the conclusion of the present convention, H.M. the Emperor of Germany pledges himself to evacuate the French departments of Marne and Haute-Marne.

ARTICLE 4.

The second and third half milliards shall be paid in the course of the year 1873, and upon the complete payment of the second half milliard the departments of the Ardennes and the Vosges shall be evacuated by the German troops.

Article 5.

The fourth half milliard shall be paid as far as possible in the concluding months of the year 1873, and as soon as this payment is executed H.M. the Emperor of Germany pledges himself to evacuate the departments of the Meurthe and the Meuse, with the fortress and territory of Belfort, provided the full amount of the fifth and sixth half milliards is furnished in securities approved by him, or in guarantees from bankers recognized by him as solvent.

Article 6.

France shall always have power to anticipate the period of discharging her debt, and, as soon as she has paid in full the three milliards still due, to claim the immediate and complete evacuation of her territory.

Article 7.

The interest of 5 per cent. stipulated for the sums still to be paid on account of the war indemnity shall cease in proportion to the payment of the aforesaid sums.

Article 8.

It is agreed that the maintenance of the German troops actually occupying the six departments enumerated above—maintenance which has been laid upon France—shall cease in accordance with their successive withdrawals in the proportion of one-third for each two departments evacuated.

Article 9.

Until the liberation of French territory is complete, the territories of the six departments evacuated in succession shall be neutralized, and must receive neither any mass of troops (other than such as may be necessary for preserving order) nor works of fortification; and H.M. the Emperor of Germany pledges himself, on his part, not to raise upon the territory at present under occupation any work other than those at present existing.

ARTICLE 10.

It is fully understood that H.M. the Emperor of Germany, if the financial engagements entered into were not completely fulfilled, would be empowered to reoccupy those of the six departments mentioned above that corresponded to the unfulfilled part of France's engagements.

Le Ministre des Affaires Etrangères.
DE RÉMUSAT.

APPENDIX No. 19 (*v. page 252*).

Note sent by Henckel Donnersmack to M. Thiers.

June 17, 1872.

BETWEEN. . . .

It has been determined as follows :

ARTICLE 1.

France shall pay the three milliards of francs still due to Germany under the Treaties of Versailles of February 26, 1871, and of Frankfort May 10, 1871, at the dates indicated below :

One milliard of francs, by February 1, 1873
The second milliard of francs, by January 1, 1874
The third milliard of francs, by March 1, 1875

ARTICLE 2.

In order to fulfil her engagements, France shall negotiate a loan of three milliards to be paid within the shortest possible period, and impose upon the subscribers or the negotiators of this loan the obligation to pay direct to the Treasury of the German Empire the sums they will have undertaken to furnish.

ARTICLE 3.

The German troops shall, as soon as the payment of one half milliard has been completed, evacuate the departments of Marne and Haute-Marne ; as soon as the payment of the second milliard is completed, the departments of the Ardennes and the Vosges, except the canton of Belfort; as soon as the payment of the third milliard is completed, the departments of the Meuse, the Moselle, Meurthe-et-Moselle, and the canton of Belfort.

ARTICLE 4.

The payment of two milliards being completed, France reserves to herself the right to offer Germany, under Article 3 of the Treaty of Versailles, financial guarantees in lieu of the territorial guarantee.

ARTICLE 5.

The evacuated departments shall be declared neutral from the military point of view, until the payment of the three milliards has been accomplished in full. Until then France shall have in them only the number of troops necessary for the maintenance of order, and undertakes not to establish any entrenched camp, not to construct any new fortifications and not to enlarge any existing fortifications. In case of the non-execution or infraction of the terms laid down in this article, the evacuated departments may be reoccupied by the troops of H.M. the Emperor of Germany.

ARTICLE 6.

All conditions established by the Treaties of Versailles and Frankfort that are not modified by the present convention remain in force, as well as the foregoing stipulations with regard to the method of payment.

ARTICLE 7.

France is authorized, upon giving notice one month beforehand, to pay at any time into the German Treasury sums on account of the payments stipulated in Article 1 of this convention, in which case these sums cease to bear interest from the day on which payment is made.

ARTICLE 8.

Payment of interest upon the amount remaining due shall be made on the 2nd of March in each year.

APPENDICES

APPENDIX No. 20 (*v. page 252*).

Draft of a Convention proposed by the German Government.

June 18, 1872.

BETWEEN. . . .

It has been determined as follows :

ARTICLE 1.

The remaining sums due to the Empire of Germany on account of the war indemnity shall be discharged by means of a loan raised by France, which shall impose upon the contractors of the said loan the obligation to pay direct to the German Treasury the sum of three milliards.

ARTICLE 2.

Fifteen days after the sum of one half milliard shall have been discharged, which shall be within two months of the ratification of this present convention, or earlier if possible, H.M. the Emperor of Germany undertakes to evacuate the French departments of Marne and Haute-Marne.

ARTICLE 3.

The second and third half milliards shall be discharged during the year 1873.

The fourth half milliard shall be discharged by the 1st of March, 1874.

The payment of the fifth and sixth half milliards shall be completed by the 1st of March, 1875.

ARTICLE 4.

After the full discharge of the fourth half milliard, the departments of the Vosges and the Ardennes shall be evacuated by the German troops.

The departments of Meurthe and Meuse as well as the fortress of Belfort shall be evacuated on the payment of the fifth and sixth half milliards.

The French Government always reserves the right of furnishing after the discharge of the fourth half milliard securities or bankers' guarantees, which by virtue of the pertinent clause of Article 3 of the Versailles preliminaries shall be substituted for the territorital guarantee, if they are accepted and recognized by Germany as sufficient.

ARTICLE 5.

As Article 6 of the draft of June 14, 1872.

ARTICLE 6.

As Article 7 of the same.

ARTICLE 7.

As Article 8 of the same.

ARTICLE 8.

As Article 9 of the same.

APPENDIX No. 21 (*v. page 252*).

Draft of Convention proposed by the French Government.

June 18, 1872.

BETWEEN HIS MAJESTY
AND THE PRESIDENT OF THE REPUBLIC.

It being recognized that, for the maintenance of a solid and final peace, the time has arrived for arranging, on the one side, for the evacuation of French territory, and on the other for the discharge of the war indemnity stipulated in the peace preliminaries signed at Versailles on the 26th of February,

1871, and by the final peace treaty of May 10, 1871, the following conditions have been determined :

ARTICLE 1.

The sums remaining due to Germany on the war indemnity shall be discharged by means of a loan contracted by France, the proceeds of which, to be three milliards, shall be paid at the times hereunder laid down.

ARTICLE 2.

Fifteen days after the sum of one half milliard shall have been discharged, which shall take place within two months of the ratifying of the present convention, or earlier if it be possible, His Majesty undertakes to evacuate the French departments of Marne and Haute-Marne.

ARTICLE 3.

The second and third half milliards shall be discharged during the year 1873; the fourth half milliard is to be discharged on March 1, 1874.

The fifth and sixth half milliards may be left undischarged until March 1, 1875, if financial circumstances have not permitted them to be paid before.

ARTICLE 4.

After the discharge in full of the third half milliard, the departments of the Ardennes and the Vosges are to be evacuated by the German troops.

The departments of Meurthe and Meuse, as well as the fortress of Belfort, shall be evacuated after the payment of the fifth and sixth half milliards.

The French Government always reserves the right of furnishing after the discharge of the fourth half milliard securities or bankers' guarantees, which, by virtue of the pertinent clause of Article 3 of the Versailles preliminaries, shall be substituted for the territorial guarantee, if they are accepted and recognized by Germany as sufficient.

Article 5.

France shall always have power to anticipate the period of discharging her debt, and as soon as she has paid in full the three milliards completing the war indemnity, to claim the immediate and total evacuation of her territory.

Article 6.

The interest of 5 per cent. stipulated for the sums still to be paid shall cease in proportion to the payment of the aforesaid sums.

Article 7.

As the German troops in occupation are to decrease in number with the successive reductions of the occupation, the cost of maintaining the said troops shall be reduced proportionately with their number.

Article 8.

Until the liberation of the French territory is complete, the territories of the six departments evacuated in succession shall be neutralized, and must receive neither any mass of troops (other than such as may be necessary for preserving order) nor works of fortification; and H.M. the Emperor of Germany pledges himself, for his part, not to raise upon the territory at present under occupation any work other than those at present existing.

Article 9.

It is fully understood that H.M. the Emperor of Germany, if the financial engagements entered into were not completely fulfilled, would be empowered to reoccupy those of the six departments mentioned above that corresponded to the unfulfilled part of France's engagements.

Le Ministre des Affaires Etrangères,
De Rémusat.

APPENDIX No. 22 (v. page 253).

Count von Arnim to M. de Rémusat.

AMBASSADE
IMPÉRIALE
D'ALLEMAGNE
EN FRANCE.

PARIS, *June* 19, 1872.

MONSIEUR LE MINISTRE,

Having read the draft convention you were good enough to send me yesterday, I have the honour to present to you a few observations arising from it.

The first Article makes no mention of the obligation to be laid on the contractors of the loan to pay the sum of three milliards direct to the Treasury of the Empire.

This clause, contained in the confidential proposals of the President of the Republic, was maintained in the first draft convention.

I suppose it is omitted by mistake from the new draft.

As for Article 4, I have already had the honour to convey to you that my Government did not think it possible to accede to the request that the departments of the Vosges and the Ardennes should be evacuated after the payment of the third half milliard.

Between Articles 6 and 7 it would be proper to insert an Article stipulating that payments not exceeding one hundred millions should be announced fifteen days, those exceeding that amount one month, before the date of payment.

I have already had occasion to inform Your Excellency that Article 7 has been in advance judged inadmissible by the Imperial Government.

It is in order to forestall any misunderstanding that I repeat this declaration.

Article 9 only mentions "financial" engagements whose non-fulfilment would give H.M. the Emperor the right to reoccupy the evacuated territories.

I suppose that here it is merely a question of a mistake easily corrected in the final version.

Pray accept, Monsieur le Ministre, the renewed assurance of the very high consideration with which I have the honour to be Your Excellency's most humble and obedient servant.

ARNIM.

APPENDIX No. 23 (*v. page 255*).

Count von Arnim to M. de Rémusat.

AMBASSADE
IMPÉRIALE
D'ALLEMAGNE
EN FRANCE.

PARIS, *June* 27, 1872.

MONSIEUR LE MINISTRE,

I have the honour to send you herewith a draft convention which I am authorized to sign. It does not essentially differ from that which you were good enough to communicate to me.

The one difference of any importance is in regard to the evacuation of the two departments of the Vosges and the Ardennes, in which, as I have had the honour to inform you already, I cannot accede to the request of the President of the Republic.

At the same time this is a detail whose importance should not be exaggerated.

Pray accept, Monsieur le Ministre, the renewed expression of the high consideration with which I have the honour to be your most humble and obedient servant.

ARNIM.

APPENDICES

Convention of June 29, 1872.

COUNT HARRY VON ARNIM, AMBASSADOR OF H.M. THE EMPEROR OF GERMANY IN FRANCE.

Stipulating on behalf of the German Empire on the one part,
On the other part M.

Stipulating on behalf of the French Republic, having agreed upon the times and the method of payment of the sum of three milliards due from France to Germany, also upon the gradual evacuation of the French departments occupied by the German army, and having mutually exchanged their powers, found good and in due form, have determined as follows :

ARTICLE 1.

France engages to pay the said sum of three milliards at the times following :
1. One half milliard of francs two months after the exchange of ratifications of the present convention ;
2. One half milliard of francs on the 1st of February, 1873 ;
3. One milliard of francs on the 1st of March, 1874 ;
4. One milliard of francs on the 1st of March, 1875 ;

France may, however, anticipate the payments due on February 1, 1873, March 1, 1874, and March 1, 1875 by partial payments which shall be of not less than one hundred millions but which may comprise the whole of the amounts due at the times above indicated.

In case of anticipatory payment, the French Government shall advise the German Government one month in advance.

ARTICLE 2.

The conditions of the third paragraph of Article 7 in the peace treaty of May 10, 1871, as well as those of the separate protocol of October 12, 1871, remain in force for all payments made under the preceding Article.

Article 3.

His Majesty the Emperor of Germany shall cause his troops to evacuate the departments of Marne and Haute-Marne fifteen days after the payment of one half milliard.

The departments of the Ardennes and the Vosges, fifteen days after the payment of the second milliard.

The departments of Meuse and Meurthe, as well as the canton of Belfort, fifteen days after the payment of the third milliard and of the interest that may remain to be paid.

Article 4.

After the payment of two milliards, France reserves the right to furnish Germany, for the third milliard, financial guarantees which, conformably with Article 3 of the Versailles preliminaries, shall be substituted for the territorial guarantees, if they are accepted and recognized as sufficient by Germany.

Article 5.

The interest of 5 per cent. on the sums indicated in Article 1, payable from March 2, 1872, shall cease in proportion as the said sums are discharged, either on the dates fixed by the present convention or before these dates after the previous notice stipulated for in Article 1.

Article 6.

In case the number of the German troops in occupation should be decreased when the occupation is successively reduced, the cost of maintaining the said troops shall be reduced in proportion to their number.

Article 7.

Until the liberation of the French territory is complete, the departments successively evacuated conformably with Article 3 shall be neutralized from a military point of view, and must not receive any masses of troops other than the garrisons necessary for the preservation of order.

France shall not raise any fortifications in these departments, and shall not extend the existing fortifications.

His Majesty the Emperor of Germany undertakes for his part not to raise any work of fortification in the occupied departments other than those at present existing.

ARTICLE 8.

His Majesty the Emperor of Germany reserves the right to reoccupy the evacuated departments in case of the non-fulfilment of the engagements entered into in the present convention.

ARTICLE 9.

The ratifications of the present treaty, by His Majesty the Emperor of Germany, on the one part,

On the other, by the President of the French Republic,

Shall be exchanged at Paris, within ten days, or earlier if possible.

In which faith . . .

APPENDIX No. 24 (*v. page 273*).

M. Thiers to M. Teisserenc de Bort.

TROUVILLE, *Wednesday morning,*
August 28, 1872.

MON CHER COLLÈGUE ET AMI,

I have indicated the settlement of September 1st as a grave moment for our colossal loan. It is certain that in this unparalleled operation speculation plays a considerable part, and that speculation at every settlement goes through a critical time, and that if the cost of carrying over become dear, the crisis may become serious. I have already persuaded M. Rouland to be lax with regard to loans on securities. I am told that this is not enough, and that, though everything promises favourably, another form of assistance is necessary : this would be the funds of the Treasury placed at the disposal of the Exchange.

But how ? M. Joubert, a most intelligent financier, who has given us valuable advice on more than one occasion, thinks we might come to an understanding with the Company of Stockbrokers for this purpose. At other times, and for less respectable motives than inspire us to-day (the success of a colossal loan made necessary by our misfortunes), recourse has been had to means of this nature.

Look into it, examine, confer with M. Dutilleul, make up your mind and let me know by telegraph what you have decided. You must consult M. Moreau, the Syndic of the Stockbrokers, and M. Alphonse de Rothschild, and learn all you can before deciding, but it is on Saturday you must move. So you have not a moment to lose.

Cordially yours,
A. THIERS.

APPENDIX No. 25 (*v. page 274*).

Minute by M. Teisserenc de Bort sent to M. Thiers.

MINUTE.

When entrusting me with the temporary charge of the Ministry of Finance in the month of August, 1872, the President of the Republic had drawn my attention to the difficult situation that might arise on the Bourse at the moment of the settlement at the end of the month. The new colossal loan of three milliards was about, for the first time, to come down with all its weight upon this settling day. Certain signs indicated that a considerable part of this loan was floating, that is to say, in speculators' hands. Were the money reserves on the Exchange equal to sustaining so heavy a load? And if money were to be lacking, to what disturbances, what dangers, what catastrophes would not our Stock Exchange, our credit be exposed?

The resources placed by the Bank at the disposal of the public by means of advances on securities appeared wholly inadequate; it was necessary to have recourse to something prompter and more effective. The President of the Republic in a letter of August 28, 1872, informed me of his decisions, which he charged me to execute.

I employed the two days I had before me in collecting the opinions of the highest authorities in the banking world, in consulting with the Syndic of the Stockbrokers, the directors of our great credit houses. No one had a very clear idea of the needs of the Exchange, no more than of the resources that could be counted upon, but there was universal anxiety. Every one was agreed besides in recognizing that in a situation so serious and so full of unforeseen elements, the State could not stand aloof; that a crisis would be disastrous, and would immediately degenerate into panic, and would strike a deadly blow at the credit of France.

The intervention of the Treasury to avoid such a calamity was then perfectly justified, provided that this intervention should take place only as a last resort and under the pressure of a fully demonstrated necessity.

We had to avoid the rock of a premature, untimely intervention which would have discouraged the efforts of private enterprise by misleading the calculations of speculators; which would have withdrawn capital seeking a high rate of remuneration from investments carried over not only for this settlement but for subsequent settlements also.

It was in view of these divers interests that, with the sanction of the President of the Republic, I fixed at fourteen centimes the carrying-over figure after which the Treasury should be empowered to begin making advances.

This carry-over price gave an interest of $5\frac{7}{10}$ per cent., which was in no way excessive at the moment. Fortunately it was not reached. The Exchange was able to satisfy all needs, and the moral effect of the Government's resolution was enough to restrain the carry-over figure between the limits of twelve and thirteen centimes which it did not overpass.

APPENDIX No. 26 (*v. page 325*).

Draft of a law for the organization of public powers, presented by M. Thiers, President of the Republic, and by M. Dufaure, Keeper of the Seals and Minister of Justice, at the sitting of May 19, 1873.

ARTICLE 1.

The Government of the French Republic consists of a Senate, a Representative Chamber, and a President of the Republic, Head of the Executive.

Article 2.

The Senate consists of two hundred and sixty-five members, French subjects, of thirty-five years of age at the least, enjoying all their civil, political, and family rights.

The Representative Chamber consists of five hundred and thirty-seven members, French subjects, of twenty-five years of age at the least, enjoying all their civil, political, and family rights.

The President of the Republic must be of forty years of age at the least, and enjoy all his civil, political, and family rights.

Article 3.

The Senate is nominated for ten years and is renewed by one-fifth every two years.

The Representative Chamber is nominated for five years and is completely renewed after the fifth year.

The President of the Republic is nominated for five years; he may be re-elected.

Article 4.

Each of the eighty-six departments of France nominates three senators; the district of Belfort, the departments of Algeria, the islands of Réunion, Martinique, and Guadeloupe, nominate one each.

Elections are decided by the direct vote of all the electors in the department, the district, or the colony, and by ballot for the departments of France.

Article 5.

Only the following are eligible for the Senate:
1. Members of the Representative Chamber;
2. Former members of the Legislative Assemblies;
3. Ministers and ex-Ministers;
4. Members of the Council of State, the Court of Cassation, and the Court of Exchequer;
5. Presidents and ex-Presidents of the General Councils;
6. Members of the Institute;

APPENDICES

7. Members of the higher Council of Commerce, of Agriculture, and of Industry ;

8. Cardinals, Archbishops, and Bishops ;

9. Presidents of the two Consistories of the Augsburg Confession with the greatest number of electors, and the twelve Consistories of the reformed religion with the greatest number of electors ;

10. The President and the Grand Rabbi of the central Consistory of the Jews in France ;

11. Marshals and Generals of Division, Admirals and Vice-Admirals on active service or in the reserves, Governors of Algeria and the three great colonies who have held office for five years ;

12. Prefects in active service ;

13. Mayors of towns of above one hundred thousand population ;

14. Officials with ten years' service as directors in the central ministerial administrations ;

15. Retired magistrates who have been attached to the Court of Cassation, to the Courts of Appeal, or have held the office of President of a civil tribunal.

Article 6.

Those indicated as eligible in paragraphs 1, 4, and 12 of the preceding Article shall, within fifteen days following the elections, declare whether they intend to accept senatorial functions. Silence will be accepted as refusal ; acceptance will entail the necessary resignation of the offices they were holding.

Article 7.

Each of the three hundred and sixty-two divisions of France, including the district of Belfort, nominates one representative. Divisions whose population exceeds one hundred thousand shall elect one representative for each hundred thousand inhabitants, any fraction beyond to count as a hundred thousand.

No change can be made in the distribution save by virtue of the quinquennial census and by a law.

Two representatives are assigned to each of the departments of Algeria, and one to each of the six colonies of Réunion, Martinique, Guadeloupe, Senegal, Guiana, and French India (Indo-China).

ARTICLE 8.

Representatives are elected by the direct vote of all the electors of the arrondissement. An arrondissement that is to nominate more than one representative shall be divided into as many sections as it has representatives. The sections shall be composed by grouping cantons together. They can be determined and altered only by legislation.

ARTICLE 9.

The President of the Republic is nominated by a Congress composed as follows : (1) Of members of the Senate ; (2) Members of the Representative Chamber ; (3) A delegation of three members chosen by each of the General Councils of France and Algeria in their annual session in the month of August.

This Congress shall be presided over by the President of the Senate.

ARTICLE 10.

When there is occasion to nominate the President of the Republic, the President of the Senate shall within eight days convoke the Senators, the representatives, and the members of the General Councils appointed.

Their meeting shall take place within fifteen days at the furthest.

The President of the Republic shall be nominated by the majority of votes.

The President of the Senate shall notify the President of the Republic elected and the President of the Representative Chamber of the nomination.

APPENDICES

ASSIGNMENT OF PUBLIC POWERS.

ARTICLE 11.

Legislation belongs to the two Chambers and the President of the Republic.

The two Chambers share alike in the formulation of the laws. At the same time, laws relating to taxation are submitted in the first instance to the Representative Chamber.

The Senate may be constituted a court to try actions against the President and the Ministers, and the Generals in command of the land and sea forces.

ARTICLE 12.

Each Chamber is the judge of the eligibility of its own members and of the regularity of their election, and can alone receive their resignation.

ARTICLE 13.

Senators and Representatives can at no time be either accused nor tried for the opinions they may have expressed in the Chamber to which they belong.

They cannot be arrested on any criminal charge except *in flagrante delicto*, nor prosecuted unless and until the Chamber of which they form part has authorized the prosecution.

ARTICLE 14.

The President of the Republic promulgates the laws when they have been passed by both Chambers. He oversees and ensures their execution.

He negotiates and ratifies treaties. No treaty is finally valid until approved by both Chambers.

He has the prerogative of pardon; amnesties can only be granted by legislation.

He disposes of the armed forces without having power to command in person.

He presides over national ceremonies; envoys and ambassadors of foreign Powers are accredited to him.

The President of the Republic and the Ministers are individually and collectively responsible for the actions of the Government.

ARTICLE 15.

When the President of the Republic considers that the interest of the country demands the renewing of the Representative Chamber before the expiration of its normal term, he shall request the Senate for authority to dissolve it. This authority can be given only in secret committee and by a majority of votes. It must be given within eight days.

The electoral colleges are to be convoked within the three days following the notification to the President of the Republic of the Senate's vote in the affirmative.

TRANSITIONAL ARRANGEMENTS.

ARTICLE 16.

When the National Assembly shall have by vote determined the date of its breaking up, the President of the Republic shall convoke the electoral colleges for the election of representatives, and further for the election of Senators, so that the two Chambers may be constituted on the same day as the dissolution takes place.

The powers of the President of the Republic shall continue until the notification of the voting of the Congress that shall have elected the new President.

The President of the Republic,
A. THIERS.

Keeper of the Seals, Minister of Justice,
J. DUFAURE.

INDEX

Alençon, 155
Alphand, M., 148
Alsace, Alsatians, 49, 50, 61, 70, 78-81, 92, 93, 96, 97, 107, 113, 114, 183, 185, 237, 270; -Lorraine, 185, 189
America, 295; Civil War, the, 208
Amiens, 96, 167
Andrássy, Count, 29, 31, 32, 51-3, 168
Antwerp, 297
Armenia, Armenian, 270
Armistice, 19, 36, 37, 58, 59, 60-3, 65, 68-78, 80-3, 85, 87, 90, 92, 93, 95-9, 101-3, 105, 107, 108, 112, 119
Army of the East, 63, 130
Arnim, Count von, 156, 184, 186, 190, 235-45, 249-55, 307, 310, 311, 313, 315
Asnières, Bridge of, 132
Assembly, Constituent, National, 10, 19, 58, 59, 63, 68, 69, 71, 73-5, 77, 81, 82, 87, 92, 97, 104, 117-21, 125, 126, 134, 136-8, 143, 144, 151, 157, 158, 162-4, 168, 169, (of 1848) 170, 171-4, 176, 177, 180, 185-7, 189, 197-204, 206-8, 213-18, 221-7, 231, 232, 234, 236, 248, 255, 256, 259, 261, 264, 265, 275-7, 278, 280-2, 285, 291-4, 297-304, 308, 309, 312, 318-23, 325-31
Audiffret-Pasquier, Duc d', 222, 223, 257, 295
Aumale, Duc d', the, 168, 215, 328, 329
Australia, 295

Austria, Austrians, 24-6, 28, 30, 31, 37, 42, 43, 52-4, 74, 89, 119, 167, 271
Army, 25, 26
Cabinet, 119
Court, 27
Emperor Francis Joseph, 25, 26, 29, 51, 167, 270, 271
German provinces of, 40
Nobility, 25
Press, 27
Austria-Hungary, 31
Austro-Germans, 25, 27, 28, 31, 167
Auteuil, 137-8, 142

Bataille, General, 128, 154
Batbie, M., 257, 298, 299
Baden, Duchy of, 31, 40, 79, 246
Bank of France, 120, 127, 153, 163, 194-7, 202-4, 206, 212, 251, 263, 279, 282, 295, 314; Board of, 195
Barail, General du, 128, 130, 133, 137, 150, 265
Barodet, M., 319, 321, 323, 325
Barthélemy-Saint-Hilaire, M., 67, 72, 102
Bavaria, Bavarian, 31, 40, 78, 90, 246; army, 62; outposts, 99
Bazaine, Marshal, 61, 62, 64, 219; army of, 64; capitulation of, 61, 64, 68
Belfort, 55, 56, 63, 111, 113, 114, 115, 120, 156, 182, 244, 246, 247, 251, 253, 255, 256, 309, 310, 312-17
Belgium, 119, 178, 305
King Leopold of, 306
Belville, 122, 147

INDEX

Berckheim, General de, 133, 265-7
Bérenger, M., 327, 331
Berlin, 27, 38, 42, 46, 48, 49, 110, 113, 184, 186, 187, 189, 234-40, 242, 243, 246, 248-50, 252, 254, 255, 270, 271, 294, 311, 313, 316
  Cabinet, 227, 250
  Court, 46, 236, 318
  French Embassy at, 318
  Treasury, 252
Besançon, 55, 56, 63, 266
Beust, Count, 24-30, 43, 51, 52, 54
Bisaccia, Duc de la Rochefoucauld-, 257, 276, 290
Bismarck, Count (afterwards Prince), 13, 14, 19, 27, 30, 36, 37, 62, 66, 67, 73-93, 95, 97-100, 102-16, 120, 127, 137, 156, 157, 184, 186-9, 234-9, 242, 243, 246, 249, 250, 252, 311-18
Blanqui, M., 88, 145
Bleischröder, M., 110, 111, 242, 249
Bocher, M., 72, 202
Bois de Boulogne, 67, 132, 133, 136-9, 143
  Longchamps racecourse, review on, in the, 149
Bonapartes, Bonapartists, 8, 9, 25, 27, 75, 76, 85, 174, 177-9, 217, 223, 275, 277, 322, 328, 329
Bonjean, President, 145, 147
Bordeaux, 102, 103, 117-20, 136, 153, 179, 266, 285, 297, 300
  Pact of, 280, 296, 297
Borel, General, 129, 131, 151
Bourbaki, General, 57, 130
Bourbons, the, 85, 86, 168
Bourse, the, 195, 278
Brest, 127, 128, 148, 154
Broglie, Duc de, 218, 257, 258, 277, 293, 322, 329-31
Brunnow, Baron, 48
Brussels, 153, 226
Budberg, Baron, 34
Buffet, M., 203, 321
Burgundy, Burgundians, 155, 230

Calais Straits, 83
Calmon, M., 67, 72, 303

Cambrai, 128, 130
Camphausen, Count, 249
Canrobert, Marshal, 128, 151, 265
Casimir-Perier, M., 173, 179, 180, 199, 224, 225, 326, 327, 331
Cassel, Court of, 85, 93
Castellar, M., 307
Central Asia, 167
Chagny, 57
Châlons, 220, 266, 267
Chamber, the French, 8, 9, 205, 225, 259, 293, 296, 304, 319, 328
Chambéry, 55, 276
Chambord, Comte de, 86, 280, 328
Champagne, 55, 155
Champs-Elysées, 106, 123, 142
Changarnier, General, 131, 257, 293
Chanzy, General, 233, 266
Charles V, 109, 238
Charles X, 117
Charonne, 147
Chasseloup-Laubat, M. de, 232, 233
Châtillon, 126, 127, 133, 267
Chaudey, M. Gustave, 145, 147
Chaudordy, M. de, 56-8
Cherbourg, 23, 127, 128, 148, 154, 274
Chislehurst, 177, 297; Court of, 178
Cialdini, General, 54
Cissey, General de, 130, 133, 134, 136, 137, 139, 141-4, 153, 180-92, 221
Clément Thomas, General, 125
Clinchant, General, 128, 130, 133, 137, 141
Clothilde, Princess, 277, 278
Cochery, M., 62, 65, 66, 81, 88, 90, 92, 94, 97-101
Commune, the, 88, 90, 128, 135, 137, 144, 146, 152, 156, 165, 221, 265;
  massacre of hostages, 105, 147;
  M. Thiers' communications with, 135; trial of insurgents, 154, 155
Constantine, the Grand Duke, 44, 45
  Paulowski, Palace of, 45
Constantinople, 89, 90, 270
  Sultan of, 270

INDEX

Corsica, Corsicans, 178, 277
  Council-General of, 178-9
Coulmiers, Battle of, 100
Councils : General, Ministerial, Municipal, Superior, of War, of Defence, 58, 122, 123, 132, 146, 155, 161, 174, 179, 189, 226, 253, 260, 265, 270, 278, 281, 302, 303, 318, 322, 324, 327, 331
Courbevoie, 133, 138, 180
Courville, General de, 137, 266
Crémieux, M., 24, 58, 59
Creusot, 269

Darboy, Monsignor, 145-7
Deguerry, M., 145, 147
Denmark, 40, 47
  Danish affairs, 25 ; Princess, 47
Departments of the—
  Aisne, 156, 182
  Ardennes, 156, 182, 251-5, 266, 310
  Aube, 156, 182
  Côte d'Or, 155, 156, 182, 256
  Doubs, 156, 182
  Eure, 156, 167
  Haute-Marne, 156, 168, 182, 251, 264
  la Manche, 168
  Marne, 156, 228, 251, 264
  Meurthe, 253
  Meurthe-et-Moselle, 156, 182, 253, 309, 310
  Meuse, 156, 182, 266, 309, 310
  Nord, 256
  Oise, 156, 168
  Rhône, 319
  Seine-et-Marne, 156
  Seine-et-Oise, 156
  Seine Inférieure, 156, 167
  Somme, 256
  Vosges, 156, 182, 228, 251-5, 309, 310
Douay, General, 128, 130, 133, 137, 138, 141, 142, 268
Ducatel, 141, 142
Duchâtel, Count, 224, 225
Ducrot, General, 72, 94-6, 128, 192, 193, 233, 266

Dufaure, M., 119, 152, 180, 214, 295, 299, 303-5, 325, 330
Dutilleul, M., 165, 193, 262, 279, 310

Elysée, Palace, the, 226, 245, 250, 252, 275, 322
Empire, the, 8, 34, 75, 76, 132, 158, 162, 163, 168, 170, 171, 174, 177, 196, 208, 217, 222, 223, 257, 282, 300, 328
Empress, the (of the French), 8, 75
England, English, 10-16, 18, 19, 23, 28, 36, 37, 52, 53, 57, 58-60, 68, 73, 74, 117, 119, 148, 161, 167, 168, 185, 194, 200, 201, 209, 218, 247, 271, 272, 279, 295, 305
  Bank of, 294, 295
  Cabinet, 8, 11, 17, 19, 58, 119
  Government, 17, 274
  Parliament, 12, 52
  Press, 149
  Prince, 272
  Queen of, 11
  Treasury, 201
Ernoul, M., 301, 331, 332
Europe, 10, 11, 14, 15, 17, 18, 20, 25, 26, 28, 31-3, 35-7, 39-42, 50, 56-8, 82, 107, 113, 119, 167, 168, 220, 227, 236, 246, 247, 279, 282, 290, 295, 300, 302, 332

Faubourg Saint-Honoré, 144
Favre, M. Jules, 7, 13, 14, 16, 19, 35, 36, 51, 67, 71, 72, 91, 94, 96-8, 112, 114, 115, 119, 120, 124-6, 155, 174, 175 ; his *Histoire du Gouvernement de la Défense Nationale*, 7
Ferrières, 36, 73, 74
Ferry, M., 67, 72
Flanders, 155, 267
Fleury, General, 37
Florence, 53 ; Conference at, 54
Fontainebleau, 121
Forgeot, General, 265, 266
Fourichon, Admiral, 57, 59, 60
Fourtou, M. de, 303, 326

380 INDEX

France, the French, 7, 8, 10-12, 19, 20, 25, 27, 31-3, 35, 36, 39-41, 51, 53, 55-9, 61, 70, 71, 73, 75, 76, 79, 81, 86-9, 93, 97, 99, 100, 102, 107-13, 115, 119, 120, 135, 136, 143, 151, 158-61, 168-71, 173, 175, 178, 183-5, 187, 194, 198, 200, 201, 209, 211, 214, 215, 217, 220, 227, 229-32, 236, 237, 239, 242, 244, 246-50, 252, 262, 265, 270, 272, 278, 280, 281, 283-92, 296-8, 300, 301, 307, 311-13, 316, 318, 322, 325, 327, 329, 330, 332

Franche-Comté, 155

Frankfort, 155, 157, 226, 294
  Treaty of, 156, 157, 164, 182, 184

Frébault, General, 268

Frederick the Great, 79, 248

French Army (forces, soldiers, troops), 29, 84, 124, 130, 134, 138, 140, 145, 147, 149, 180-2, 199, 229-34
  Cabinet, 104, 170, 176, 179, 180, 260, 292, 321, 326-9, 331
  Fleet, 23, 83
  Outposts, 94, 99
  Press, 105, 152, 220, 236, 271, 275, 324
  Revolution, the, 277, 288
  Treasury, the, 120, 163, 166, 212, 264, 274, 279

Frossard, General, 128, 266, 267

Gabriac, M. de, 33, 44, 184

Gambetta, M., 57-64, 68, 69, 71, 85, 99, 100, 118, 222, 275, 293, 304, 323, 324

Gazette, The Official, 71, 303

Germain, M., 200, 205, 206

German Army (forces, troops), 55, 82, 103, 113, 127, 155, 156, 191, 192, 310
  Emperor, 167, 187, 188, 227, 234-7, 239, 248-51, 253, 270, 271, 311-14, 316, 318
  Empire, 117
  Empress, 318
  Federal Council, 246
  Fleet, 83

German (*continued*)—
  Government, 157, 167, 184, 185, 187, 189, 227, 312, 313
  Press, 79
  Reichstag, 316
  Staff, 81, 95
  States, the little, 89
  Treasury, 183, 185, 237, 250

Germanic Confederacy, Northern Confederation, 34, 78, 79
  Emperor, 40, 41

Germany, Germans, 11, 26, 27, 37, 40, 56, 79, 83, 84, 90, 107, 108, 110, 112, 113, 115, 156, 158, 182, 183, 185, 186, 228, 234, 236, 238, 240, 241, 244, 246, 252, 255, 262, 263, 270-2, 279, 282, 294, 295, 307, 309, 311-13, 315, 316

Gladstone, Mr., 12-15, 17, 19, 168

Glais-Bizoin, M., 57-9, 100

Goltz, von der, 89

Gontaut-Biron, M., 235-8, 246, 249, 270, 271, 312, 314-18

Gortchakow, Prince, 33-9, 41-4, 46-8, 50, 54, 58, 64

Goulard, M., 226, 303, 304, 319, 321, 325, 326

Government, the French, 9, 10, 14, 17-19, 25, 27, 31, 32, 34, 35, 39, 46, 57, 87, 97, 121, 123, 126, 131, 146, 152, 156, 158, 163, 170, 176, 177, 185, 189, 197, 198, 204, 206, 207, 213, 217, 219, 221, 222, 233, 243, 248, 249, 256, 257, 262, 273, 275, 276-8, 281, 292-4, 298, 299, 302, 303, 307, 312, 315, 316, 318, 319, 321, 325, 328-31
  Imperial (the late), 9, 10, 93
  Of France, 68, 117
  Of National Defence, 9, 19, 90, 101, 118, 119, 221
  Of Paris, 18, 19, 24, 47, 58, 59, 62, 68, 71-6, 91-3, 95, 97, 98
  Of Tours, 54, 61, 64, 73, 74, 99, 100

Gramont, M. de, 25, 26, 29-31

Grand Elector, the, 79

Granville, Lord, 8-20, 168

Grenoble, 136, 177, 276, 277, 293, 294, 296

INDEX

Grévy, M., 60, 198, 209, 276, 277, 320, 321
Guise, François de, 109

Hamburg, 294; Bank of, 263
Henckel, M., 110, 111, 242-5, 252
Hermitage, the, 38, 44
Holland, 305
Hunebelle, M Jules, 132
Hungary, Hungarians, 26, 27, 30, 31, 90, 167

Imperial, Prince, the, 8, 77, 328
Imperialists, 322
Indemnity, 93; amount of, 107, 109, 113; matter relating to, 155-67, 182-5, 193, 197, 234, 235, 237-56, 264, 272-4, 279, 282, 309, 310
Issy, 132, 133, 136, 137, 139
Italy, Italians, 28, 37, 43, 52-6, 74, 119, 161, 168, 178, 305, 306
  Cabinet, 56, 119, 306
  Government, 306
  King Victor Emmanuel, 53, 55, 56, 63, 306
  Parliament, 54, 56
  Unity of, 168

Joinville, Prince de, 168
Journal des Débats, 259
Journal Officiel, 165, 283
Jura, the, 55, 156, 182

Kerdrel, M. de, 257, 291, 292
  Committee, 294, 295, 304
Kern, M., 111, 112, 211
Kiva Expedition, the, 271
Krantz, Captain, 128, 129, 140, 142, 148, 154
Krupp, Herr, 269

La Bergerie, 127
La Muette, 138
La Roquette, Prison of, 147
Ladmirault, General de, 128, 130, 133, 137, 138, 140-2, 144, 153, 265
Lambrecht, M., 119, 153, 179

Langres, 55, 63, 266
Lanza, Signor, 54
Larcy, M. de, 119, 180, 260, 304
Le Brettevillois, General, 137
Le Flô, General, 67, 119, 153
le Havre, 83, 96, 265, 274
le Mans, 96, 155
Lecomte, General, 125
Lefranc, M. Victor, 153, 180, 225, 276, 302, 303
Legion of Honour, 130, 132, 145, 269, 318
Legitimists, 86, 169, 174, 211, 212, 275, 280, 299, 322, 328
l'Etoile, 137; Arc de Triompe in, 142
Loire, the, 92, 120, 266; Army of, 63, 68, 99, 101
London, 7-9, 12, 33, 48, 54, 60, 194, 218, 272, 294, 295
  Foreign Office in, 8, 17-19, 23
  French Embassy in, 7, 14, 19, 257
Lorraine, 49, 50, 61, 70, 78, 80, 81, 92, 93, 96, 97, 107, 109, 111, 112, 115, 237, 270
Louis Philippe, 117
Louis XIV, 79, 202
Louvre, the, 145, 165; State Office at, 122
Lucerne, 280
Luxembourg Gardens, the, 125
Lyons, 55, 63, 74, 103, 136, 207, 212, 266, 321; camp of, 56; Central Mayoralty of, 319, 321, 323; municipality of, 319; inhabitants of, 319
Lyons, Lord, 16, 20, 57, 60, 209, 295

MacMahon, Marshal, 128, 130, 137-42, 144, 150-2, 177, 193, 215, 220, 221, 265-7, 328, 329, 332
Madrid, 307
Maintenant, M. de, 295
Malakoff, taking of the, 131
Malta, 247
Manteuffel, General Baron von, 190-3, 235, 237, 246, 311-13, 315
Marne, the River, 267
Marseilles, 74, 136, 266

382 INDEX

Martel, M., 198, 321
Metternich, Prince, 29, 31, 75
Metz, 36, 49, 58, 67, 72, 79, 80, 82, 85, 92, 93, 96, 107, 109, 111–13, 153, 219, 228, 317; army of, 19, 35; capitulation of, 62, 64, 67, 68, 71, terms of, 85; siege of, 55
Meudon 132, 180, 181
Mexico, 306; King Maximilian of, 306
Mignet, M., 67, 72
Moltke, Count, 66, 77, 94, 100, 112, 114, 115, 236
Monarchy, Monarchical, Monarchists, 52, 75, 89, 117–19, 136, 171, 173, 175, 198, 227, 256, 259, 280, 290, 292, 294, 300, 301, 325, 328
Mont-Valérien, 36, 67, 83, 121, 126, 127, 140, 141
Montaudon, General, 57, 128, 153
Montchanin, 57
Montluçon, 57
Montmartre, 122, 144
Montretout battery, the, 133, 137, 139, 141, 267
Montrouge, 132, 133
Mortimer-Ternaux, M., 134, 136
Moulins, 57
Mulhouse, 183

Nancy, 107, 191, 234, 237, 246, 311, 315
Nantes, 136, 275, 276
Napoleon III, 25, 75, 85, 89, 93, 117, 130, 177, 220, 221, 277, 278
Napoleon Bonaparte, 12, 301
Napoleon Prince Jérôme, 178, 277, 278, 321
National Guard, the Republican, 90, 118, 123, 124
Neuilly, 126, 127, 137; Pont de, 133
Nevers, 57
Nikolsbourg, Treaty of, 89
Normandy, 83, 96, 155

Okouneff, M., 48, 64
Olozaga, M., 307
Orléans, 60, 61, 62, 65, 66, 99, 100, 121; Orléanists, 86, 134, 173, 174, 202, 213, 328

Orléans (continued)—
  Bishop of, 62, 86, 99, 247, 248; palace of, 68
  Princes, 86, 87, 168–70, 178, 217
Orloff, Prince, 270-2

Paris, Parisians, 8, 15, 18, 21, 23, 26, 34, 39, 42, 43, 47, 48, 50–2, 55, 58, 59, 62–6, 68–72, 75–7, 82, 83, 87, 88, 91, 92, 95–8, 100–6, 109, 111, 115, 118–21, 123–5, 127, 132, 134–7, 139, 142–5, 149, 155, 180, 184, 218, 224–7, 229, 230, 235–8, 249, 262, 264, 266, 267, 272, 275, 310, 313, 315, 316, 319, 322–4, 332
  Army of, 130, 133, 151
  Burning of, 145
  Capitulation of, 175
  Entry of Prussian Army into, 105, 106, 108, 109, 115
  Evacuation of, 155
  Foreign Ministry at, the, 67, 71, 123
  Forts of, 74, 90, 94, 134, 156
  German Embassy at, 240
  Headquarters at, French, 67
  Hôtel de Ville, 72, 75, 76, 90, 98, 145
  Insurrection of, 121–47, 221, 227, 300
  Revictualling of, 59, 69–71, 76, 77, 87, 90–6, 98
  Siege of, 55, 124, 129–42, 153, 220
  Treaty of, 271
Paris, Comte de, the, 86
Passy, 138, 142
Picard, M., 67, 90, 94, 119, 124–6, 152, 153, 173–5
Picardy, 96, 155, 267
Piscatory, M., 67, 72
Place de la Concorde, 123, 142, 144
Place Vendôme, 144
Point du Jour, 133, 137, 140–2
Poitiers, 57
Poland, Poles, Polish, 32, 33, 79
Pont de la Chambre des Députés, 124
Pouyer-Quertier, M., 119, 155, 164, 165, 186–90, 193, 200, 211, 262
Pope, the, 306

INDEX

Portugal, 119, 307
Pothuau, Vice-Admiral, 119, 129, 180
Potocki, Count, 51, 53
Prague, 89, 90, 104
President of the Republic, title of, adopted, 173, 174
Prussia, Prussians, 10-13, 16, 23, 25-30, 35-8, 40-2, 45, 46, 49, 51-3, 55, 56, 61, 67-9, 71, 72, 74, 79, 81, 83-5, 87, 89, 95, 100, 103, 105, 109, 110, 120, 126, 132, 139, 148, 149, 151, 152, 155, 167, 168, 182, 227, 228, 230, 240, 241, 248, 252, 254, 267, 268, 310, 313, 315
   King of, 27, 50, 58, 64, 65, 79, 80, 81, 87, 89-93, 105, 108, 114, 116, 119, 311
   Prince-Royal, Crown, 94, 101, 108
Prussian camp, 9, 16, 19
   Court, 9, 94, 249
   Government, 19, 242, 243, 253, 254
   Headquarters, 13, 14, 58, 59, 62, 87, 98
   Outposts, 94
   Press, 27
   Treasury, 186, 241
Pyat, M. Felix, 72, 88, 90

Reffye, Colonel de, 268, 269
Reichshoffen, 128, 228
Rémusat, M. de, 175, 176, 235, 245, 246, 252-5, 303, 313, 316, 318, 323, 324, 327
Rémusat, M. Paul de, 66, 81, 175, 180
Republic, Republicans, 9, 25, 28, 34, 75, 85-7, 89, 117, 118, 135, 136, 169-73, 176, 197, 221, 225, 227, 258, 276, 282, 284-90, 297, 298, 300, 301; Conservative-, 259, 286, 289, 301; of 1848, 87; of 1789, 288; system, 320
Rhine, the, 80, 247; Bas-, 92; Haut-, 92; provinces, 269
Ricard, M., 173, 177
Ricotti, Signor, 54
Rivet, M., 172-4
   Constitution, the, 174, 308
Rivières, General de, 266, 267

Rome, 56, 235-7, 246, 325; Church of, 300; Court of, 270
Roon, Count, 112, 249
Rouen, 83, 154, 167, 267
Rouher, M., 161, 217, 223, 224, 329
Roussy, M. de, 310
Royalist, Royalists, 118, 276; Press, 275
Rue Haxo, the, 147
Russia, Russians, 23, 26-9, 32, 34, 36, 38, 41, 43-5, 47, 48, 50-3, 57, 58, 62, 68, 69, 74, 100, 119, 167, 271, 272
   Baltic Provinces of, 40
   Emperor Alexander, 32, 33, 36, 38-40, 43, 46, 47, 58, 64, 167, 270, 271; daughter of, 272
   Imperial Council, 46
   Tsarevitch, the, 44, 45
   Tsarina, the, 45, 47

Sadowa, 25, 89
Saint-Cloud, 125, 132, 137
Saint-Denis, 139, 267
Saint-Germain, 128, 129, 180; Faubourg, 142, 144
Saint-Marc Girardin, M., 221, 257, 259, 260
Saint-Pélagie, 147
Saint-Petersburg, 21, 23, 32, 33, 44, 46, 53, 54, 59, 100, 246; Winter Palace at, 38
Saint-Vallier, Count, 191, 192, 312, 313, 315
Sanson, General, 129, 142
Saône, the, 55, 56; Haute-, 55, 156, 182
Satory, camp of, 125, 133, 144, 180, 181
Savoy, 107; dynasty of, 300
Saxony, 24, 40
Schouwalow, Count, 272
Sedan, 93, 128, 177, 229
Seine, the, 67, 72, 83, 123, 124, 126, 133, 155, 265, 267; Prefecture of, 303
Sella, Signor, 54
Senard, M., 53, 54, 56
Senate, the, 75

Sèvres, 67, 94; bridge of, 67, 72, 88, 94; outposts, 69
Silesia, Silesians, 32, 230, 243; frontier, 26
Simon, M. Jules, 67, 118, 119, 124-6, 175, 188, 325, 326
Spain, Spaniards, Spanish, 271, 306
Carlists, 307
Government, Republican, the, 307
King Amadeus, 306, 307
Strassburg, 36-8, 49, 80; army of, 19; capitulation of, 38
Stuttgard, 33
Switzerland, Swiss, 52, 55, 101, 111, 113, 119, 178, 183, 278

Tann, General Baron von der, 62, 66, 73, 99
Teisserenc de Bort, M., 200, 260, 273
Thiers, Madame, 41, 73
Thiers, M., 31, 50, 58, 64, 72, 215, 218, 221, 329
Government of, 188, 197
Message to the Assembly, 281-92, 296, 299, 302
Thile, von, 249
Times, The, 7
Tissot, M., 7, 8
Toul, 36, 316
Toulouse, 74, 136, 266
Tours, 23, 48, 51, 57, 59, 60, 63, 66, 68, 69, 73, 85, 97, 99, 100, 155, 232, 266
Archbishop of, 23; palace of, at, 23, 61
Délégation de, 51, 56, 59, 60, 61, 70, 98
Trocadéro, the, 142
Trochu, General, 67, 70, 95, 105, 220, 248
Trouville, 264, 265, 267, 268, 270, 272-5, 277

Tsarkoé Sélo, 33, 38, 41, 44, 47
Tuilleries, the, 145; Court of, 31, 34
Turin, 24, 55
Turkey, 119

Valazé, General, 129, 154
Vanves, 132, 133, 137, 139
Vauban, 201; *Dime-Royale* of, 201
Verdun, 36, 113, 266, 316, 317
Verona, 24, 25
Versailles, 50, 62, 66, 72, 85, 91, 97-9, 100, 102, 104, 108, 115, 117, 119, 121, 122, 124-9, 136, 139-44, 148, 151, 155, 157, 158, 180, 191-3, 197, 218, 220, 223-6, 232, 234, 238, 245, 251, 266, 305, 323, 327, 328
Château de, 144, 148
German Staff Office at, 66
Peace Preliminaries signed at, 157
Treaty of, 175
Vienna, 24, 26, 28, 31, 33, 51, 53; French Legation at, 24; Hôtel Cours d'Autriche, 24
Villeneuve-l'Etang, 127
Vincennes, 180, 181, 268
Vinoy, General, 122-7, 130, 131, 133, 137, 138, 141
Visconti-Venosta, Marquis, 53, 54, 306
Vitet, M., 172, 173, 257, 260

Waddington, M., 327, 331
War Expenditure, Table of, 159
Warsaw, 32, 33, 51
Winterfeldt, Herr von, 67, 72
Wittgenstein, Prince, 66
Wolowski, M., 200, 202
Würtemberg, 78, 246

Zorilla, M., 306